Max-Erich Sommerfeld
13 and 3 Summer Lilacs

Max-Erich Sommerfeld

13 and 3 Summer Lilacs

The Lean-Transformation of an Engineer

Bibliographical Information of the Deutsche Nationalbibliothek:
This publication is listed in the Deutsche Nationalbibliographie of the Deutsche Nationalbibliothek; detailed bibliographical information can be accessed under http://dnb.dnb.de .

The automated analysis of the work to extract information, particularly patterns, trends and correlations in accordance with $ 44b UrhG ('Text and Data Mining') is prohibited.

Copy Editing: Fennah Podschies

Layout and Publishing: BoD · Books on Demand GmbH, In de Tarpen 42, 22848 Norderstedt
Printing and Production: Libri Plureos GmbH, Friedensallee 273, 22763 Hamburg

ISBN: 978-3-7597-9361-4

Table of Contents

About the Author

Max-Erich Sommerfeld was born on August 14, 1957, and studied Mechanical Engineering and Economics in Berlin. Married since 1989, he accumulated extensive experience in industry throughout his long professional career.

He began his career in various companies in Berlin before focusing on long-term roles with two renowned firms. Over 32 years, he acquired comprehensive knowledge and expertise in Manufacturing and Lean Manufacturing. In March 2020, he retired and has since used his time to travel and share his knowledge and experiences.

In this story, largely based on true events, he intertwines the world of Lean Manufacturing with his own professional experiences. To respect the privacy of those involved, names and locations have been changed for a respectful portrayal of events.

For better readability, this book consciously avoids gender-specific language. Of course, all readers are equally addressed and invited to engage with the content.

Foreword

'Movement is beneficial' – a simple phrase that carries profound significance in our lives. It reminds us that movement is not only physical, but that it also pertains to change and development.

We see movement in nature, when the lion chases the gazelle; an eternal dance between predator and prey that maintains the balance in the savannah. Sometimes the lion wins, sometimes the gazelle is faster. But regardless of who triumphs, it is always about movement and survival.

We see it in our own lives when we face new challenges and evolve. And we see it in organizations that must thrive in a constantly changing world.

This book is the story of a journey; a journey through the last 16 years of my professional life. It is the story of a Lean advocate navigating a world of change and continuous improvement. It is a tale of highs and lows, encounters and insights, small steps, and giant leaps on the path to becoming a Lean Sensei.

The narrative begins with my immersion into the world of Lean Manufacturing – a world shaped by both production processes and deep insights into human nature. On this journey, there are unexpected and surprising events that make these 16 years without changing companies highly varied. In this story, I emphasize the focus on the development of employees to identify waste and to achieve continuous improvement.

Throughout this journey, I have learned that movement can be physical, mental, and organizational; indeed, it must be! The principles of Lean Management serve as a guide that helps us embrace the challenges of change and transform those into opportunities.

This book is aimed at all those on their own journey of transformation, whether as young engineers, experienced leaders, or simply curious minds. It demonstrates that there is not always a fixed plan and that sometimes we just need to keep moving forward in order to grow and learn, and also to avoid being left behind.

The journey into the world of Lean begins here. May it inspire you, move you, and remind you that movement is beneficial.

Introduction

As a child of ten, starting in 1967, I sometimes spent a few hours alone at home after school. My father owned a taxi company and usually didn't come home until the evening. My mother worked at a restaurant by Woolworth. Occasionally, I would go there to grab a bite to eat. I often saw a tall man with a full beard and his wife there. They would have a light snack in the afternoon, drink something, and then leave. They were very quiet people, although their appearance made them stand out a bit. My mother always told me never to look like that man. Such a person should never be a role model for me. The long hair, such a beard; it looked unkempt and disreputable. Unknown to me at that point, I would have a significant encounter with him again later in my life.

After eating, I would go home and do my homework. Once I had finished, I would play outside or, if the weather was bad, occasionally listen to the missing persons announcements on TV. The war had ended only 22 years ago, but this span of time seemed unimaginable to me; I was only ten years old. Yet for those searching for their missing relatives, it must have felt like it happened just yesterday. After the missing persons reports, the stock prices would follow on the black-and-white test pattern on the first channel. I listened, even though the names and numbers meant little to me: Gelsenwasser, Hamborner, Haus der Aussicht, Harpener. I always found these names fascinating. I had no idea that one of these names would accompany me throughout my life.

In 1971, I graduated from elementary school and went on to the Bertha-von-Suttner-Gymnasium, only two streets away from our apartment. It had a proper, large sports field. I was excited and genuinely looking forward to this new school. On the day of the enrolment, many people gathered in the assembly hall: new students with their families, all the teachers, and a few older students. The classes were divided, and I ended up in the 'b' track. I already knew some classmates from elementary school. When the teacher was announced, I suddenly saw a tall man with a full beard stand up in the hall. It was the man who always ate with his wife at Woolworth (the one I should never take as a role model!). He was now my homeroom teacher at the gymnasium. My mother was incredulous; I found it somewhat amusing.

From this point on, learning was no longer as easy as it had been in elementary school. My parents had no higher education and could no longer support me with my studies. It became even harder a year later when my mother passed away. She was small and her heart was weak, likely a result of her war experiences, perhaps also on account of smoking. However, my father and I somehow managed. He worked, drove his taxi, and I studied and played sports. Physical activity is good, as my father had taught me. He had been a successful cyclist before and after the war and was still very fit in his mid-sixties.

Finally, I graduated with my Abitur, but couldn't find an apprenticeship, so decided to study mechanical engineering followed by economics. The lectures ran from morning until late afternoon. For breaks, I got myself rolls and brought butter, toppings, and jam to the university. Every morning, I would stop at the bakery around the corner to buy my rolls. Eventually, my classmates started ordering from me, and it kept increasing. I didn't mind; I really liked the young dark-haired saleswoman. One day, I mustered the courage to ask her out for dinner. We are still together today. We have been a couple for 46 years and married for 35 of those years.

At that time, Germany was still divided, and there were only a few industrial enterprises in Berlin. In 1981, our professors offered us an excursion to the Federal Republic. We visited numerous large companies in Essen, Duisburg, Mülheim, and other places. One of these companies was called FR-HDA. The HDA stood for Haus der Aussicht. There, we were shown modern milling and grinding machines, as well as new technologies for the production of highly complex turned parts for intricate industrial products. The machine park was state-of-the-art. I finally learned what was produced at the Haus der Aussicht company; the company whose name I often heard in stock market reports as a child. They made high-quality gearboxes.

I completed my studies with great success. However, leaving Berlin after my studies was never an option. During my second degree in economics, I was involved in a food company as part of my student thesis. This company produced instant products and packaged cocoa. The topic of the thesis was 'Preventive Maintenance'. We had an initial meeting with our professor. He lived in a spacious house with a beautiful garden in Berlin-Hermsdorf. Just before we left for the company, he picked fresh flowers from his garden and wrapped them in paper. We were curious and asked for whom this gesture was intended. His answer was simple, "Wait and see, gentlemen!"

At the company, we were greeted by the friendly secretary of the managing director, Mrs Ballauf. When she received the flowers, she beamed with joy and thanked him several times. She then led us into the conference room, where Mr Miller, the managing director, was already waiting for us. We introduced ourselves, and after just a few minutes, Mrs Ballauf re-entered the room, this time with a cup of coffee. Mr Miller thought it was a good idea and asked if she could bring a cup of coffee for our professor as well. Her answer surprised us all, including Mr Miller, "This cup is for the professor. Would you also like one, Mr Miller?"

The message was clear; always maintain a good relationship with secretaries, receptionists, or doormen! If you earn their appreciation, doors and gates will open for you.

After graduating, I started my first job as an engineer in a food company together with my friend and fellow student. In the first few years, I switched companies a few times; time passed quickly. In 1988, I started working at a company in Berlin that was involved in mechanical engineering. It was my first long-term position after completing my studies. We planned a new plant on a greenfield site in southern Berlin. It was not an easy task at the time, but we found a suitable plot. The plant was planned and built according to the principles of material flow, which was not common at the time. Not all areas in the new plant were accessible by crane, which was also astonishing in 1990. We used CAD planning for the layout design. Many group leaders couldn't fully interpret these representations. They needed to see actual models instead. So, we decided to use a Lego-like building set at a scale of 1:25. With these building blocks, one could see the overall picture well, unfortunately this representation didn't allow for quick changes or simulation of the material flow.

This meant that many participants ended up agreeing to things they didn't fully understand. So, despite the involvement of employees and group leaders, the plant had a somewhat shaky start. In the following years, we had many consulting firms on site. All confirmed that we had done well, although recommended that we intensify or even apply Lean elements such as Value Stream Analysis, Kanban, Supermarkets, 5S, etc. At that time, I didn't fully understand these concepts and thought they were only suitable for mass production in the automotive sector. One of the consultants strongly recommended value stream analyses to me and gave me materials for self-study.

Lean-Manufacturing, Explained Briefly

At this point, it might be useful to say a few words about Lean Manufacturing and explain some of the terms that the many consultants at the company piqued my interest in. The explanations of tools and behaviors that follow in the next chapters will then become clearer in the overall picture. They are, so to speak, puzzle pieces that complete the picture.

The core aim of Lean Management is to create an environment where employees think and act independently, identifying and solving problems. To achieve this goal, it is crucial to develop employees before changing processes or products. The knowledge of the employees is the most valuable asset of the company. This approach ultimately leads to improved processes and products by optimizing the value chain. Employees independently identify and reduce waste by implementing their ideas. Value stream analyses and the application of specific

Lean tools facilitate the uncovering of waste. However, I will mention it only briefly here. A more detailed explanation will follow at an appropriate place to keep the readers' interest.

It is sobering to realize that a proportion of less than 1% of value-adding times in the lead time of a product is not unusual. Just think of your last visit to the doctor: you call, get an appointment in two days, drive an hour to the practice, wait another thirty minutes, and then spend ten minutes with the doctor. Three of those minutes are probably taken up by conversations and notes. Then you drive back home. There were seven minutes of value-added for the customer in a lead time of about 50 hours. That is 0.23 percent!

Similarly, in production, there is quite a bit of waste that could be avoided. The eight types of waste are as follows:

1. Over-production: producing products without a customer order
2. Waiting: of machines, materials, and people
3. Over-processing: doing more than the customer expects
4. Unnecessary movement: in the process
5. Transport: through production
6. Inventory: of materials
7. Defects: scrap and rework
8. Unused employee knowledge

Avoiding such waste or eliminating problems and deviations is a change for the better; and that is precisely what Kaizen means in Japanese: Kai (change) and Zen (for the better), not to be confused with the Bavarian expression 'Koi Sinn' (no sense)!

A Kaizen process[i] begins with recognizing a deviation from a standard or a problem. Employees from different levels come together as a team to analyze the problem and develop solutions. Then, an action plan is created using the PDCA (Plan-Do-Check-Act) principle. Who will do what, when, and where? During implementation, progress is monitored and measured. If the improvement works, it is embedded into the existing standard and becomes the new standard. After a set period, the success of the process is reviewed. The insights gained flow into the continuous adaptation and improvement of the process. Kaizen fosters a culture of continuous improvement, where small steps lead to lasting efficiency gains.

The methods for identifying and narrowing down waste and problems are varied. Here are some that will be explained in more detail later:

- Value Stream Mapping
- Pareto Analysis
- Spaghetti Diagram
- 5 Whys Analysis (the children's method)
- Fishbone Diagram
- Swimlane Diagram

Similarly varied are the tools to solve the problem. Here are a few that will be explained further in the course of the text:

- Kanban
- Supermarket
- Andons (signals that indicate, for example, a need for material replenishment)
- 5S (Sort, Set in order, Shine, Standardize, Sustain)

- SMED (Single Minute Exchange of Die)
- TPM (Total Productive Maintenance)
- Standard Work
- Shadow Boards
- Mixed-Model Line

The application of these tools is supported by principles and behaviors, of which the following is just a selection:

- Develop people first, then processes – 'People-Centric Lean'
- PDCA (Plan, Do, Check, Act)
- Go Gemba, go to the place where value is created
- 9-Step Problem Solving
- A3
- Hoshin Kanri
- 3P (Production Preparation Process)
- MDI (Manage Daily Improvements)
- Managing means improving, not just administrating
- Use the brain of the factory
- Servant Leadership

To keep it fresh in your mind, here comes the most important part at the end of the lists; the cultural change.

When you start applying selected methods and tools, you must also initiate and drive the cultural change within the company in parallel. Cultural change in a company is a lengthy process that can take years, whereas the tools you find useful can be implemented within just a few weeks or months. The category of Cultural Change in Lean Transformation refers to the changes in corporate culture necessary to successfully implement Lean management principles. Lean is not only focused on processes and efficiency, but is a philosophy that requires a profound change in the way people work, communicate, and approach problems.

Here are some aspects of Cultural Change related to Lean:

- Focus on the customer and creating value for the customer is central. Employees must understand how their work affects the customer and that it is the customer's money that ultimately secures their wages
- A core element of Lean is continuous improvement. In the context of Cultural Change, employees must be encouraged to continuously seek opportunities to improve processes and their work
- Lean encourages viewing mistakes as opportunities for improvement. In this positive error culture, problems are seen as shared challenges that need to be addressed and solved. Blame is avoided
- Open and transparent communication is promoted. Employees should feel free to express themselves, share their ideas, and raise concerns to create a learning organization.
- Lean fosters collaboration and teamwork. To achieve common goals, employees from different levels work together as a team. Hierarchies are broken down
- Respect and appreciation for employees are crucial. Lean principles emphasize that people are not just resources, but play a decisive role in the improvement process

Cultural Change is indeed one of the most demanding aspects of Lean Transformation. It requires profound changes in the thinking and behavior of supervisors at all levels, as well as the employees. The goal is to create an environment where continuous improvement and adaptation become the norm.

Without a lasting change in these aspects described above, there will be no sustainable and successful company transformation.

I have distilled this overall complex topic into a few central questions or statements for myself and chosen them as my guiding principles:

- The customer pays the salaries and wages, not the company. Because if we have no customers, there is no money.
- Do our products solve the customer's problems or tasks?
- Do we develop the employees first, before the processes?
- Have we specified the desired state so clearly that deviations can be quickly identified?
- Managing primarily means improving. Improving, in turn, means identifying and solving problems
- Do our employees recognize deviations, i.e., problems, in the production process, and can they solve them?
- Am I a servant leader, helping employees implement their ideas, thus using their knowledge, the knowledge of the factory?

If you heed these statements, ask yourself these questions, and work on being able to answer them with 'yes', you are on the right path to transformation. However, it will be a long journey and surely it will not always be straightforward. The wisdom of Franz Kafka also applies in this situation:

'Paths are made by walking'[ii]

It is a plea for action, for setting out; because movement is beneficial.

I read the materials recommended by the consultants very carefully and concluded that they were the right path – no matter what industry one was in. Unfortunately, in my position, I did not have the opportunity to initiate such projects. Some attempts brought me responses like, "First bring down the set times and rework costs before you start such projects." The long-term thinking and belief that Lean projects and behavioral changes could jointly solve problems were missing among the senior executives. The prevailing REFA mindset of time standards and piecework pay dominated, no matter what ideas I proposed: 'Kanban? We're already doing that!' 'Value stream analyzes are conducted by others; you take care of the preliminary work', or 'Preventive maintenance blows our budget', were often heard. There was no way to implement these approaches in this conservatively thinking company. Lean, it was thought, should only take place in production, without giving employees the necessary decision-making power over their tasks. Self-regulating systems were seen as a threat to established power structures and were therefore not an option for those involved.

Up to this point in my career, I had encountered different types of senior executives. There were the paternal figures from the first two companies who set the direction while leaving the path open. Then there were the factual executives who strictly adhered to the company's internal management guidelines, valued punctuality, and allowed a lot of freedom in implementation. And finally, I knew the visionary, whose goal was always clear and who promoted everything that served his vision. Mistakes were seen as learning opportunities, with the request not to repeat them. All had their own style, yet none of them was so obsessed with power that they oppressed or mistreated their employees.

However, the culture I encountered in the aforementioned mechanical engineering company was something I had not expected. The monthly meetings with the management were beyond my imagination. They often escalated into a wild spectacle, with the manager shouting furiously and banging his fists on the table so hard that the cups rattled on the plates. In his eyes, we were nothing more than idiots, incapable of anything useful. Sometimes he even admitted that he was probably the biggest idiot of all for having hired us. In those moments, I had the feeling that there was a tacit, silent agreement in the meeting room. Yet even this occasional feigned self-reflection did not lead to improvement. Those who opposed the established regime found the opportunity to develop themselves elsewhere after a few months.

Neither my studies nor previous positions had prepared me for such behavior. My wife had studied social sciences and explained to me that this was narcissist behavior. Narcissism in corporate leadership can have severe impacts on people and the organization. Our manager was a classic example of narcissistic leadership. His stubborn adherence to his own ideas and suppression of dissenting opinions created a toxic work environment. In such cases, not only do the employees suffer, but so does the company's performance.

The behavior of the narcissistic manager unsettled his executives. They were afraid of his verbal attacks and did not trust their own decision-making abilities, leading to a lack of initiative and innovation. Younger executives or people with initiative left the company in time, or were dismissed. Some older managers tended more towards resignation. They were in the final phase of their careers and heading towards retirement. Three of them had just gone through the bankruptcy of another large company. They had no option to change, and the fear of financial risks had broken their resistance. This, in turn, hindered the company's adaptability, leading to poorer business results and limiting competitiveness. I already mentioned the statement 'movement is beneficial'. This organization was paralyzed and did not move; failure was only a matter of time.

Another sign of a narcissistic leadership style became evident during breaks. Just ten minutes after the clattering of cups and plates in the meeting room, he would show off the new dance steps he had learned over the weekend in the kitchen, as if nothing had happened. This behavior, in the context of narcissistic leadership, can be seen as manipulative. Narcissistic leaders often have the ability to use their behavior strategically to elicit specific reactions from their employees. In this case, showcasing dance steps in the kitchen could be interpreted as an attempt to distract from the real problems and challenges within the company. On the other hand, he probably wanted to endear himself to us, as he was, in fact, dependent on us. Until the next meeting, almost everyone followed his instructions blindly, which was one reason for the company's failure. At the next meeting, he needed us again – this time as scapegoats for the failures. The cycle began anew, and it was loud and dreadful.

In hindsight, this narcissistic behavior amounted to bullying an entire group. At that time, one could of course complain about such behavior, whether to the Works Council or the HR Department. However, one thing was clear: you should always have a new job contract in hand before raising such accusations. For never had a member of senior management left the company as a result of such allegations. It was always the lower-ranking employees who felt the loss of a trusting working relationship. The Works Council always ensured that the people in production achieved as many percentage points as possible in performance-based pay. My impression was that they didn't care much about the management level as they weren't unionized.

Like many others, I belonged to the group of people who more or less unconditionally carried out what the manager instructed. The plant was only a few kilometers from our newly built house, and the company's pay was good. Although I had tried several times to find work elsewhere and even received offers from Rendsburg, Hamburg, Bremen, and Kassel, my wife and I decided against it. We didn't want to commute and give up our accustomed way of life. In Berlin, we had many long-standing friends we had known since our student days and with whom we shared numerous experiences and regularly did things together. The pressure wasn't strong enough, and at that time, there was no serious threat of the company closing down. We didn't feel the burning platform; it was just very loud once a month event. The customers wanted our products – they were top-notch, but expensive, and the demand was stable. However, demand was unfortunately not increasing.

I managed my stress by starting athletics in 1997, specifically the decathlon. No matter who was in what position there, performance was always recognized. It helped me unwind, although it did not solve the problem. The loud meetings with the

Managing Director continued. The company's success, one might almost say, remained predictable. In 1998, the ailing machinery company, as the board of the parent company once described us, was sold to a subsidiary of a foreign corporation.

Usually, large companies suffer from decrepit conditions, as a result of outdated plants where efficient material flow cannot be realized, or as a result of worn-out machines and facilities that urgently require costly investments for renewal. None of these aspects applied to us. Our plant and 80% of our machines were less than ten years old. However, there was apparently insufficient volume to operate this multi-million-dollar site economically. Additionally, Berlin lost its special status with the reunification of Germany. It was only a matter of time before the 16% Berlin subsidy on trade tax would be eliminated—another factor that would financially disadvantage the site.

Subsequently, numerous meetings with the new owners' managers took place, but brought hardly any noticeable improvements to the overall situation. For reasons I couldn't comprehend, the management remained in office. Within just ten years, the once publicly traded company with 6,000 employees turned into a limited liability company with only 800 employees. The only thing we still possessed was very good products that stood out in the market as a result of their quality and performance. Would we gain an advantage through the expanded distribution channels? Or did the new parent company merely need the knowledge of how to make better products? If the company had been a cheese, one would have said, 'it's starting to stink, let's go!'

By the summer of 2004, I had already been working at this machinery company in Berlin for sixteen years. I was almost on my way to an international athletics competition in Aarhus, Denmark, when the rumor spread that my long-time superior and protégé of the management would be replaced by a new Plant Manager. This was several signals at once. The management was effectively overruled and had to make a sacrifice. Their influence was waning. My boss, with whom I had a good relationship and who always protected me, was now to do something else. In his place, a manager selected by the new owners would now come in.

Kanban and Supermarket

With a Kanban, which means 'signal carc' in Japanese, one can take products from a Supermarket. The Kanban card functions like money, signaling the need to restock or re-produce an item. Here are the basic rules:

- No material exists withou: a Kanban card
- Kanban cards are counted and numbered
- Without a Kanban, no material is produced or re-plenished
- Only the quantity specified on the card is produced or replenished, no more, no less
- Only defect-free products are passed on
- No Kanban card leaves the cycle and goes to the office

'Supermarket' – everyone has been there. You go, take the products you need, go to the cashier, and pay. You hand over money. If you need the same items tomorrow, they will be there, because the shelves will be restocked. What was consumed will be replenished from the storage, and then reordered for the supplier. Translated into a manu-

Berlin

When I returned from the competition in Denmark in mid-August, my former boss had indeed been reassigned to the Quality Department. My new boss was a 'cleaner', brought in by the new parent company. The Managing Director now saw his chance to get rid of me. My protective shield was gone! He made it clear that I was at the top of the new boss's list to be 'dealt with', which meant being fired. It was more serious than ever, filling me with fear and threatening our very existence. In September, after my summer vacation, there was a management meeting where it was announced that by the end of the year, two people from our group would be leaving the company.

I immediately realized I would be one of those two people. A week later, I received an invitation from the HR Department for a meeting. The Head of HR, Ms T, couldn't understand why I was being given an offer to leave the company, although she was obliged to present it to me. The offer included a severance package and coaching that would last until the end of the probation period at a new job. Ms T could do nothing more than initially delay the process, hoping it would fall through.

It was a nice attempt, but to cut a long story short, the plan worked until October. After that, she too had to show results to avoid problems. The usual procedures followed. She said the company wanted to get rid of me and advised that I consult a lawyer immediately. I first visited the company doctor as a result of a ringing in my ears, then a specialist, and finally a lawyer. Confidentially and very directly, they threatened me with bullying. The Works Council said, "Take the money and leave. We can't help you." The lawyer also recommended getting as much as possible and dragging the process out as long as I could.

All the positive self-talk couldn't change the situation. Our system, our existence, began to wobble. Normally, a stable situation rests on four pillars: family, finances, home, and friendships. Now, our finances and thus our home were at risk. Family and friends would remain; if we couldn't solve the financial problem, our home would change. If we could solve it, I would probably no longer work in Berlin and would be separated from my wife and friends during the week. If I stayed in Berlin, I would face a 30% salary cut, which wasn't a viable solution either. A dilemma emerged, and it was clear that we would have to make sacrifices somewhere. Initially, it felt like a situation where after low tide in the North Sea, the sea had not returned; it had just gone. This was incomprehensible and unimaginable.

I agreed to the coaching in November, and my lawyer successfully renegotiated the severance package. My contract was now set to end on June 30, 2005. For each month I left earlier, I would receive an extra half month's salary. There was an option to extend this arrangement for another six months, until December 31, 2005. I regularly attended coaching sessions at the renowned Outplacement Agency. The focus was initially on how to apply successfully, how to create concise thirty- or ninety-second presentations, and on psychological support during this extraordinary situation. I had a great coach and was well-prepared for interviews and a new job. Then I had another idea. I contacted my former college friend Hans, who ran a plant in the automotive sector and was well-versed in Lean principles. Although he had no vacancies, he invited me to visit his plant.

Lean

What I saw there deeply impressed me; a Supermarket filled with car door panels; each pallet equipped with a small sign. On a board, one could read the sequence in which the pallets had to be loaded onto the trucks. This was the sequencer. Naturally, the truck was loaded in the reverse order of how the customer had to have the parts. Thus, the first part to be unloaded was also the first to be delivered to the assembly line.

In the plant, there was a production line where the small signs from the pallets (which were taken from the supermarket by forklift drivers and loaded onto the truck), were hung on thin steel cables. This was the sequence of orders to reproduce the removed material and refill the warehouses. It was a 'full replenishment system'; the warehouses were refilled.

This became my goal. I wanted to introduce such a system in Berlin, in a small area, without prior approval. I conducted a small value stream analysis and found a relatively short, internally-running process of welding and painting that still always caused missing parts on the assembly line. Ideal for a trial because the complexity of the parts was very manageable, with eight different assemblies! I only had one shot, and everything had to be perfect. On the computer, I simulated the production of the assembly, the painting process, the pre-assembly, and all transport processes in fifteen-minute intervals. I tried to push the system to its limits with unilateral loads, or by removing Kanban cards, to block it. If there was a blackout, I continuously optimized it until no more problems occurred. Only then did I create a plan and invited the six employees of the affected areas. Their supervisors were not invited. I had to take this risk.

They would never have agreed to a system change or even this experiment. The affected employees in the plant knew about my situation and supported me in this endeavor.

Two of the colleagues were initially very sceptical. I heard, "I am the Production Controller here and set the orders!" Others were more open to the idea and welcomed it. These were the people from the assembly line, who regularly lacked material and had to reschedule the entire line's assembly sequence as a result. Their motivation was the hope for improvement. One of them was neutral and went along with the majority. Eventually, we agreed on a trial period of six weeks, with weekly meetings to discuss the results.

After just two weeks, it was clear; the system worked. Even the two initial sceptics who opposed it had changed their minds. The other employees were also in favor. In the following weeks and months, there were never again shortages in the assembly as a result of this component. The number of Kanban cards regulated the circulation stock of the assemblies, and we managed to reduce it by an impressive 45%. To top it all off, the former sceptics asked me if I could introduce such a process for other assemblies as well. It made their work-life easier, and they now had more time to address other problems.

2005, Berlin

During the period of separation, my new boss and I actually found a respectful way of dealing with each other. He had to get rid of me – that was his task, and he admitted it. Nevertheless, I assured him that I would continue to deliver my performance. He had to provoke me several times, even setting traps to create scenarios where he could issue me with a formal warning. However, I never showed any misconduct. Always correctly equipped with safety gear, I appeared in the production area to address an accusation. The allegation was always refuted, mainly by the production staff, with whom I had a very good relationship. The Industrial Engineering Department was never at fault. After three attempts, he stopped trying; it was a small, unspoken truce we agreed upon. He also had to manage an entire plant, so couldn't just focus on trying to burden me.

At some point, I noticed that he moved a bit stiffly and sluggishly. He was usually very agile, brisk, assertive, and quick on his feet. When I asked him about it, he said he was suffering from back pain. I arranged an appointment for him with my physiotherapist, who treated decathletes. The treatment was successful, and his pain was gone after a few sessions. A few weeks before my planned departure at the end of June, we had a conversation in his office. His desk was always neatly organized, and a small brass paperweight in the shape of a cannon held down the few loose papers in his inbox.

We talked about my situation and my impending departure. He almost seemed concerned that I hadn't found a new job yet.

Then he said something unexpected, "I know I aimed at the wrong target. It couldn't be helped." At that moment, he turned the paperweight so that the barrel of his small brass cannon pointed at the Managing Director's office. We both had to grin. I immediately took advantage of this mood. As I didn't have a signed contract or a job offer at that moment, I asked my 'current boss' to extend the termination agreement by six months. This was an option my lawyer had successfully negotiated. After consulting with the coaching agency, he agreed to my request. We had a fair deal in this unfair situation. Well, the part about 'no prospects' was a bit of a fib at that point. However, I had no contract!

After about thirty applications, I received my first invitations to interviews in the spring of 2005. None of the companies were in Berlin; they were all far in the west. There was a medium-sized, family-run company in Hattingen that manufactured pellet presses, a larger company in the printing industry in Mönchengladbach, and a company in the Bergisches Land that belonged to a large US corporation. It was HDA-ÄÄtch, formerly FR-HDA or Haus der Aussicht. On the day of the interview in the Bergisches Land, as I took a taxi from the train station to the company, many things seemed strangely familiar. The small castle, the 360° highway exit, and the factory grounds. Right after the gate, we turned right and drove directly to the hall I had visited on a field trip after my studies.

During the job interview at HDA, the interviewers showed me the milling and grinding machines from the 1980s that were used to process the gearbox shafts and gears. I immediately remembered the field trip during my studies. What was once the latest of the latest had aged. These machines were to be replaced by new investments. That would be one of the pro-jects if I got the job. However, it wasn't that far yet. Now I had a job prospect at the Haus der Aussicht. That somehow fit.

The interview was in March, but the company didn't get back to me. In May, I inquired about the status and mentioned that I had two other offers. After that, everything happened very quickly. Can you guess where I ended up? Well, after a hastily arranged second interview, I was w th HDA, the company whose name had accompanied me since childhood. Within a few days, I received the signed employment contract and sent it back signed by fax.

Two weeks after extending my termination agreement by six months, I had a new job contract and resigned as of June 30 – six months before the newly agreed termination date. This little manoeuver earned me three full months' severance pay as a nice bonus. My current boss grinned a little. It wasn't his budget, and I would quickly disappear from the company's pay-roll so he was satisfied.

Everything now had to move very quickly for us. My first work-ing day was supposed to be July 1, 2005. I had never worked outside Berlin before, and I had never had my own apartment. My wife and I had to find accommodation for me, preferably furnished and near the company premises. Thanks to the hous-ing brokerage in the Bergisches Land, this worked out very quickly – by mid-June, I had an apartment. On June 29, I trav-elled to the Bergisches Land with my packed car.

2005, Bergisches Land

> 'Develop people first, then the process'. This concept is a fundamental principle in Lean Management, often referred to as 'People First' or 'People-Centric Lean'. It emphasizes the importance of employees and their engagement for a company's success. Your employees are the brain of the company, its most valuable asset on the journey to earning customers' money. If you have a great product, but your employees have limited or no access to training and development, it's like a tiger without teeth. It looks impressive, and it makes an impact for a while, but it won't be long before it starves.

The Bergisches Land

June 29th was the day I said goodbye to my wife in Berlin. She went to work a bit later than usual that morning, and I left our home. We had been living together for 22 years, and now we were both very sad. It wasn't just that moment – the entire 550 kilometers journey to the Bergisches Land was filled with sadness and felt like an ordeal. Several times, I wanted to turn back, but that wasn't an option. In the afternoon, I arrived in the western Bergisches Land. After unloading the car, I went shopping. The first weeks of separation were awful. My wife and I agreed that this commuting would last no longer than three years. To make the frequent travelling as pleasant as possible, I bought a 'Train card 50' for first class and travelled back to Berlin every other weekend to see my wife.

First, I took the urban rail to Düsseldorf. The ICE then took me quickly, though not always punctually, to Berlin Central station, where my wife was already waiting for me on the platform. On the alternate weekends, my wife visited me in the Bergisches Land, staying in my furnished Chippendale apartment. It was located on the outskirts, about a kilometer from the forest, in an upscale residential area with single-family homes. A good pizzeria was a 5-minute walk away. There was a sauna on the outskirts, just a 10-minute drive away. Despite the professional challenges, my new residence in this region gave us the opportunity to explore a new environment and for me to settle in.

Together, my wife and I discovered the surprising beauty of the Bergisches Land and the Rhine-Ruhr area on weekends. This area, located in the western part of Germany, is a region known for its rolling hills, dense forests, and picturesque villages. It's an area rich in history, with numerous castles and medieval towns, offering a glimpse into the past. Despite its rural charm, the region is home to several significant industrial businesses, contributing to its diverse economy. The area is also popular for outdoor activities like hiking and cycling, providing ample opportunities to explore nature. With its' blend of natural beauty and industrial presence, the region offers a unique and balanced experience. We attended local events, often walked along the Rhine, and met up with old holiday acquaintances. You know how it is... On vacation, you meet great people while playing volleyball on the beach, have a few drinks together in the evenings, and exchange contact details on the last day. In most cases, you never see each other again. However, now it was different – we did see each other again. I lived in the same region where many of our holiday acquaintances were from, in the area of North Rhine-Westphalia.

Eventually, the train rides to and from Berlin became too long, and Sundays always ended too early. We would leave home at 4.15 pm, the ICE departed at 5.03 pm for Düsseldorf, I arrived at 9.10 pm, and caught the urban rail at 9.26 pm. Thirty minutes later, I was at my destination and in my apartment by around 10.15 pm. In the fall, my wife suggested that I should consider flying from Tegel and Düsseldorf. I started looking for flight connections: €29 with Deutsche BA, 55-minutes flight time – that was the future. Plus, there were those green-blue chocolate hearts offered upon disembarking, which were later taken over by Air Berlin – and which in the future would turn red.

The Restart

I was employed at HDA-ÄÄtch as the Manager of Industrial Engineering, just as I was in Berlin. My superior was the Production Manager, and my position was at Level 7 within the entire company hierarchy, with Level 0 being the Executive Board and Level 3 being the managers for the European factories. At that point, I hadn't yet contemplated which path I should take, or what level I could aspire to. My focus was on the here and now, on the beginning. The responsibilities I held encompassed eighteen employees. Together with them and in collaboration with other departments, our task was to design the manufacturing processes, covering everything from the NC programming of all machines in the factory to the preparation, selection, and procurement of machining tools. Fixtures and auxiliary tools were also part of our scope. When introducing new products, it was also our responsibility to coordinate the prototype as well as the pre-series production.

The intensification of Lean principles was not at the top of the agenda initially, although the company nevertheless expressed interest in it. It was mentioned during the interviews, but no questions were asked about it. I was still at the early stages of my Lean journey and had experimented in Berlin with Kanban. It had worked, and I ultimately wanted more.

On my first day at work, there were flowers and a laptop on my desk. Only later did I notice them, as after the formalities, a meeting required my attendance. It was already about replacing the milling and grinding machines for production – the ones seen during an excursion to the Ruhr region and adjacent areas after completing mechanical engineering studies. Now, my task was to assist in procuring the next generation and automating the entire cell with a portal robot. Everything felt very exciting and new. If I were a mouse, I would have said, "The cheese smells good!"

Another project was already underway when I started at HDA-ÄÄtch in early July. New products had been designed. It was now about prototype manufacturing, workplace design, fixture construction and procurement, as well as the timely introduction of gearbox production. My employees were highly experienced and skilled NC programmers, but not project managers. Nevertheless, they had done great preliminary work. The department head, who had always taken care of this, had been seriously ill for months, and no one knew if he would ever return. Unfortunately, he did not, and the reactions at the cemetery showed how close and trusting their relationships had been. A sad chapter right at the beginning.

For me, the saying 'the first shot must hit' applied, so I invested all my energy to successfully continue and complete the project. It worked, and I had a successful start in my new job. A few weeks after starting, the vacation plan for my department for the following year had to be created. To my surprise, the employees expected me to do it, as it had always been done by their ex-boss. We discussed it, and eventually, I told them that they were all 'more than 3 times 7'. They were capable of writing NC programs for a machine park worth over €100 million, and almost all of them had families with children. So, as a team, they could create their vacation plan themselves. I shared my criteria with them and they agreed, "Create a matrix with the machines and the names of the programmers. Then mark who can program which machines. All machines must be covered by at least one programmer during the vacation period. Then create the plan."

They took matters into their own hands and met three times over the next fourteen days. In the end, the plan was ready, and the workshop confirmed that it was acceptable to them. It was great, and my employees thought it was even better because they had done it themselves and succeeded. They felt confident that they could continue to make decisions for themselves in the future, although there would also be situations where I would rely on them to implement something. In such cases, they should simply carry out the task without discussion. I didn't find the term 'executive matter' suitable, so instead, we called it 'don't ask, just do!' Through the vacation plan, I had gained a good deal of trust from these employees. One of the Lean principles; 'Develop people first, then products and processes', had also worked. They agreed with this approach. It was a pretty good start, both for me and for them.

My Lean-Transformation

In my evening leisure time, I pondered where and how Lean ideas could be implemented in the new company. This was a lesson brought from my previous firm. As the Head of Industrial Engineering, it became my mission to actively apply Lean tools. Being one step ahead, implementing these ideas myself, and independently utilizing the instruments was not only more efficient, but also faster than waiting for a Lean leader to drive the implementation forward. In Berlin, this approach was denied to me. However, here in the Bergisches Land, I was not going to allow it to happen. My department should serve as a role model and leave behind the reputation of classical, outdated work preparation.

As a farewell at the company in Berlin, a comprehensive overview of the tools was compiled. SMED, TPM, Kanban, JIT, JIS, Supermarkets – so many instruments in the Lean toolkit had already been applied in Berlin. Besides the instruments, some basic behavioral rules were also followed. The principle of developing the employees first was immediately applied, giving them the opportunity to create their own vacation plan. I was now very motivated to apply other tools from this toolkit. Eventually, the time would come. I just had to be patient. An Arabic proverb says, 'patience is the key to paradise'.[iii] Patience is also one of my middle names, unfortunately not the first or second...

For me, it was a phase of immersing myself in a different professional environment. Every day, every hour, I discovered something new. In addition, I took a lot of time to get to know the processes and the people in the company, to understand how the company functioned and how the people thought. With each passing day, I felt more comfortable in my role, the company, and the region. It was an adventure to take on new challenges, and I felt like I was always learning – something I hadn't felt at my old employer in Berlin for a long time. It was also immensely important that my wife enjoyed coming to the Bergisches Land, despite the hardships. The weekends were always like a brief getaway from everyday life for her.

End of the Year

Whether on the train or in the plane, I used the travel time to prepare for the upcoming week and to distribute tasks within the team. My employees always had something new to choose from, and they also found it a bit amusing. In any case, they liked that on Monday mornings, in addition to their daily tasks, they always received new ideas and problem statements. Many saw it as an opportunity to develop themselves. It wasn't just the employees who benefited from these preparations. I also benefited because I was always thoroughly prepared for the weekly meeting on Monday mornings at 8.30 am. with the production manager. In this meeting, called the 'P-Meeting', all department and group leaders, as well as maintenance and myself, presented the situation and the status of projects and production orders for the week in their respective areas. Production requested the necessary support, I required capacities for the prototypes, and deadlines were coordinated. The discussions were informative, but it took a long time for everyone to have their say. During this time, the actual operation was left alone. This was met with little enthusiasm from the group leaders, especially on a Monday morning at the start of the week. It often happened that there were problems with the first orders while the supervisors were in the meeting. Then they were disturbed by phone, or even had to go 'briefly' to the workshop to make situational decisions.

On my many train journeys in July 2005, right after my start with HDA, I saw the summer lilac blooming for the first time on the edge of the tracks. It still provides nectar to the butterflies even in late summer. That was similar to my situation. At 48 years old, I had also arrived in the late summer of my career, and I found nectar at HDA after the plant had withered in Berlin. Besides the ballast of the track system, it almost looked like an attempt at reconquest. I wondered how many more times I would see this lilac bloom. We had originally planned to do this commuting for a maximum of three years.

2006

> 'Managing means improving' is another central statement in the Lean field, which emphasizes continuous improvement and optimization. If you don't make improvements and instead settle for the status quo, you fall behind compared to others. It's like 'swimming against the current'. If you stop, you drift backwards. However, improvement has an important prerequisite: You need to know what the normal state is in order to recognize deviations, or problems, and ultimately solve them.

The Beginning of the Year

The year 2006 began. Finally, we had the opportunity to embark on our long-awaited vacation. My probationary period was over, as was the supervision by the employment consultancy. You could say, 'the sea was back, and the cheese smelled good!' After the turbulent eighteen months – marked by my job change and the move to the Bergisches Land – we longed for relaxation and recuperation. Our choice fell on the Canary Island of La Palma in the Atlantic.

La Palma, also known as 'Isla Bonita', is one of the Canary Islands renowned for its breathtaking natural diversity and spectacular landscapes. The island is home to the Caldera de Taburiente National Park, which, with its volcanic formations and deep ravines, offers fascinating insights into geological history. The beaches, including the black sand beach of Puerto Naos, invite you to swim even at this time of year with water temperatures of 22°C. La Palma is also famous for its numerous hiking trails that wind through lush forests and impressive volcanic landscapes. The island greets visitors with its uniquely pleasant climate, giving one the feeling of early summer in January. Colorful houses and the musical backdrop of merengue and salsa at beach bars and on local radio add a lively, Caribbean-like touch to the island. The variety of Canarian culture combined with these elements creates a unique blend that makes the island truly special.

We had previously visited the island several times with friends for hiking, and this time we found our lodging with a warm-hearted family in Todoque on the west side of the island. It was a small complex with four holiday homes and buildings for the owners. Everything there was always so relaxed. It wasn't what we had previously imagined the Canaries to be. There was no mass tourism, no high-rise buildings. It was an enchanting, green island. The temperatures were ideal for hiking on trails lined with lush green forests. This harmonious getaway provided us with new energy for the coming year – another year of commuting between Berlin and the Bergisches Land.

The Factory in the Bergisches Land

Everything comes to an end, even vacations. Mid-January, we returned well-rested, and I travelled back westward. The project for the automated gear line was now picking up speed, thanks to approval from the parent company in Tomado, USA. I had found my solid role within the team. As part of Industrial Engineering, we were responsible for creating the requirement catalogues for the machines and designing the cell layout, integrating it into the already quite densely-filled factory hall. Additionally, moving other machines to create the necessary space was also part of our tasks. The layout had to be continuously adjusted like a sliding puzzle, so that eventually a contiguous area for the new line would be available. It sounds simple, but it meant that some machines had to be taken out of service, relocated, and brought back into operation. As a result, these machines were down for several days and couldn't produce. Procuring the tools and fixtures, as well as programming, would follow later in the project. Our tasks were indeed varied, and the program was challenging. The collaboration with the Facility Manager and the Procurement Manager went exceptionally well. Compared to my previous company, HDA was truly a team.

Another workplace challenge arose, as the production hall wasn't air-conditioned. The summer heat, exacerbated by the production process, worsened the situation. The control units of the machines contained highly sensitive circuit boards that reacted to high temperatures and overheated. This caused some of these machines to fail on the few hot days of an otherwise average summer. Replacing the components took several days, turning a hot day into a whole week of production outages.

To make matters worse, the necessary replanning led to material shortages, causing further production interruptions. As a result of this chain of problems, the planned production quantities couldn't be met, putting significant pressure on management. Production and maintenance reported to the Production Manager, who was also a team member of the gear line project. There was a lot to handle. Up until eighteen months ago, he had held my position. His real and undeniable strength lay in production-oriented product development with engineering, project work, and detailed production knowledge.

His boss, the Plant Manager, remembered my hiring interview, in which he had also participated. I had mentioned that in the Berlin plant, maintenance was also under my responsibility. He wanted and had to improve the situation and asked me to develop a concept for preventive maintenance for the plant—and quickly. I found it very good that he brought up the idea. In Berlin, I had developed a similar concept. Unfortunately, it was never implemented as a result of budget constraints. Now, at HDA, the Plant Manager wanted it, which made a difference. The challenge was gladly accepted. Below is a brief overview of TPM.

TPM (Total Productive Maintenance) is a systematic method for maintaining and improving production equipment, especially machines, to ensure minimal downtime. A TPM project for machining machines aims to increase the overall performance of these machines and extend their lifespan. This significantly contributes to cost efficiency and thus to the company's competitiveness.

Key steps in a TPM project include:

- *Training the team*: All employees of the selected machines are trained to recognize problems early and fix minor issues themselves
- *Evaluating the current state of the machines*: Determining downtime, maintenance needs, and wear factors is necessary

- *Autonomous maintenance:* Machine operators take over simple maintenance tasks such as regular cleaning, lubrication, and checks
- *Planned maintenance:* Regular maintenance schedules are created to carry out preventive maintenance work, thus minimizing downtime
- *Continuous improvement:* TPM focuses on identifying and addressing problems and failures promptly, while also developing long-term solutions
- *Measurement and evaluation:* Success must be measured. Downtime, the time between two failures, or the repair duration are possible parameters
- *Reward and recognition:* To motivate those involved, successes and improvements are rewarded and recognized

The concept was based on my previous work in Berlin. Through timely calls to the important machine manufacturers of my new employer, I could quickly obtain non-binding cost estimates and downtime for the maintenance work. The companies welcomed this inquiry – not least because they would earn money from it. In fact, they had already proposed regular and more frequent maintenance in advance. Apparently, they had trouble constantly performing short-notice repairs at HDA and thereby disappointing other customers.

With the incoming offers from the companies, I quickly and accurately drafted a plan for the plant and was able to present it. The Plant Manager found it coherent, and the costs of €250,000 per year didn't deter him. He immediately saw lower expenses for unplanned outages and, of course, the higher output of the machines, leading to higher profits for the site on the other side of the equation. Then he asked if I would also take

49

responsibility for the implementation. My answer was a decisive yes, coupled with the caveat that I would also need to take responsibility for the area, and not just the project to avoid conflicts of interest. There was a reason why there was no TPM at HDA yet.

The Plant Manager understood my concerns, and after a week, he informed me that both the management and the European Manager had given their consent. However, the agreement not only covered the concept and the necessary budget; it also included the organizational change resulting from this restructuring. From then on, I was to report directly to the Plant Manager and additionally take responsibility for maintenance. Within a year, I thus rose to a Level 6 manager with over thirty employees and a budget of €12 million. This personnel change, as explained to the rest of the team, was a redistribution of the particularly high load across multiple shoulders. This allowed the Production Manager to focus on meeting production targets and the Facility Manager on the large gear line project. It was, in the broadest sense, a Lean decision. No one person should carry as much burden and responsibility as possible, but as many shoulders as possible should bear equally high loads. It was, so to speak, a level-load at the management level.

During the week, I was alone in the Bergisches Land. In the evenings, I occasionally worked at home on the preventive maintenance project. I analyzed the data on machine downtimes in detail, read Lean books on preventive maintenance, and assigned priorities to the machines. Everything served the preparation of discussions with Production; they were my customers. Of course, my thoughts also were about how to balance my private life in Berlin and my demanding work schedule. It was really essential to me to continue paying attention to my health and fitness to meet the high demands. Regular exercise – you know, movement is good – sufficient sleep, and a well-stocked refrigerator became my loyal companions during this busy time. It was also crucial not to travel home tired and worn out, possibly sick, and then use the weekend to recharge. We still wanted to do enjoyable things and meet friends. Frequently I jogged for an hour in the evenings or went to the sauna. Physical fitness helped me in all aspects, both professionally and personally.

The final offers from the companies for regular maintenance services matched the cost estimates I had calculated in my concept. In an extended meeting, I presented these to the employees involved, and we immediately coordinated the dates for the service work. The Production Planning Department developed an updated production plan based on the improved machine availability and the planned downtime for maintenance.

This plan was quickly implemented. The first service work began in late summer, followed by additional machines in the fall. Of course, there were expected comments like, "We always did this between Christmas and New Year. Once a year is enough. We didn't lose any production then." However, we remained steadfast and implemented the concept consistently, as annual maintenance is often not enough for 25-year old machines, and they fail beforehand with defects. This autumn was different. The systems ran excellently until the Christmas period, when another major maintenance was due. The production quantities were reliably and better planned, thanks to the regular maintenance. The Lean principle for this approach was:

Frequency and Magnitude: The more frequently you check or correct something, the smaller the deviation from the target will be. This means the magnitude of the deviation from the target is reduced because you check beforehand. If you produce a batch of a thousand pieces and check the batch at the end, you can have up to a thousand defective parts in case of a quality problem. If you check the first five and then every fiftieth, there can be a maximum of fifty defective parts.

That doesn't just sound better, it is better!

Lean

Among the numerous significant projects in production, there was another critical issue affecting the entire site: the Lean transformation of the plant. The appropriate program for this came from the parent company in the USA. This transformation went hand in hand with the approach of Operational Excellence (OpEx).

> *OpEx* aims to operate in such a way that the company's strategy is implemented excellently. It is a holistic, company-wide strategic approach that promotes efficiency, continuous improvement of processes and workflows, quality, productivity, and thereby ultimately the competitiveness of the company.

The Lean transformation affects all functions of the plant, not just production. Quality, order control, productivity, work safety, inventory management, and so on are closely intertwined. The cultural change in the thinking of all employees, including supervisors, is the foundation for the start of a successful transformation. Therefore, Cultural Change and Lean itself are key categories in an OpEx assessment. As I mentioned earlier, I had already described the Cultural Change at the beginning. The Lean category is aimed at assessing the implementation and effectiveness of Lean principles within the company. Here are some aspects that are often considered in this category:

- *Lean Principles and Methods:* This evaluates the extent to which the fundamental principles of Lean management are understood and implemented in the company. This includes things like waste elimination, continuous improvement, pull principles, value stream mapping, etc
- *Implementation of Lean Tools:* An examination of the specific tools and techniques used within the framework of Lean. This includes things like 5S, Kaizens, Kanban, Poka Yoke (error prevention), etc
- *Cultural Aspects:* How well is the company culture aligned with the Lean philosophy? Are employees able to practice continuous improvement, and is there an atmosphere of teamwork and open communication?
- *Applicability to Different Areas:* Is Lean applied only in production, or has it been extended to other areas such as purchasing, logistics, administration, quality, and even marketing?
- *Results of Lean Implementation:* What measurable improvements have been achieved through Lean initiatives? Increased delivery reliability, shorter lead times, productivity improvements, quality improvement, higher employee satisfaction, etc

- *Sustainability:* This assesses the extent to which Lean practices and principles are anchored in the company and integrated into daily operations. Or are they just short-term initiatives?

Overall, the Lean category aims to assess the maturity and efficiency of Lean implementation within the company and identify opportunities for further optimization. The results of the various functions of the plant are a consistent consequence of these central aspects of Cultural Change and the Lean category.

At HDA, we were still far from implementing Lean ideas. Traditional thinking in batch sizes with high quantities was still the priority, but this was soon to become history. Evening meetings were scheduled to forge plans for the future. The team also invited me to these meetings to jointly design the visions and future image of the company with my colleagues. Participating in such discussions was new to me in this context, and it marked another significant step on my path to Lean transformation.

Before we could develop our visions, it was crucial to meticulously describe the current state. This was aptly named 'Ugly Baby', to emphasize that we should have no reservations about brutally disclosing and documenting the actual condition. A comprehensive inventory in all functional areas – from inventory management to maintenance to order control – was necessary. This way, we could recognize the point in our change process where we stood, identify necessary behavioral changes to improve, and understand what had hindered us so far. The task was complex and extremely demanding, requiring deep knowledge and a clear understanding of processes and interrelationships. However, even just dealing with the Ugly Baby posed a challenge for some team members. They hesitated to label the current state as improvable or 'ugly', because it would document that not everything had been perfect so far. A balancing act began – perhaps a bit easier for me as a newcomer than for the managers responsible for decades in the company.

Based on this current state, we began to describe what the future picture should look like. Where would we see ourselves in one, two, and three years? What behavior and Lean tools would we use? How should the company's key figures develop through these changes? A kind of video emerged, in a way a short film with four consecutive images. Of course, some crucial points regarding the key figures were predefined. A large plant like HDA should turn over inventory forty times a year after completing the transformation. The on-time delivery rate of orders, measured by customer request, should be 97%, and there were many other target specifications. Achieving these goals presented a very exciting and challenging task. To avoid losing touch with reality, we regularly coordinated with other colleagues in the plant. The milestones and steps to get there should be considered realistic by as many as possible.

The meetings where we formulated the future image of the plant took place in the evenings after the day's work. Initially, I engaged somewhat cautiously and did not want to be too bold right away. After two sessions, I realized that I could contribute more with my thoughts. What surprised me a bit, almost frightened me, was the fact that I was somewhat ahead in this company with my limited knowledge of Lean Manufacturing. When it came to Kanban and a Supermarket in one of the vision sessions, I heard from the responsible managers, "Explain it to us, show us how it works! Then we'll do it."

The first thing that came to my mind was that no one had explained it to me. I had worked it out myself, even though it was not within my area of responsibility. First, I read about it, then I looked at it, and finally, I installed it myself. 'Only where you have walked by foot have you truly been',[iv] says Johann Wolfgang von Goethe. In this sense, I followed this principle. In contrast, they preferred to be carried on litters. Learning a new tool, experimenting, and acting independently did not seem to fit with their work culture. The willingness to make mistakes and learn from those was not in their nature. Without the openness to accept mistakes, you cannot be a role model, especially when it comes to introducing an error culture based on Lean principles. Without this culture of learning from mistakes, the necessary cultural change becomes a real challenge. An Albert Einstein quote also fits quite well; 'Hoping for change without doing anything is like standing at the station and waiting for a ship'.[v]

After a few months of intensive work and exchanges of ideas with part of the workforce and upper management, we had a vision in mind. We were proud of the joint discussions and decisions and presented it to the management and group leaders. Now that it got serious, some of those who had previously agreed with us made a U-turn. There was approval, although others brought us doubts and resistance. Killer phrases like, "All well and good, but who is going to pay for it?" or, "We've tried that before, it doesn't work in our plant!" dampened our enthusiasm and brought us back to reality. We had a divided team in front of us. Our visions, which we had designed with so much passion and involvement of others, seemed to meet insurmountable skepticism and rejection from some. The scepticism hit us from both sides of the hierarchy, from above and below.

We had the impression of being surrounded by thick layers of clay that allowed nothing to penetrate. It was as if we were trapped in the singularity before a black hole. Attracted by the power of the superiors, our strength was not enough to move away and towards the goal. The principle of acting in the spirit of Lean, 'managing means improving', was difficult to implement at this location.

When we presented our visions to Ashley, the Global OpEx Leader of the ÄÄtch Group, and discussions with him ensued, I again heard this helpless sentence, "Explain to us how it works, and we will do it!" It was quite something to say this to me as a newcomer to the company. In the moment when these words were said to the Global OpEx Leader from the USA, it became clear to me that there was indeed a dangerous attitude in some areas; no desire to learn, try out, and take responsibility for something new. Perhaps it was even fear of the consequences of failures. For the leadership style was still not characterized by a positive error culture. However, there was no way out, the transformation had to be started. It became a journey over rocky paths, where we turned back again and again to look for a better way.

A few weeks later, it became known that there would be another personnel change at HDA. The Plant Manager had just managed to get me extended responsibilities for the maintenance area before he was approached to leave the company. On the one hand, it was a sad moment for me; on the other hand, he was also the person everyone else feared when goals were not fully achieved. Whereas Berlin was about thinking and believing in set times and piecework, here the thinking was in piece numbers. If necessary, production continued even without customer orders, just to maximize the capacity utilization of the plant and the bottleneck machines. A fatal behavior in terms of Lean, inventory, and cash management.

The search for a new Plant Manager began – one who would actively support the path of transformation. This search took several months. Candidates came and went. In the meantime, we were coached by an Englishman who ran a plant of the ÄÄtch Group in Slovakia. Ron originally came from Birmingham and was a very patient and calm person. He was also somewhat stout, and his movements were rather deliberate; but he was authentic. He regularly came to us in the Bergisches Land. In one of the meetings, a sentence from him reminded me of my professional end in Berlin, 'Two will not join the party in the future'. This time, I was sure I was not one of these two.

Ron coached us in the Lean transformation, as well as in our team dynamics. There were times when arguments arose within the team, and we learned how to strengthen our collaboration. Some positive changes occurred in our work atmosphere during this period. It was very impressive to me how Ron engaged with us on the subject and how he influenced us to gain support and resilience. I couldn't help but envision myself in such a role someday in future, when I would be nearing the end of my career. Dreaming, after all, is permissible.

Alongside the 'Big Transformation', there were also smaller requirements and ideas from the parent company aimed at supporting the overall process. Achieving a successful Lean transformation requires several essential prerequisites. This was recognized even by American society. Before contemplating implementation, people must undergo training. It takes twenty to forty percent of active supporters of the Lean mindset in a given area to generate momentum. The critical mass must be attained to allow this process to become self-sustaining. Otherwise, there's a risk of the campaign losing momentum and fizzling out.

Before tackling process, improvements and describing standard situations, there must first be order and cleanliness. Or do you prefer chaos as the standard? To achieve order and cleanliness, Lean Manufacturing offers a tool called 5S.

5S is a method for managing cleanliness and orderliness in workplaces. It consists of five steps:

- *Sorting (Seiri):* This involves sorting out unnecessary items and materials at the workplace, keeping only the essentials
- *Set in order (Seiton):* After sorting, the remaining items and tools are systematically organized. Everything has a designated place, adhering to the principle of 'a place for everything, and everything in its place'
- *Shine (Seiso):* This step entails thorough cleaning of the workplace. Cleanliness is crucial for maintaining a good working environment and for identifying deviations
- *Standardizing (Seiketsu):* This involves establishing standards and rules for maintaining order and cleanliness at the workplace
- *Self-discipline (Shitsuke):* This is the discipline to continuously uphold these standards and seek improvements

However, a stable 5S process seemed distant, not only in our factory, but also in other areas of the ÄÄtch Group. Hence, we initiated a 'Five-Star Audit' in preparation for 5S in the factories.

It was akin to 5S 'Light'. Through this, employees engaged with the topic. In the five categories of orderliness, cleanliness, safety, environment, and process quality, there was a questionnaire that could be developed internally. Each question could be answered with a simple yes or no. If a question was answered negatively, it provided valuable insights for improvement. Addressing these points naturally led to better results. Once we managed to achieve a success rate of 90% or more over a 4-week period with internal and external audits, we could apply for a certification audit. If successful, the department would be awarded a coveted star.

Particularly notable in my department was the tool and measuring equipment preparation, overseen on an interim basis by Mr K. Everything was meticulously clean and neatly labelled, making the area a role model even before the introduction of the five stars. Nevertheless, some colleagues in the factory mocked it. "Too much effort for cleanliness, it's still a workshop, not a laboratory", were the comments of some colleagues. People in the Bergisches Land can be pretty direct. My opinion differed. Given the precision tools and measuring equipment we stored there, capable of tolerances of +/-0.001 mm (a thousandth of a millimeter, roughly equivalent to 1/50 of a hair), perfect conditions were indispensable. The Five-Star Audit provided the ideal means for me to collaboratively create these conditions.

We decided to first collectively reach the 90% mark, and I supported the department wholeheartedly. Whatever they needed to improve order and cleanliness was procured from a budget allocation. When we finally achieved this goal, we involved auditors from the company. Team leaders, cell leaders, and department heads came weekly for an external audit in the department. We aimed to obtain an unbiased assessment. After two more months, it finally happened; the department maintained a 90% or higher success rate for four weeks, even with audits from colleagues from other departments and supervisors.

For the star award ceremony, we invited the Production Manager to a final audit. And it worked! The pride felt by the team was unparalleled – as they say in Berlin, *proud as Bolle*. Some still mocked us for this 'childish' initiative, but perhaps a hint of envy was also present. As recognition of the outstanding achievements, I wrote a brief article for the 'ÄÄtch News' – the weekly company news published on the website – introducing the team along with a photo and highlighting the department. As the location was rarely featured in this global news, the article garnered much attention and commentary. And, of course, pizza was delivered to the factory, because successes must be celebrated!

During the next visit of the Global Operations Manager to our factory, he naturally wanted to personally meet this special department and its dedicated employees. Had he read the news, or was it Lynne, his secretary, who tipped him off? Never before had a President from the company's U.S. division visited this department. They always wanted to see the machines that produced the products. Now, he was looking at the people who made this possible through their work. Everyone looked forward to this moment and finally received the long-awaited confirmation; our tool preparation was the neatest and cleanest worldwide – the foundation for the outstanding quality of our HDA products. From then on, every request for this department was promptly approved. The mocking smiles of the other colleagues slowly turned into approving ones, naturally also from the Works Council. It is worth mentioning that Mr K, who not only impressed with the Five-Star Audit, but also with his outstanding performance, was promoted by me to Group Leader. His commitment had more than paid off. In terms of future changes, it also didn't hurt that Mr K was the nephew of a Works Council member.

The principle of the Lean mindset, 'managing means improving', had proven to be a valuable tool for me. We described a standard, identified deviations, identified them as problems, and ultimately solved them. This earned us and the site a reputation for being ready to embark on new paths. My personal Lean transformation slowly took shape, and of course, I wanted more. We followed a principle: when starting with Lean, choose a tool that brings you success; because successes motivate you to want to achieve more.

End of the Year

Throughout the year, I continued taking the late flights from Düsseldorf to Berlin-Tegel on Fridays. Along the railway track, the summer lilacs blossomed again from July onwards. It was the second time, and I remembered that we originally planned to commute for only three years. Deutsche BA was taken over by Air Berlin – even the chocolate hearts found their way into the new planes - except now they were red. At some point, I acquired a frequent flyer card and could use the priority lanes. It made traveling a bit more pleasant because the queues at the airport, especially during holiday periods, became shorter and more predictable for me. From Berlin, I received other news.

The company management has decided to close the traditional but struggling company in Berlin. It felt like I had left at the right time. Movement is indeed good.

Our year-end brought us once again to the enchanting island of La Palma. We knew that relaxation and outdoor activities in nature, along with a very pleasant climate, awaited us on this island. On a hill, we rented a villa with breathtaking views down to the sea. The house was situated at about 600 meters above sea level. Banana plantations were not nearby, which was always important to us. In this street of Tacande de Abajo, we had now stayed for the second time. The street ascended steeply. Just before reaching our accommodation, we always passed a junction – a dirt road as a dead end, which descended a bit and was lined with some houses. No property was visible, everything was just green, resembling tropical parks. Every time we drove past it, our curiosity was aroused. How about going down this path once to see if you could also rent a villa there? Someday we would follow this call, someday...

2007

> 'Movement and speed', these are the things that ensure your 'survival'. A quote from Christopher McDougall's book 'Born to Run' captures it aptly: 'Every morning in Africa, when the sun rises above the savannah, the gazelle wakes up. She knows she must run faster than the fastest lion to avoid being eaten. Every morning in Africa, when the sun rises above the savannah, the lioness wakes up. She knows she must run faster than the slowest gazelle, or she will starve, and so will her cubs. Whether gazelle or lioness, when the sun rises, it's time to RUN to survive', or as I always say, "Movement is good."

Translated to the business world, this means two things. You must be faster or become faster in implementing ideas, improvements, or new products than others. You must also continuously drive change. Stopping is like standing still in the morning. Then you'll either be 'eaten' or 'starve'.

The Beginning of the Year

The year 2007 began, and the tasks for the lean transformation were now clearly defined. Not just by the team itself, but also by the parent company in Tomado near Detroit, which was now waiting for the implementation of the measures. 'Show us how it's done' was no longer an acceptable answer. Now it was time to 'do'. To achieve the goals this year, significant changes had to be made. This required changing entrenched, seemingly immutable processes and altering our own behavior. Old beliefs and thought patterns do not lead to new approaches and solutions. To support the team and provide it with security, the company was eagerly searching for a new Plant Manager. Also, the largest investment project in years – the automated production cell for gears – was in full swing. To meet customer demand, the old machines had to be stabilized in terms of their availability and output. My TPM project was more important than ever. It was a very busy and exciting starting point at the beginning of the year.

The Plant in the Bergisches Land

The search for a new Plant Manager concluded promisingly when a tall, young, dynamic Lean expert of Turkish descent was hired in January. Up to that point, he had been a Department Head for Strategic Projects at a car manufacturer in southern Germany. His drive and desire for change promised a whole new era for the management team. After a surprise promotion, I had already been part of this team since the end of 2006 and I had my hands full; however, my new boss immediately gave me additional tasks. My task with first priority now was to create a machine registry for the plant. The existing plant layout resembled a patchwork quilt.

Over the preceding 25 years, a modest number of innovations and investments had generally been implemented wherever free space was quickly available. Optimizing the material flow had never been a priority. As long as the processing time of the parts was shorter, the manufacturing world was in order. 'The little bit of transport is handled by interna logistics', was apparently always said. It felt like there were about a hundred isolated solutions across the plant. Although internally there was talk of only four 'flow lines', the associated machines and facilities were scattered throughout the entire plant. Production lines were more virtual than physically real flows. The flow pattern of the products, represented by lines in the layout, strongly resembled a tangled ball of yarn.

In a layout of the plant printed on A0, which displayed all facilities, the age of the machines was visualized using colors. Machines older than twelve years were marked in red, while yellow indicated those between eight and twelve years old. Green was for machines up to eight years old. After capturing the current state, the layout featured large red areas, several yellow zones, and only a few green areas. Our goal was to reduce the average machine age to eight years. This task was enormous, as were the numbers, as the current average age was eighteen years.

Discussions within the team about which machines should be replaced first and which later were nerve-wracking. Everyone had their own interests. Ideally, everything should have been replaced immediately, but the financial means were naturally not available. It ultimately required decisions about which machines should be replaced first, where new technologies could be introduced, and whether there were areas where cross-departmental synergies could be utilized. After all, the technology landscape had significantly advanced over the preceding 25 years. Stagnation is regression, and catching up requires a lot of effort and money.

To establish a basis for decision-making, we first prioritized the product lines. What are the 'bread-and-butter' products that generate profit for the plant and cover fixed costs well? Then we looked at the position of the machines in the value stream. Which machines were the bottlenecks, and were there alternatives? After creating a list that prioritized the machines to be replaced, we summed up the necessary investments for each year. The presentation of the required investments was done in the form of annual investment plans.

In parallel with the lists, we created a new layout for each year, offering a glimpse into the future. In the PowerPoint presentation, the seven pages appeared like a video, showing the development of the layout from 'red' to 'green'. After about six years and an investment of around €120 million, the layout would mostly be green. Wow, that's a substantial amount! People began to question the feasibility of this plan. Was it even realistic? Would the ÄÄtch Group provide this money? The Ugly Baby was apparently also a very expensive Ugly Baby!

As a team, we were still euphoric. This new boss created facts and described the actual situation without sugar-coating anything. It was the behavior we needed to not only develop our vision, but also implement it. This made our disappointment even greater when the era of this new manager came to an abrupt end after only eight weeks. An apparently unfortunate misunderstanding or incident between him and the HR Manager led to his immediate dismissal. We barely had time to take a farewell picture in his office when this episode was already history. The team, which had just moved into a state of awakening, did not understand this and was now unsettled again. Liam, the Chief Financial Officer (CFO) of HDA, temporarily took over the position of Plant Manager, while another position seemed to be planned for Ron, the Plant Manager from Slovakia, who had temporarily overseen us the previous year.

Liam was a calm, tall young man from southern Sweden with clear ideas about investments and financial conduct. He always had an open ear for suggestions from employees, and his way of dealing with them was factual, caring, and calming. It was exactly what the team sought after the turbulent changes of the preceding weeks and months. In everything he did, one could sense that he also wanted to effect change, but in a more measured way. However, he lacked experience in manufacturing or plant management, and he was not a Lean expert. He knew this, and so did we. Often, common sense is enough, and Liam had plenty of it! It was a compromise that the company made with his appointment.

After his personal introduction, he invited me and the Production Manager to a confidential meeting. He explained his ideas and emphasized his trust in our technical expertise. Liam saw himself as the CFO and team coach, while the two of us were the technical experts. The agreement was simple: if we needed investments or wanted to introduce changes in the process, we should agree and come to him together. If we convinced him of our ideas, he would procure the necessary funds. He knew the pathways and pots better than anyone else.

This cooperative approach proved extremely effective and worked well right from the beginning. Step by step, we advanced in transforming the plant. It wasn't fast, but nonetheless it still moved forward. We stabilized the company's production and output. After six months, the corporate management decided to confirm Liam permanently in the position. Now, a new CFO was being sought. There was another side effect for all managers. With this decision, the Plant Manager moved into the position of the Executive Board and reported directly to the European Manager. Thus, my colleagues in the management team and I suddenly found ourselves at level 5. Wow, only two years in the company and already two levels up! In Berlin, that had taken me twelve years.

In these eventful six months, further significant personnel decisions were made, not just for HDA. Some unannounced million-dollar deals by HDA, including the acquisition of a supplier and the property with halls, seemed to have been too much for the parent company. Although it clearly saved the company taxes, it was formally the profit of the ÄÄtch Group that had been invested in these actions and therefore could not be paid out to shareholders as dividends. As a consequence, the European Manager was replaced. His position was filled by Ron, the Plant Manager from Slovakia.

This decision proved to be a blessing for HDA, as he had previously coached and mentored us. He knew everyone on the team, was aware of our strengths and weaknesses, was familiar with the plant and its processes, and had a much deeper understanding of HDA's largest customer. This was the plant in Slovakia, to which a large portion of HDA's transmissions were delivered. Coaching with us now reached a higher level, also accompanied by other expectations of us. We felt supported and guided by him — we were, so to speak, his baby, even if it was still a very expensive Ugly Baby in transformation.

At this time, the first construction work began for the auto-mated gear line in our plant. This posed a significant challenge, as in a plant with manufacturing tolerances in the thousandth of a millimeter range, no dust could accumulate without compro-mising product quality. And this dust inevitably resulted from concrete work and in large quantities. A thousandth is, as previ-ously mentioned, quite small. Concrete dust is about thirty times larger than the manufacturing tolerances of the gears and housings. We were keenly aware that we had to meet many re-quirements to prevent a decline in quality.

As a team, we mastered this task brilliantly. We installed extrac-tion systems and worked with a lot of water during all concrete drilling and grinding work. We also took care of the machine ap-provals for the new cell and the implementation of the meticu-lous scheduling. The facilities had to be delivered and commis-sioned in a precisely defined order, as a result of their size. The crane always had to have sufficient maneuvering space. The support of the Design Department also proved crucial, as in some cases components had to be redesigned in the area of the end face. This was the only way we could ensure that produc-tion in the new system ran smoothly.

Anyone who has worked in production and tried to get changes to drawings from the Design Department, which are not directly related to the main function of the product, knows how chal-lenging it can be for a designer to make such drawing changes. In this particular case, it involved implementing a face groove and two mounting holes in the blanks to ensure that these com-ponents could be manufactured reliably and accurately in the grinding machine process. Thanks to dedicated collaboration,

71

everything pointed to an on-time and successful commissioning of the new system.

SMED

Another experience with the application of Lean tools brought me a friend in the company. At one of the machines, gear shafts were pre-milled before their final contour was created by turning and grinding. This machine was the bottleneck in the process. To achieve the required number of gear units, pre-milled blanks had to be purchased. HDA even used pre-casted blanks. This, of course, was expensive. At HDA, they tried to increase the output of the milling machine using traditional methods. Different tools, feeds, weekend overtime, and more. These measures brought marginal changes, but not the hoped-for breakthrough.

Marginal improvements are generally a good method. After all, Kaizens – small, one or multi-day projects, aimed at specific improvements – have exactly this goal within continuous improvement. However, Lean Manufacturing also has a desire for significant, large-scale improvements. These are called Kaikaku. This milling machine was to undergo such a Kaikaku. We didn't want 3% more, we wanted 15% more!

The production manager informed me of what he considered 'really bad news', and he meant it very seriously. Support from the USA was coming; a Green Belt named Amal with Indian roots. He said, "If support comes from the USA, we haven't done our job right." It sounded from his mouth like an accusation but also like an admission. Instead of recognizing the opportunity of this valuable help, the HDA team saw it as a threat. It revealed the fundamental problem – the refusal to accept outside help and to grant insights into processes because they feared becoming transparent. This detailed knowledge of the processes was considered the lifeline of the site. However, my experience taught me that sometimes that could at most be the ventilator that only keeps you alive for a while.

Here is a brief summary of SMED.

- The SMED technique[vi] was developed by Shigeo Shingo, a Japanese engineer and consultant for Toyota, in the 1950s and 1960s. The SMED method aims to minimize the time required to change over machines. Changeover times are the periods that arise between switching products on a machine. The method focuses clearly on distinguishing between internal and external changeover steps
- The term SMED stands for 'Single Minute Exchange of Die'. Shingo's primary goal was to reduce the changeover time of a machine to less than 10 minutes, i.e., to a single-digit value. Therefore, 'Single Minute'. It should be noted that this originally applied to press machines that manufactured fenders from steel sheets. Changeover traditionally took about 4 hours in companies, even in Japan. By applying the SMED technique, Toyota managed to drastically reduce changeover times, thus increasing production flexibility and reducing production costs
- The core idea behind the SMED technique is to improve the efficiency of setup and changeover operations by converting direct times into indirect times

- Direct times are those directly associated with the core process, i.e., the time needed to change or adjust a machine before it can produce again. These direct times cause the machine to stand still and produce no products. An example from motorsport is the tire change on a Formula One car. While the tire is being changed, the car cannot drive and stands still
- Indirect times, on the other hand, are those that can run in parallel with the core process without stopping the machine. This means that certain preparations and adjustments are made before the actual changeover, allowing the machine to run as long as possible and lose little time from stoppage. As a result, the changeover process can be faster and more efficient. The fitting example is preparing the spare tire and placing the screwdriver for the tire change. During this time, the race car is still on the track

By converting direct times into indirect times, machine downtime is minimized, and production time is maximized. It doesn't necessarily mean that the effort for changeover is reduced; it is just carried out at other times that are less critical. This was a conflict with HDA's thinking. Shorter changeover time had to mean less effort in their definition. This was not always the case with SMED and still led to a significant increase in productivity. You could produce more.

The parallel to the tire change here is this. Previously, during a pit stop, the 4 tires were changed one after the other; everything was 'direct time', with the person with the tool moving around the car. Today, 4 screwdrivers are provided for 4 mechanics while the racer is still driving, and only then does the car come into the pit. It costs more money but takes only a quarter of the time, and it is obviously worth it. What was once considered direct time is now indirect time. Previously, a pit stop took more than a minute as many necessary steps were only taken during the stop. Through parallel preparations, direct times were converted into indirect times, and the actual stop now takes only seconds. The race cars lose less time in the pit and can quickly return to the race. These differences often decide victory or defeat in a race.

Back to our project. Amal arrived. Nomen est omen, as 'Amal' means 'hope'. So, what could go wrong? We worked together on the milling machine and applied the SMED technique. There were a variety of ideas and suggestions during brainstorming sessions that we conducted directly at the milling machine with the operators. For example, we set up a Kanban system with a small supermarket for milling tools and procured tools for aligning the tools. In just two weeks, we achieved an impressive 20% reduction in machine downtime. We exceeded the goal.

Nevertheless, it was always a tough battle. Every idea with one-time costs was always questioned by the department head, who had internalized budget thinking, "Are we really saving the changeover time, or are we just shifting it from direct to indirect and spending money on it? This blows the budget!" Our hope was finally fulfilled. With combined efforts, we managed to significantly increase the output. Amal lived up to his name. Not only did Amal and I get along well professionally – we also harmonized personally.

When the weekend came, I wanted to do something with my wife, Amal, and his wife Aditi. However, my ex-boss was worried about such a close bond with Amal. Regardless, we decided to make the best of it. We went on trips to a lake, took a steam-boat ride, and dined together. On Sunday afternoon, my wife and Aditi said goodbye. Amal and I went to the sauna. His enthusiasm was evident, and he later assured me that he had never experienced and would never experience such infusions as in the Bergisches Land. He was particularly taken with the oil application during the infusion in the sauna. So, Lean not only brought the solution to problems, but also a valuable friendship.

One more Time: Develop People first!

Amid all these developments, we still had our regular business to handle – smaller projects and various other tasks concerning the staff. One employee in my department was an absolute specialist in programming the measuring machines that were used to gauge gear shafts, gears, and gearbox housings. He knew which points on the flanks of the gears and on the housings were critical, how to approach these points with sensitive sensors, and under what conditions the measuring machine, operating in the thousandths of a millimeter range, ran most reliably. He had Polish roots and spoke perfect German, but only a few words of English. Another branch of the ÄÄtch Group had a problem with an identical measuring machine in a plant in Cincinnati, Ohio. They asked us for weekly support teleconferences.

For several weeks, we conducted these conferences together. They described their problem, asked questions, Stanko responded, and I facilitated the meeting by translating; I was not the measuring machine expert! Eventually, the crucial question

76

came: could Stanko come to Ohio for a week, with paid compensation? I promised to check and inform them shortly. With the team and the former head of the department I discussed this idea. He was sceptical and seriously worried that Stanko might get lost or something might happen to him in the USA. Despite these concerns, I asked Stanko if he felt up to it. Of course, he said, "Yes." We informed the colleagues in Cincinnati, Ohio, of our decision and began the preparations: ESTA visa, flight bookings, and so on. The colleagues on-site were very happy and assured us they would pick Stanko up at the airport and bring him back.

In the penultimate teleconference, we learned that a sales employee in Cincinnati originally came from Switzerland and spoke German. Franz Frieh lived up to his name; he was so free and helped out as an interpreter. What can I say? The trip was a complete success, and more were to follow. Stanko visited the USA more often and learned quite a bit of English in the process. He had become a different person – more confident and prouder of his experiences. This was also reflected when a plant in China heard about how well Cincinnati was supported by HDA. It is very rare for a Chinese plant to request support, however Cangzhou now also wished for Stanko from Germany to help with their measuring machine problems.

When Stanko looked at me questioningly, I said, "You are a sought-after man, that's great. Enjoy it and make the most of it; we will cover your absence internally. It is also a success for HDA that we are asked to send employees around the world to help others with their problems." He looked at me questioningly not because he was unsure, but because he did not want to neglect his work. He was simply happy and travelled far and often, even to China – a wonderful development for him.

Lean

In our Lean transformation, we were now making some real progress. The Ugly Baby that described the current state had now become a plant in its first year of transformation. Now, something had to happen, in a positive sense. Ideally, not just a cosmetic operation, but actual streamlining measures! On the one hand, it was about implementing the written programs, and on the other, monitoring the metrics to see if they were moving in the desired direction, as a result of the measures taken. This was crucial for what the parent company wanted to see, "Show me the result, show me the money!" as often demanded by the Americans.

Quality indicators, machine availability, and thus production volumes were on the rise. Workplace safety was also showing a positive trend. However, there were other parameters like inventory and turnover frequency as well as delivery time and delivery reliability of important products, which hardly changed or even developed in the wrong direction. The higher quality and improved output led to an increase in order intake. This, in turn, initially extended delivery times and reduced delivery punctuality if you take the customer's desire as the basis. Although higher order intake was rather a luxury problem, the customer naturally felt dissatisfaction. The discussions internally and in teleconferences with the bosses from the USA became increasingly heated. Internally, people even spoke of 'barbecue meetings', where people got grilled. It was only funny for those who were not in the spotlight. Unfortunately, what did not happen was the consistent implementation of the investment plan to continuously rejuvenate the machinery. A few small machines were approved, but then no more. This made some people thoughtful and did not make the task easier.

During a coaching meeting, Ron explained to us that other plants had a so-called 'Green Cross' in the production areas. It served to visually represent hazards or, in the worst case, accidents involving employees. It was a monthly calendar in the shape of a cross. Every day without an accident was filled in with a green marker. If there was an incident, the day was red, and countermeasures had to be taken. This sounded simple to me. Putting a checkmark was not a huge effort, and the countermeasures had to be implemented in any case. After Ron's explanations, the team and Production Managers discussed where these crosses should be placed, who should update them, and agreed that the Works Council should be involved first. After the meeting, I went to my office, designed such a green cross in Excel, and immediately hung the printout on our board in the area of Industrial Engineering.

The next morning, I explained to the employees what it was about, why it was important, and asked them to maintain it for a while. For the first time, I said, "Don't ask, just do it!" Everyone immediately remembered their new freedoms. They agreed, supported by my good rapport with the Works Council, which also quickly approved it as a pilot project. Before his departure, I called Ron, the European Manager, that morning, showed it to him, and asked if that was how he had imagined it. He was amazed at the quick implementation of about twelve hours.

This was not only very quick for HDA standards but also in comparison to other plants. Later, I learned from colleagues that this little story shaped my nickname in the USA. They saw me as 'the fastest man in the Bergisches Land'. They did not know, of course, that I originally came from Berlin and also did decathlon! They found out later during visits to us, as a small magnet sign from Berlin with the text hung on my whiteboard in my office, 'Attention, you are leaving the American sector!'

In this phase, the play with my maintenance project (TPM) was relatively easy. I received the budget for maintenance, the work was carried out, and the machines could not help but produce more reliably. In my considerations, I added evaluations that showed the downtime of the machines per month and formed a table from it, where the worst-performing machines were at the top—the so-called 'Flop Ten'. Special measures were taken for these machines to move them into the non-critical area of the table. Success metrics were not only reduced downtime, but also MTTR (Mean Time To Repair), ie, the time until the machine runs again after a failure notification, and MTBF (Mean Time Between Failure), ie, the time until the next failure of the machine after a repair. This approach was very well received by both HDA and the Americans.

The development was closely monitored. The Global Vice President visited again towards the end of the year. Donald was known to be notorious for his questions, and he called it his 'Walk of Fire'. Normally, he did this with the levels above me, and it lasted up to an hour. Even experienced Plant Managers broke out in a sweat. Such a fire is just hot! He led them with questions in a targeted direction, and in the end, they could only accept and commit to a goal. This goal was very, very ambitious, more of a vision. No one should ever have to achieve this goal within that year; it was a kind of game. However, they were often reminded of their commitment at an appropriate time. For me, he had – more as a demonstration effect towards the other HDA colleagues – a 'light version' ready. He asked me a few questions on the topic block 'machines, repair metrics, and availabilities' without me having to commit to a goal. He just wanted to check if I had the knowledge ready, even in such situations. As I was deeply involved in the matter, all answers matched one hundred percent. He said something like, "I am delighted!" I later often heard this sentence from colleagues.

My Lean-Transformation

As if it were a test, just before his departure, he made me an offer; I could opt for an abbreviated version of the Lean Six-Sigma Black Belt training, as I was already performing similarly to a Black Belt in my current role and had some Lean experience. This offer greatly honored me. Typically, one earns a Green Belt first, gains experience, and completes two projects. Then, the Black Belt training starts with another two projects, and after two and a half years, certification is achieved. My training was to be completed within one year. Nevertheless, I asked what impact this might have on my career. I did not want to spend my future dealing with statistics and probabilities. His answer made my decision easy. If a technical position with international responsibility in Europe became available, there would be a good chance for me of being selected for it. This statement rounded off the offer, and I accepted.

Another significant realization crystallized within me during all these small and large projects; the faster changes occur, the more progress is made in continuous improvement. There is a cycle applied for changes, known as PDCA. The PDCA cycle stands for 'Plan-Do-Check-Act' and is a fundamental concept in Lean management used for the continuous improvement of processes. The faster this cycle turns, the quicker our car metaphorically drives up the road of improvement, transforming the organization. It is not the right approach to search endlessly for the perfect solution. If I can achieve eighty percent of the goal in just twenty percent of the time, I already gain an advantage when planning the next steps in the right direction. After two not perfect but quick rounds, I have already achieved ninety-six percent. Both change and speed are crucial components of successful management. The old saying 'don't let the perfect be the enemy of the good' applied, and still applies!

My interest in Lean and the courage to try new things on a small scale paid off. Compared to other colleagues in the company, I was one of those experienced with Lean tools and increasingly eager to apply them. For me there wasn't the production pressure that my colleagues on the shop floor faced. That was certainly a significant advantage for me. I had learned what a SMED event is and how it works, I had implemented 5S in my department and handed it over to the employees as a continuous process, and TPM had also been started. My personal Lean transformation took a turn with this special offer of Black Belt training. Until now, I had gained experience with Lean tools in a zigzag course on my own – as situations demanded. Now, all the target buoys were strung together like pearls, and I received an event card: 'Pass Go and collect your Lean toolbox!'

In the coming year, I was to participate in extensive training at various locations in Italy, southern Germany, and at our site, each in week-long blocks. Of course, this would have enormous impacts on managing my department and the HDA projects. I initially discussed the upcoming training with my boss. Liam was the first to recognize the many opportunities this training presented for the site and agreed on the condition that I would work as a Black Belt for HDA for two years afterward. In all honesty, he had no chance to oppose Donald's proposal. We had a deal, and I had goals for the coming year that would help me achieve my bonus and steer my professional future in new directions.

A new Island

In May, we took a vacation to Tenerife for a change. Our goal was to explore another island of the Canaries. We wanted to discover something new and explore the green side of Tenerife. Not the side where sunburned, pot-bellied, red-skinned people from another island drank beer and roared loudly. Away from the hotel complexes and the well-known beaches, we booked a finca in the quiet bay of Masca. The space in such a narrow gorge is very limited, and the roads and paths are steep. Therefore, we had to park our small rental car on the roof of another house. Fortunately, there was no parking space on the roof of our vacation house!

The island revealed its impressive and green side to us, inviting us to extensive hikes. The finca we chose was located in a dreamy, secluded, and peaceful spot, providing us the perfect escape from our hectic daily routine. However, our tranquility in this valley was briefly disturbed on a Sunday morning by squealing tires and roaring engines that woke us up. A rally was taking place through the curves and switchbacks of the gorge. By noon, the circus was over, and as a result, some damaged guardrails had to be replaced. Nevertheless, we enjoyed this vacation to the fullest and returned refreshed.

A new Home

On my drives to the airport in July, I saw the blooming summer lilac for the third time. We realized that commuting should come to an end in a year. However, my prospects in the company were promising, and the job market in Berlin had not significantly improved. So, we decided to keep the second residence. We were, so to speak, going into overtime. This meant we required a long-term solution for my living situation. The furnished Chippendale apartment was quite small, and we had no chance to bring in our personal cozy style. My wife suggested buying our own apartment. Although I was initially hesitant, I soon realized that it was the only right decision. Instead of rent, we would pay a small maintenance fee and have the chance to get money back at the end of the commuting era.

It was astonishing how quickly my wife found a suitable property in the small local ads of our town – a charming fifty-square-meter apartment on the edge of the city. The house had a ground floor and a first floor. The apartment was upstairs. There were only six units in the building. A shared garden was also available. We did not haggle much and bought the apartment immediately. We first completed some renovation work. Then, we worked together to beautify and furnish the apartment with a new kitchen and some selected pieces of furniture.

After I had cleaned and painted the two basement rooms that belonged to my apartment, I drove to Berlin to fetch my fitness equipment by car. In the basement I set up a small fitness area. The apartment soon felt more like a cozy home, and I enjoyed that the small center was only a kilometer away. Not only were the shopping facilities close, but also green, park-like belts stretched through this area. Several times a week, my running route began right at my door and took me through green spaces, past meadows and woods with gentle hills, over small side streets, then back to my apartment, followed by a nice bath – a perfect end to the workday.

Surprising Year-End

The entire company was doing brilliantly worldwide, almost too brilliantly. The company's account held about $16 billion. This posed the risk of becoming a takeover candidate. If an investor bought the ÄÄtch Group, after the breakup of the conglomerate and the sale of individual divisions, these sixteen billion would be left over, at least! Shortly before the end of the year, there was also a press release from the USA in the ÄÄtch-News and reports in the business sections of some magazines. A major takeover deal between two American companies was announced. We, the ÄÄtch Group, had now acquired a company.

Our management had gone Christmas shopping just before the holidays.

For more than $14 billion, the American automatic transmission manufacturer ZUAG Company was bought. The ZUAG Company had achieved sales of around $8 billion with 32,000 employees in the current year, compared to nine billion US Dollars for the ÄÄtch Group. The combined group's sales would be $17 billion in 2008. Together, the two corporations employ more than 68,000 people in approximately 120 plants worldwide. Synergy savings were calculated at around $350 million annually. The integration of this business field would prove to be a significant challenge for everyone in the coming months.

Familiar Year-End

Although we had a wonderful time on the island of Tenerife in May, our winter vacation led us back to La Palma. This small island had taken a special place in our hearts, and offered us an oasis of tranquility every time. With so much hustle and bustle, travel activities, and new experiences throughout the year, we found it very pleasant to have a fixed point for the year's end that guaranteed us relaxation besides our home. And this island provided just that. We now knew our way around, knew where the roads, hiking trails, restaurants, and facilities were. Once a year, we hiked up a mountain called Pico Beyenado. It was 1,860 meters high, and the view of the Cumbrecita and the Caldera was always a great experience.

The Cumbrecita on La Palma is an impressive crater rim in the Caldera de Taburiente. This natural formation offers breathtaking views of the surrounding mountain ranges and the national park. The caldera itself is a massive crater surrounded by green slopes and steep rock walls. A paradise for hikers, with unique landscapes and diverse flora. Definitely a place that impressively reflects the beauty of La Palma!

The hike lasted a total of six hours. It was at times sweat-inducing and in many ways breathtaking. We enjoyed the time in this enchanting environment and were once again captivated by the island's beauty.

2008

> 'Go to Gemba' if you want to identify problems and are interested in solving them! Gemba walks are a crucial element of Lean practices, significantly aiding in the detection of deviations from the normal state in work areas. The term 'Gemba' is Japanese, meaning 'the real place' or 'workplace'. During a Gemba walk, leaders, managers, or other employees go directly to the site of action, where the actual work and value creation for the customer take place. So, leave your desk, leave your office!

The Beginning of the Year

Refreshed and full of enthusiasm, I embarked upon 2008, which undoubtedly promised some changes. At HDA, we were already in the second year of transformation with the factory. The second major challenge was to successfully commission the new automated gear line. In addition to these tasks, my Black Belt training and the two associated certification projects were also on my agenda.

Lean

The weeks of my training in various ocations flew by, and I delved deeper into the fascinating world of Lean management. This demanding yet highly varied phase was characterized by expanding knowledge, acquiring new skills, experiences with new tools from the Lean toolbox, and building new contacts. Each of us in this training was considered a 'high potential', otherwise the company wouldn't have invested in us. At 51, I stood out a bit and was considered something of a 'senior high potential', as most in the class were significantly younger. One thing was clear; in the future, we would all take on different roles within the ÄÄtch Group. We pledged to support each other in this future, regardless of the position we would be in. Thus, a very interesting network began to emerge. Sometimes we would simply meet at meetings, conferences, or other trainings at the ÄÄtch University in Prague (yes, the company had that, too). The training at various locations in Europe provided me with comprehensive insight into the problems of others, as well as how these problems were solved there. The exchange of experiences with like-minded individuals at other ÄÄtch Group locations was invaluable. The discussions we had during this time were on equal terms. The myriad possibilities that Lean management offered thrilled me. I no longer had to decide to apply this knowledge – it was now expected of all of us. However, at this point, I already knew that my working life in future would not be limited to HDA.

The Plant in the Bergisches Land

Already in the first year of the transformation, it became clear that the plan for conversion of the plant into a Lean factory was stalling in some segments. Nevertheless, we had reached the desired metrics in a few categories. Based on these parameters, a deliberate competition took place between the plants. In this internal ranking of Operational Excellence, we had laboriously worked our way into the upper half. It was a small success considering where we started from. However, a large plant like

HDA was expected to achieve more. In Lean, every gear meshes with the other, and for us, the gearbox manufacturer, there was a grinding in the gears. The challenge now was to clean the gears causing the grinding while the operation was still running.

There were issues in materials management. We observed the stagnant metrics of turnover rate and missing parts. So many times, in connection with Kanban and Supermarkets, I had heard the phrase from colleagues, "Show us how it's done, then we'll do it!" My hope that they would figure it out themselves had by now evaporated. Now suddenly, there was a chance to introduce such a system for gears. Liam announced that we would be getting a young man from Italy for six months; his name was Fabio. He was a participant in the Accelerated Development Program (ADP) and was still looking for a project for his Green Belt training. A brief explanation of the ADP process:

> An *Accelerated Development Program (ADP)* refers to an expedited development process for young people. It aims to prepare young talents specifically and intensively for leadership positions. In this process, promising young talents have the opportunity to gain a wide range of experiences and skills in a fairly short period to prepare them for more challenging positions within the company. This can be achieved through rotations in various departments and countries, specialized training, mentorship programs, and targeted projects.

I immediately suggested to Liam the topic 'Kanban and Supermarket for gears from the small gear manufacturing cell'. This was the area with high volume, frequent missing parts, and consequently, low turnover rate of materials. Liam liked the idea and suggested it to the Supply Chain Manager. He had always wanted us to show him how it's done; now we would do just that. Fabio would work in his department and be guided by me; he still had no idea how to proceed with this topic, yet he wanted to take credit for the success under his leadership. For him, the question was relevant; what's the correct saying? 'Let me work or let I work?' Both are wrong; 'Let others work!' Insofar as it related to him, that was the correct answer.

And so, Fabio analyzed the range of parts, the batch sizes of production and assembly, the lead times, the required safety stock, essentially everything needed to introduce Kanban and a Supermarket. Then we had an overview of how much space we would need and started with layout designs of the Kanban-controlled Supermarket, which would operate on the FiFo principle.

> *The FiFo principle* stands for First In, First Out and is a method of inventory management. In a FiFo system, the oldest inventory is used or sold first to ensure that products do not become obsolete or spoil. This process should occur without crossing or returning material flows, a key principle of flow design.

The available space for the Supermarket was ideal, directly adjacent to the gear line where the parts were manufactured. The operators of the cell already pushed the loaded carts into this area, but not sorted as we intended. So, there would be no additional transportation required. We knew the number of different parts and thus how big the Kanban board would need to be, and we also knew the trigger points for reproducing the gears.

As a result of this Green Belt work, we had a Supermarket area with aisles for withdrawing gears and empty carts, with rows operating on the FiFo principle and labelled with types. We introduced visual markings for production. Everyone could see whether the reorder level was approaching or had already been reached. They could see it on the floor, and on the large Kanban board; they could see details about it. To make it clear to the employees that the Kanban cards they booked when withdrawing had a monetary-like function, we placed a payback sign above the barcode reader, similar to in a Supermarket. The Kanban cards were sequentially numbered and signed, like banknotes. The Kanban board also had specific zones in traffic light colors for each gear. If the cards were in the green zone, production could decide to produce a batch. If a card was in the yellow zone, they had to start producing that product within 24 hours. If a card landed in the red zone, they had to inform the supervisor immediately. In the first few weeks, the process was audited daily. Errors in implementation were eliminated through explanations or actions.

It was a great system that led to a 35% reduction in inventory and reduced missing parts situations for assembly by 95%. Now we had explained it, installed it, and demonstrated it! However, behind closed doors, you could hear phrases like, "That's all well and good, but I am the Production Scheduler and I dictate the orders!" Well, if something is important to you, you'll find a way; if it's not, you'll find an excuse.

It wasn't just us; it was grinding at many sites of the ÄÄtch Group. So, the rumor soon spread that the headquarters in Tomado was working on a new program to accelerate the transformation process. It was supposed to be called 'Lean

Accelerator'. This process would last six weeks in each plant and enable a significant step toward Lean Manufacturing and Operational Excellence in specific areas of production. This goal was to be achieved through daily project work over the entire six-week period, with all the support available.

It surprised no one that Toddville in Ohio was slated to be the first plant to undergo this initiative – after all, it was only about forty miles from the company headquarters in Tomado and couldn't evade such programs. The responsible parties – primarily Donald, my sponsor – mobilized all available resources of experts from the headquarters in Tomado and neighboring plants. I was also invited to participate. With my experiences, I was to subsequently co-lead this process at HDA over the course of the year, with two colleagues taking turns.

However, before it was our turn, the plant had to tackle a major challenge: getting the new automated gear line with the portal robot up and running. After several postponements, it finally happened in late spring; the first large gears went through the system. I have spoken about this cell many times before. Let me briefly illustrate the effect of the system to you. In the previous manufacturing, gear production consisted of five process steps. These were turning the blanks, rough milling of the profiles, grinding the outer diameter, finish grinding the profile, deburring and washing the finished gears. Typically, a batch size of 12 to 24 pieces was set. Without manual intervention in the sequence at the machines, it took about a week for such a batch to be completed through all the machines. This was mainly as a result of the waiting times in front of the machines, as they were never immediately available, and the material often lay unused, waiting for transport, and of course, as a result of the machine changeover times.

In the new gear line, a linear robot took over the transportation, with a maximum of two different batches in circulation. Once the last piece of a batch was manufactured at the machine, it was retooled. The other machines continued operating during this time. Within just 24 hours, a batch was completely processed and ready for assembly. This resulted in saving a whole four days of lead time! As an added bonus, the pure processing times were on average 20% lower.

It was impressive to see how confidently the linear robot, supplying the five machines arranged in a line with gears, grasped the various (up to 100 kilograms) heavy parts, and the speed and precision with which it delivered them to the clamping system of the machine. Of course, there were teething problems in the system, but fortunately these were mostly minor issues and corrections. The key criterion was the progress in the performance of the system. Unfortunately, there were also hiccups here. The development did not pick up the desired speed, and America pushed for a WAR (With All Resources) to be conducted to accelerate the ramp-up of the system. We explained to them that using the abbreviation WAR, which translates to 'war' in German, was not a good idea in a German context, so instead suggested a High Impact Team (HIT). Fortunately, they understood the reasoning behind this proposal, and so it became a HIT, even though it wasn't a record but rather a line. Liam chose me as the Leader and Moderator of the team.

The daily agenda for the meeting at the machine followed the PDCA (Plan, Do, Check, Adjust) principle, as follows:

- Review of the plan from the previous day and the quantities achieve
- Identification of possible deviations and development of countermeasures
- Determination of the plan for the next day and review of the preparations for it
- Exchange of hints and ideas
- Status of the implementation of ideas

To attract special attention, I ordered a ship's bell from purchasing, which I rang promptly at 9.30 every morning. The ringing sound echoed throughout the entire factory hall, and the purchasing department's comment was, "No one has ever ordered a ship's bell here, let alone received one." My response to that was, "You have to change things. There's always a first time!"

We were at the scene, Gemba. Through our agenda, we were able to identify problems, because there was a plan from the previous day and there was reality. Any deviation from the plan was a problem. We first asked the employees for their ideas, and then throughout the HIT, we received daily hints from them. The fact that these hints were taken seriously and addressed by management gave them the confidence to openly share their thoughts with us. The Works Council was initially somewhat displeased because every idea from the employees was supposed to go through the 'committees' and be evaluated, which was a very cumbersome process. We didn't have that time. The Works Council did eventually understand that and let the PDCA wheel continue its rapid rounds.

Gradually, the performance of the gear line improved. It was about time because in June, I was scheduled to travel to the USA to participate in the Lean Accelerator at the Toddville plant and to take away as much as possible from this process, as well as from what was implemented. It would be my third trip to this plant and lead me to experiences that we could make very good use of at HDA, just a few weeks later.

Toddville, USA

The colleagues at HDA had been right about many of their concerns regarding this site. This I had already noticed during my second trip to this plant. Toddville lagged behind in terms of quality, overall process understanding, and the sustainability of implemented measures. There, often only superficial changes were made that did not endure. The products manufactured there did not have the tight tolerances that we could achieve at HDA. We were different from Toddville, and this should remain the case in the future. A key experience for me was a question from an American colleague from Industrial Engineering, "How do you manage to have newly hired machine operators for grinding machines understand their functionality so quickly and operate the machines alone?" My answer was, "We only hire trained grinders, and training in Germany takes three years." His response gave me confidence that this plant, this country, and this system would not pose a short-term threat to HDA. He said, "We don't have specialized training for grinders. We hire people who feel capable of handling the task. Unfortunately, this often goes wrong. Besides, employees with a three-year education are way too expensive. That would drive up production costs."

Up to that point, I couldn't have imagined that people in responsible positions could think in such a short-term way. The underlying idea of the American Dream was 'from dish-washer to millionaire'. Anyone can do anything and become a millionaire regardless of their social status and education. Even actors and peanut farmers can become President of the United States. Social ascent is possible for everyone. It can also go wrong. Not everyone achieves what they think they can.

Yet the Lean Accelerator was supposed to quickly change everything for the better. That was management's plan. What I experienced there was essentially a flood of the plant with experts, new ideas, and projects within a very short time. There was hardly any room for testing and reflecting on changes. The presence of Black Belts, Green Belts, Presidents, Vice Presidents, and Regional Managers of all kinds was overwhelming. Essentially, it seemed that all parts of the headquarters related to Lean, Manufacturing, Procurement, or Quality had been relocated to the plant. Anyone who wasn't at the top of their game had to go to Toddville. Much else fell by the wayside. Actually, I felt a little sorry for the employees in the plant's production. Nevertheless, or maybe because of that, the progress made did not meet management's expectations. So, the whole thing was extended by two weeks. An immense effort and outlay in personnel, when you add everything up.

I was there for a week and could only gather a small part of the possible experiences. However, I left with the firm decision to approach things at HDA in a much more sustainable manner. My confidence was high that this would succeed, as we had no fear that the entire headquarters with all he VIPs from Tomado would fly in to the Bergisches Land. In that respect, we had control over how much chaos and hustle we would spread.

Additionally, I decided not to invite any external participants for duck hunting. I had declined in Toddville as well and instead went out on Lake Erie with another colleague on his boat. Wakeboarding was more preferable to me than shooting ducks.

The Plant in the Bergisches Land

One of the tasks in preparation for the Lean Accelerator was to design a project banner. Other sites chose their products and elements from the Lean field for their banners. Our choice was to depict an ICE train in connection with a gear profile, accompanied by the text 'Lean Accelerator'. The entire design was kept in our company colors of red and white.

Many, including ourselves in the end, wondered why we chose an ICE train. Well, firstly, the ICE was one of the fastest means of transportation, and furthermore, at HDA, we manufactured the parts that caused the train to release its brakes. It was only through our technology that the ICE could achieve its impressive speed. This connection to the term 'Accelerator' was simply perfect for us.

Parallel to all this, my training began, and I started the Black Belt projects that I would need for certification in the end. The topics of my projects were, of course, 'TPM' and 'internal logistics of material provision'. Much of the training material would flow into these projects; that was the goal. The first two weeks of training took place at HDA, followed by other locations near Imola in Italy and then again in southern Germany on the edge of the Black Forest. One of the course participants was Rick, formerly the Gear Department Manager in Toddville. He and I knew each other from my visits to Toddville in preceding years. Originally from Manchester, he had left his football career behind at Bolton Wanderers. As a young man I had also played football in the third league in Berlin and continued to jog regularly. We were both still in top athletic shape, which gave us a common bond.

A special part of the training program was that I had to pass on my newly acquired knowledge as a trainer to a group of future Green Belts. This group was extremely diverse, consisting of participants from both home and abroad. At that time, the principle in the company was: 'If you want to advance in the company, you have to go through a Belt training programme!' And here we were. On the one hand, there was me, passing on my new knowledge, and on the other hand, there was the class of young people who still had a long professional future ahead of them and wanted to get their Green Belt. Among the participants was Ann-Marie, the HR Manager for Europe. We knew each other from some meetings at HDA, as well as from the first Belt trainings. The first two weeks had the same content for both Green and Black Belts, so it became a joint event.

The content of the training was very diverse, and we also did some fun exercises. Once, we sat and lay on the floor shooting lightweight plastic balls through the conference room with small catapults to determine dispersion characteristics and the influence of various factors. Nevertheless, there was a lot of dry statistics involved, and I secretly hoped that I wouldn't have to deal with it too much later on. However, a major advantage was that I could already apply the newly learned knowledge to my work at HDA and in preparation for the Lean Accelerator. My two projects on the TPM concept and the internal logistics from the warehouse to the workplace benefited from this.

In the fall, it was time. After the Lean Accelerator weeks in Toddville and Italy were completed, we started in the Bergisches Land. Of course, we didn't have the same support as the plant in the USA. Thank goodness! No one travelled from America. Nevertheless, we had to report on various projects daily. We had an internal report-out in German, and conference calls with the USA twice a week.

Before the Accelerator, we conducted extensive basic training for the employees to ensure they were we l-prepared for the event. In addition to Lean basics, 5S training and practical exercises were conducted. This officially kicked off the event and initially laid the foundation for a clean, organized, and efficient work environment. Each workstation was thoroughly analyzed, cleaned up, and unnecessary items were removed. The necessary tools and materials were arranged neatly and easily accessible. This was visually supported by floor markings or shadow boards - not everyone may know what a shadow board is:

- The Shadow Board is a facility for organizing tools, as well as measuring instruments and other aids required to perform activities at a workplace. Each item has its place on the board, which can be identified by the outlines, or the shadow, of the tool. Anyone passing by can see at a glance whether, how many, and which tools are in use, or whether they are missing at the end of the workday

- As the tools are not stored in drawers but in labelled or pictorially marked places, the time-consuming search is eliminated. The rule is: everything has its place, and a place for everything. This also reduces the loss of tools. Furthermore, order promotes safety in the workplace as nothing is left unsecured that could accidentally fall. It was amazing to see how much these seemingly small changes initially improved the visual impression of the workstations, then productivity, and finally workflow

We divided into different groups to work on various aspects targeted and in parallel. One team focused intensely on workplace design and material flow in the workshop. Here we relied on spaghetti diagrams to visualize movements and create more efficient processes.

- The spaghetti diagram (spaghetti chart) is used to visualize workflows and material flows
- The movements of the employees are depicted as lines between the various positions of the workstation. Using the spaghetti diagram, transport routes and employee movements can be visualized. It facilitates identifying these types of waste and serves as a basis for improvements
- After documenting all movements, the sheet often looks like a plate of spaghetti, hence the name. It was great that parts of my second Black Belt project could be implemented here. Close collaboration with the team enabled us to quickly implement change requests and new ideas—a real win-win situation for the site and for me

Another team focused on optimal and timely material presentation at workstations. By delivering smaller quantities more frequently with a so-called small train, we were able to reduce the space requirement at the workstations. Here, Lean principles such as 'Frequency and Magnitude' as well as 'Pull' and 'Supermarket' played decisive roles in making material supply more efficient.

In a nutshell, a 'small train' refers to a method of material provision. Materials are preassembled in small quantities and loaded onto trailers, which are then assembled into a train that travels past workstations, delivering the materials according to a set schedule. Simultaneously, the train retrieves empty containers. The materials are divided into time slots, called patches, to ensure that only minimal quantities of material are stored at workstations, minimizing space requirements. This approach aims to achieve nearly continuous provision, ideally delivering only the amount needed at the time of demand, aligning with the Just-in-Time philosophy to reduce waste.

Regardless of the solution devised, it always starts with the employees. 'Develop people first, empower the people'. This approach is vital for fostering empowerment, granting employees the freedoms needed to implement ideas. For instance, consider the material provision process from the warehouse to manufacturing. Initially, the process relied on paper orders placed in a box, emptied by warehouse staff at the end of the day. The next day, orders were retrieved from the high-shelf warehouse and delivered to workstations. However, this often took too long, resulting in materials arriving late. To address this, a board was introduced, dividing the working week into five-day and four-hour segments. This allowed manufacturing supervisors to request materials with a four-hour precision, and with a 24-hour lead time. Despite this improvement, discussions arose among stakeholders. Some claimed that orders weren't placed on the board in time, while others argued that the warehouse didn't process requests promptly.

To overcome this mistrust and build trust, it was crucial to thoroughly document the process at the interface to prevent disputes. Once the realistic 24-hour lead time for the warehouse was confirmed, autonomy was granted. The next day, they agreed on a stamp clock. Each material request was time-stamped before being placed on the board. This clarity restored trust gradually. Furthermore, by allowing them the freedom to implement their own solution without suggesting one, they had the chance to devise a unique solution.

Each team focused on visualizing information and statuses in the workplace. Red-green signals were introduced to indicate the current status of the cell at a glance. Additionally, green pylons were introduced to signal transport, while a red pylon indicated a quality issue that needed to be addressed. Yellow pylons signalled that material was required for the next production batch.

Through close collaboration and exchange among the three teams, many changes were implemented, driving the Lean process forward in the factory. This continuous improvement culture empowered every individual to take responsibility for the quality of their work. Ultimately, understanding that it's the customer who pays the employees underscored the importance of customer satisfaction and the role of each employee as a small entrepreneur within the larger production chain.

My Lean-Transformation

At the end of the year, I had to take the final exam for the Lean Six Sigma Black Belt certification. The exam took place in December, and we worked on it as a team. In the end, we all received our certificates and were happy about our achievements. Unfortunately, my supporter in the USA, who had offered me this special opportunity, had to leave the company at short notice. Apparently, his decisions regarding the Lean Accelerator in Toddville and the resulting costs were not entirely in line with the company's philosophy. Donald was now Roger. In three and a half years, I had witnessed three Global Vice Presidents. It's a position in which I wouldn't wish to find myself.

Even though he was no longer with the company, I called him, thanked him once again, wished him a happy holiday season, and shared my successful completion with him. In just ten months, I had successfully completed the entire process and finished two projects. Now I had redeemed my event card and held a Lean Six Sigma Black Belt certificate, my ticket to another level, in one hand. In the other, I had the Lean toolbox. Donald was very happy for me.

Sometimes, things really move fast at the ÄÄtch Group. Material presentation at the workplace, a small train for provision, 5S, the principle of 'Frequency and Magnitude', TPM – I could test or deepen everything. And it always came down to people who had to do all this, ideally wanted to do it. Involving them is an indispensable necessity for managing, which means 'improving'.

In conclusion, it's worth noting that the best strategy is worthless if nobody implements it. At the same time, it's not productive to implement isolated measures without having an overarching strategy. You need the ideas and commitment of the employees, and for that you need a clear strategy. Without one of them, nothing remains in the end! Zero times a hundred and a hundred times zero yield the same result: zero.

What else happened

In the summer, it happened again. During train rides, I saw the purple lilac for the fourth time. Three years had passed, and I was sure it wouldn't be the last bloom I saw during train rides. After all, I hadn't had my own apartment for very long, and the prospects at the company were getting better and better. With all the projects and training, the year flew by for me, in more ways than one. I had completed over a hundred flights – the training events in Europe, trips to America, La Palma, and every week to Berlin and back. Slowly, I began to make contacts with others at the gates, who, like me, stood there every week. Often, we sat next to each other on the plane. Eventually, we started to arrange meetings. The circle of acquaintances had expanded, yet the commuting remained.

2009

'Invert the Triangle' is a term often close y associated with the reversal of the traditional corporate hierarchy. Yet, at its core, it is about empowering employees to become co-creators. They are most familiar with the processes, know their weaknesses, and possess the best ideas for improvement. Understanding their thoughts and proposed solutions is invaluable. It's also referred to as 'using the brain of the factory'. During Gemba Walks, they should not only ask their employees for ideas, but also encourage them to ask their colleagues in production for their suggestions. The end goal comes closer when the Gemba Walk is used to discuss ideas already proposed by employees on a board. Then, they can hold their managers accountable for supporting employees in implementation. The manager becomes a servant leader, aiding the employee in conducting their own Kaizens. This might be unfamiliar for some. However, it's also part of 'Invert the Triangle'.

The Beginning of the Year

Once again, we returned refreshed and rejuvenated from our favorite vacation island. As early as autumn 2008, it became apparent that the year 2009 would bring some changes once again. Both of us were eager and excited about what was to come. In order to work wholeheartedly as a certified Black Belt for HDA, I had to relinquish my traditional leadership position. It was the first time since 1985 that I wouldn't have any personnel responsibilities. A Lean consultant and friend had once told me during an evening gathering, "The true leader isn't the manager with their employees, but the coach who has no employees and must convince team members of everything they want to achieve." My perception of career and influence began to shift. I was now facing this exciting challenge head-on.

The Plant in the Bergisches Land

When my vacated position was to be filled anew, I had the intention to participate in the selection process. My idea was to be part of the decision to appoint the future employee with whom I would be discussing projects in the Bergisches Land in the future. However, the HR Department had a different idea. They took the easy way out. My former boss regained my position. He was the one who had concerns about Stanko's travel activities and didn't want me to go to the sauna with Amal. Searching for the reason behind this decision, I adopted an 'oh well' attitude. That's life, I thought to myself. In any case, my focus was on my new role.

At the same time, the plant was struggling with a growing backlog of orders for high-quality gearboxes. This meant very long lead times for customers. The sales department was the first to feel the discontent, followed by HDA as the supplier. These gearboxes generated high margins for the site and were of immense importance to the Slovakian plant of the ÄÄtch Group in Brezno. Here, a €10,000 gearbox was used to build a €300,000 station, with the gearbox being the centerpiece of the entire unit. To put it in everyday terms; HDA provided the engine, and Brezno turned it into a car. However, HDA was in a dilemma.

They could sell a gearbox to the ÄÄtch Group's sister plant in Brezno with a pre-agreed profit margin of 10%, or they could sell the product to external customers outside the ÄÄtch Group with a significantly higher margin. While the latter option was much more attractive for the site, it also meant Brezno would generate €300,000 less in revenue with each gearbox.

Resolving this conflict, drastically reducing lead times, and increasing capacity became my first Black Belt project for HDA and for the ÄÄtch Group. We had weekly conference calls with the USA and Brussels, with Liam providing strong support, and we truly functioned as a team. Together with Product Management, Marketing, Sales, and Manufacturing, we analyzed the reasons for the backlog, developed appropriate measures, and discussed possible organizational changes. In close collaboration with sales, we also defined new standards for the products, set minimum stock levels for specific products, and worked on reducing the internal lead time of the gearboxes. To achieve this, we utilized value stream mapping.

First, let me explain briefly:

- The first crucial step involves an in-depth analysis of the current state. Initially, the customer pace is precisely determined. To illustrate, let's consider a highly simplified example. Suppose the customer desires:
  ⇒ 200 parts per month, with 20 working days and one shift of 480 minutes each. This leads to an expectation of
  ⇒ 10 parts per day in 480 minutes. Thus, the takt time (customer pace) amounts to
  ⇒ 480 minutes/10 parts = 48 minutes per part.

⇒ Next, we analyze the duration of each process step. If they are shorter than the customer pace, they can meet the demand. On the other hand, any step taking longer becomes a bottleneck. Therefore, an extremely thorough examination of all processes is crucial. We asked questions about cycle time, setup time, machine availability, batch size, inventory levels, and much more for each step in the product manufacturing process. The goal was to understand how much time and resources were actually available for our product at each workstation.

Of course, this simplified calculation doesn't apply in a complex manufacturing operation. You have multiple product lines that may pass through the same workstations. You might have different shift models, and facility availability can vary. All of these factors influence the available time for 'our' product.

This was my first project after the rapid Black Belt training. As at the beginning of my employment at HDA, I aimed to ensure that the first shot hit the mark. With great care, we created a comprehensive overview of all workstations, their working times, availabilities, and all factors as described above. Although it wasn't initially intended, I documented all data in an Excel file and linked processes using formulas. This technical refinement allowed me to calculate various scenarios online and identify bottlenecks in real-time. Thus, I remained one step ahead and could provide precise forecasts. Suddenly, I possessed an extremely detailed understanding of the complex interconnections in manufacturing this product line. Through this detailed value stream analysis, we quickly identified the process steps whose cycle times exceeded the customer pace and focused on gradually optimizing them.

The success wasn't solely driven by the great ideas of managers in our weekly meetings. Around forty dedicated employees were involved in producing this product line. Forty employees have forty times more ideas than one employee. Moreover, nobody knows the process and its problems and potentials better than the colleagues who execute it, so we involved them closely. Some were familiar with this form of participation from the project with the ship bell the year before. The bell couldn't be overlooked in the plant. It took some time to break the ice and overcome the mistrust, but then the ideas flowed.

We implemented whatever was feasible. Every bottleneck was attacked. A new one always emerged, yet at a higher level. That was the goal of continuous improvement. The PDCA cycle spun quickly to ascend as swiftly as possible with our change mobile. Increase production volume, decrease lead times – those were the core objectives. PDCA was the engine; the dashboards in manufacturing were the gauges. Eventually, we realized that the magic triangle had shifted. Employees had ideas, I took care of the implementation in their interest, and also had massive support from Liam, my boss, while he handled anything related to sales or finance.

Now, the Lean principle, 'Invert the triangle', had worked excellently in my first Black Belt project. Step by step, we reduced the backlog. In the weekly conferences, we could now present results, not just the next actions. It was an extremely successful project that propelled HDA into the upper quartile of productivity. Liam was beaming from ear to ear – and not only when his boss came and congratulated him on what had been achieved. It was simply joyful to see how we had managed to eliminate the problem.

The second Project

When our executives in the USA acquired ZUAG Company at the end of 2007, everyone understood the magnitude of the integration challenge (well, perhaps not everyone). ZUAG Company's products were comparable in quality to the highest-quality products of HDA. Here too, there were manufacturing tolerances in the thousandths of an inch. Initially, after the takeover, everything continued as usual with the operations, and the initial integration efforts focused on the IT side. However, efforts to achieve synergy improvements, estimated at $350 million annually, began.

It turned out that the long-established site in Colorado Springs, USA, was to be closed. Production was to be shifted to Toddville, the darling of the parent company. However, simply moving the USA machines from Colorado to Toddville would have compromised the quality and reputation of these products, if not completely destroyed them. Because Toddville was known for one thing: they could do everything, but without stable quality! It's no wonder the plant had been called 'Shoddville' by HDA colleagues. This sparked an outcry at ZUAG Company in the USA and also at the European plant, which further processed a large portion of the gearboxes. This plant was located in Strasbourg, France, near the German border, and about five truck hours away from the Bergisches Land. In contrast,

Toddville was about six weeks away by sea freight. What a strong argument for producing the European volume in the Bergisches Land!

Therefore, we endeavored to establish close cooperation between us and this plant, where ZUAG gearboxes were installed into customer stations. The concerns of the French site about sourcing products from Toddville were significant; the plant's reputation preceded it. We agreed to obtain an older ZUAG product for our service – not to inspect it, but primarily to dismantle it, measure it, scan the gear profiles, and verify manufacturing capabilities at HDA. We examined everything, obtained drawings from Strasbourg, and were confident that they could be manufactured in the Bergisches Land using existing as well as new tools. The gear profiles closely resembled those of one of our gearboxes. The pre-milling tool could already be used without modification. We invited colleagues from Strasbourg, and there was no need to convince them greatly. During their tour, they quickly recognized that we had the required expertise to manufacture their products. Presenting and building the required capacities in terms of machines and personnel became our joint task.

It became my second Black Belt project for HDA. Together with Strasbourg, we began developing a business case. Production volumes, already existing and thus usable machines and tools, required machines from Colorado Springs, data transfer, personnel requirements, ramp-up of production capacities, transport costs, lead times – we worked out everything together with the French colleagues and felt very good about it. Then there was the information that Roger, the new Global Operations Vice President, would visit HDA in March. We had a coup planned.

The plan was to place a pallet with the disassembled ZUAG product in the hallway, so we would stumble upon it and have to talk about it! On the day of the visit, the meeting started as usual in the conference room. During this meeting, Roger personally handed me the Lean Six Sigma Black Belt certificate as Donald's successor. He expressed the wish to see me involved in a significant project or in a leadership role someday. 'Vamos a ver', was my thought. It won't fail because of me.

During our tour of the plant, we stumbled, as planned, halfway over this one pallet that shouldn't have been there. This was, of course, a violation of Lean and 5S, however, it was there and couldn't be otherwise. Roger immediately recognized that it wasn't an HDA gearbox. We explained the situation to him and presented the draft business case we had prepared. He was surprised and genuinely interested. Then we asked for his permission to order some milling and grinding tools to conduct experiments. The prospect of reducing the global lead time of these products by about six weeks quickly elicited an, "Okay, go for it." from him. However, it wasn't just the lead time; it was also the associated reduction in inventory turnover that appealed to him. If we could turn six weeks into one week, that would mean $7.5 million less inventory and thus free up cash flow for the ÄÄtch Group.

Now, contact had to be established with the plant in Colorado Springs. He agreed to this request as well, yet we should avoid letting the Toddville plant know about it. Those were very exciting weeks at that time. The following week, we had the first teleconference with the Colorado Springs plant. Through our explanations and sending some drawings, we gained the position of the 'savior of the brand and quality' of their products among the ZUAG Company employees. They also inquired with their colleagues in France and received consistently positive feedback about us. In contrast, employees from Toddville had the image of being the brand's undertakers. The quality of the products produced in Toddville did not match the level of tightly-tolerated devices from Colorado Springs. These profound discussions, like the ones we were about to have, had not yet begun between Toddville and Colorado Springs. The colleagues from Ohio tried to deduce everything from drawings. It was a fatal mistake.

In the meantime, we received the ordered tools at HDA. We were now able to produce a sample batch and did so in coordination with Colorado Springs. All parts were measured in detail, and we sent the records along with the parts to Colorado Springs. There, the parts were measured again, and the colleagues confirmed the quality of our batch. We were listed as a certified supplier for Colorado Springs before Toddville had conducted any tests in production. After many weeks of discussions in teleconferences about gear manufacturing, it was now about housing manufacturing. The colleagues were fully convinced by now that we were the right choice. They suggested that we should preferably visit them. A visit to the plant, videos, tours, and discussions would be much more effective than working it all out in teleconferences. The process needed to be accelerated. Our travel request was approved, and we were sure we were in business.

Colorado Springs, USA

The journey to Colorado took place in September, accompanied by Rainer, the most experienced NC programmer from my former department. Immediately, discussions arose within the 'old' management team about why I should make this trip instead of the new, former Head of Industrial Engineering. Yet, it was clear that this was my Black Belt project, and Rainer represented Manufacturing. Thus, we planned the trip together, appreciating the vigorous support from the secretariat. We were determined to make the most of this opportunity. This applied in multiple ways. As an NC programmer, one doesn't often travel, perhaps only to a trade fair, machine acceptance, or a programming course for a new controller; however, to the USA, to Colorado, one wouldn't typically go. Rainer was very pleased about this opportunity. There are experiences in a career that happen only once; this was one of them.

Our travel route took us from Düsseldorf to Los Angeles, and then to Denver. From there, we drove by car across a plateau at the foothills of the Rocky Mountains. We traversed icy and snowy roads on this journey. Upon arrival in Colorado Springs, we were warmly welcomed by our contact person from the teleconferences and introduced to the employees. The atmosphere was friendly and inviting. It was palpable that they saw us as partners in this important endeavor. We exchanged ideas, made notes for implementation, and seized every opportunity to learn, absorb, and document as much as possible.

Time flew by during these days as the hours in the plant were fully scheduled. We shot videos of housing processing, received detailed information about the tools, and analyzed the NC programs. In the evenings, we dined at a nearby French restaurant. In this rather conservative region of the once 'Wild West' of the USA, the restaurant offered the dish 'Chest of Édith Piaf', a delicious creation of tender turkey breast, crisp vegetables, and a seductive béarnaise sauce. Well, Édith Piaf died in October 1963, so a comparison was not possible. The quality of the restaurant was also evident in the side dish; rosemary potatoes instead of French fries. Even during such dinners, we discussed machining problems with colleagues and received valuable insights. In short, things that were not in the drawings. Our knowledge advantage over Toddville was hardly catch-uppable.

We made very good progress during these days. On Wednesday evening, our supervisor suggested that we take a trip on Friday before our departure. As the Rocky Mountains were in sight and driving distance, he proposed that we visit Pikes Peak in the Rocky Mountains. Upon arrival, we took the cog railway from Manitou Springs to the summit of the 14,000-foot mountain. The view from up there was breathtaking, yet it was also very cold. We both were not really equipped with winter gear; however, we endured half an hour up there before descending. On the way back, we visited the Red Rock Canyon. We were equally impressed by the impressions and hospitality.

Then our paths diverged. Bob drove back to Colorado Springs, and we continued our journey, first by car to Denver. There, we stayed at a hotel with a large and warm swimming pool and a steam bath. We greatly enjoyed this after such a strenuous week. The next morning, we headed back to Düsseldorf via Vancouver. The year had been so exciting up to that point that I only noticed the summer lilacs by the railway tracks in autumn. It was the fifth. Time flew by, and my wife and I, we bravely ran along. Our planned 3-year sprint of commuting seemed to have become a mid-distance race for now.

The Plant in the Bergisches Land

Upon our return, we shared all the gathered knowledge and interesting aspects of housing and gear manufacturing with the team. Rainer and I agreed that we had brought back all the information needed to manufacture ZUAG gears at HDA. That this was feasible, we already knew beforehand. The colleagues in Colorado Springs saw it the same way, but now we had all the details. Together with the management, the controller, and representatives from the Strasbourg plant, we finalized the business case and submitted it. Technically, it was submitted by Strasbourg. We hoped that the sector management of ZUAG Company could sell this endeavor better than HDA.

To keep it brief: the business case was rejected. This and another decision were already predetermined. The Toddville site was to be promoted, not HDA. Over the following months, all machining machines were successively dismantled in Colorado Springs and transported to Ohio. These moments were frustrating, especially for the teams in Colorado Springs and Strassbourg, who had worked so hard to open doors for us. Of course, it was also disillusioning for us. The only thing left for us was occasional orders for ZUAG gears, because Toddville unsurprisingly failed to meet the demand in terms of deadlines and quality.

My first Black Belt project continued to be successful. The backlog of gear orders was reduced to the target level through numerous individual measures. Instead of 12 weeks, the delivery time for standard products was reduced to 2 weeks, while for non-standard gears, it was shortened from 18 weeks to 4 weeks. This allowed sales to confidently approach the market. The world had turned around, and we could increase customer satisfaction through fast and punctual deliveries. Now, we awaited the promised major boom, as this had originally been the main argument of sales: We could sell 30% more if the plant only had more capacity and shorter delivery times.

However, the market response was less than modest. A company named 'Lehman Brothers' suddenly faced financial problems and triggered a global financial crisis. The real estate bubble burst, leading the economy of many countries into recession. Affected were the food sector, the aviation industry, and construction companies, exactly the clientele that necessitated our high-quality products for their applications. Our euphoric hope quickly burst. Instead of increased order intake, we experienced the opposite - a declining order intake, another extreme on the list of problems. A continuously declining revenue over several weeks without improvement forced us to reduce costs at the site. It happened, what nobody wanted and what nobody had on the radar: HDA rapidly slid into short-time work. The location could no longer afford two Black Belts and a Lean Leader. Two out of the three of us had to go. That was a harsh quota.

With the Lean Leader, they had not been satisfied before, especially manufacturing had complained. He always emphasized that he could only advise. Everyone else had to do the work. Fundamentally, that is true, but one should exercise some finesse and actively accompany the inexperienced group leaders

on their journey. He did not do that. He had not quite understood the concept of a Servant Leader. My Black Belt colleague
was employed for another four months, then he also left HDA.
Apparently, I had always set off early enough in the morning,
hunted a gazelle, and survived this crisis. Exercise does indeed
do good. Consequently, I additionally served as the interim Lean
Leader in our plant. My mission now also included accompanying the team on their journey until we found a suitable successor. The search dragged on, perhaps deliberately, a bit. During
these months, I conducted numerous meetings with the team
focusing on the application of Lean tools.

Liam was always present, and after one of these sessions, he
asked me to stay for a few additional minutes. He had realized
that the team was not yet ready for the next steps. The momentum of the Lean accelerator had not transferred to other
departments. Previously, the remaining critics had rejected innovations, because they should do it themselves; now, they resisted again with seemingly firmly anchored statements from
the textbook: 'This won't work' or 'Lean is too standardized and
doesn't promote innovation'. In one or another conversation
with colleagues, I naturally heard the classic line again, "Show us
how it's done, and we'll do it!" I quoted the saying, "If you want
something, you'll find a way; if you don't, you'll find an excuse."[vii]

That hit the nail on the head. To get the team to want it now,
Liam asked me to organize a workshop on Lean at the annual
staff meeting. He wanted to involve more people, also through
his support and commitment. It would be great if everyone
would row together, ideally also in the same direction as us.
The focus of the workshop should be on material reach and the

Lean tools that could influence it. We still suffered from excessive stocks and far too low material turnover speed. Amongst professional peers, this turnover speed is an indicator of how far a Lean transformation has progressed in a plant.

I suggested to my boss to acquire ten copies of a Lean novella in advance, which should serve as compulsory reading before the meeting. The story illustrates the practica application of Lean methods in a real work environment while conveying the fundamental principles of Lean thinking. Through the narrative, an attempt is made to present the complex Lean concepts in an easily understandable and appealing manner. It is a popular resource for those who want to better understand Lean principles and integrate them into their way of working, just like at HDA. In the meeting, based on this novella, parallels were to be found first, and then ideas for the plant were to be developed. Liam immediately agreed and ordered the books. When we distributed them at the weekly meeting — along with the request to read them before the staff meeting — it caused a small uprising among the relevant participants who said, "Are we in school here? I'm an adult and decide for myself what I read!" Some team members were still not enthusiastic about taking initiative. They preferred everything to be served on a silver platter. Lifelong learning was not their thing, either.

The staff meeting, organized by Liam and the HR manager, took place at Münster Castle. A few Wilsberg crime dramas had already been filmed there. We continued filming our transformation video at this location, and I'm not sure which story had more twists and turns. Overall, we spent two nights there and had a nice accompanying program. In addition to the presentations and workgroups, there were some group events in the garden. The team bonded further, with more colleagues now convinced of the Lean ideas, yet not all. Some still struggled with the idea of being role models and not just followers. Shouldn't leaders always be that, "Yes, but only for the right things." was their response, and they chuckled. These were the people who, for many years, had placed new machines in a patchwork pattern in the production line and with whom you could play 'Killer Phrase Bingo' in a meeting and always win after fifteen minutes. 'We've tried that, it doesn't work', 'You can't do that in our production', 'That blows the budget', etc.

A few weeks after this wonderful staff meeting, rumors spread that our great boss Liam would be leaving the company for a new role within the corporation. This uncertainty was naturally not conducive. The team, which had largely just decided to embrace the Lean path more intensively, experienced renewed uncertainty. At the end of the year, Liam personally informed us that he was to take on a European role in finance, which had become vacant and had to be filled anew. It was a well-deserved reward for his very successful work as a manager in the Bergisches Land, a foreign discipline to him as a merchant.

He had held this position for a record-breaking almost three years. Now, a newcomer was coming in to lead the team again. Jean, our European Vice President, helped with the appointment. He brought in a young man from his former employer who was ripe for the next career step. Until he arrived in February, we continued our weekly conversations with Liam as usual. At the next meeting, I took the opportunity to inquire about our agreement. I reminded him of the originally envisaged two years that were supposed to be served as a Black Belt for the site. He smiled and said I could look for other positions, as he was leaving too! Liam was as fair as ever.

Show the Ticket

Later that same evening, I glanced at our company's internal job portal to just get a feel for its layout. Yet, at that moment, an intriguing position in Europe for an engineer caught my eye. The Global Product Management was seeking a Manager for VA/VE in the ESA (European Served Area) region. Eight facilities across Italy, France, Germany, Slovenia, and Slovakia were to be overseen. The head of this department sat in the USA, with managers in each region except Europe. VA/VE wasn't entirely new to me; I had some experience from my time in Berlin.

Value Analysis (VA) and Value Engineering (VE) are methods aimed at enhancing value in products or processes. While VA focuses on analyzing existing products to identify and optimize unnecessary costs or resources, VE goes beyond. VE aims to create innovations by improving or redesigning functions in line with customer needs, thereby increasing the product's value to the customer.

The advertised position required an experienced Project Engineer with knowledge of design, manufacturing, and Six Sigma Belt training. Except for design experience, I met all the criteria. So, I applied, armed with the ticket from my Black Belt training. Donald had said there is a good chance for me if an international position became available, and Roger had expressed interest in seeing me in an international role. I was eager to see if these statements would hold true now that the opportunity had presented itself. The HR Manager at HDA was pleased, even though my application came just nine months after starting as a Black Belt for the plant. Familiarity often breeds favoritism. If someone from this plant were to land an international position, it would be a testament to successful talent development. Well, we both would be happy to see her achieve this success!

In previous years, in my former role in Industrial Engineering, I had worked on two development projects with a colleague from the USA. He was a strict, wiry Program Manager named Robert. After our joint projects were completed, he eventually disappeared from sight. It was said he fell ill. His heart couldn't cope with the stress, and others took over his projects. Now, after a long time, he was back, assuming global responsibility for the VA/VE process. He had left the stressful deadline-driven business with new products, and now operated more in the strategic realm.

The position for Europe had not yet been filled; it was being managed from America. His global team consisted exclusively of design engineers. As a result of the two projects with HDA, he remembered me fondly; however, Robert wasn't sure if he should fill the role of Regional Manager with a Lean-oriented Manufacturing Engineer. Honestly, I had some doubts myself about whether this was the right position for me. It wasn't my plan to leave the manufacturing sector after having just acquired the Lean toolbox. The question arose: What would I do with my newly acquired knowledge in product management? However, I recalled that Lean, when applied correctly, isn't confined to manufacturing; it should encompass all areas. Also, the saying 'don't let perfect be the enemy of good' applied to my situation. If I could just get my foot in the door, other options would likely present themselves.

Moreover, my view on the situation in the Bergisches Land with Liam's impending departure had a different perspective now. Nobody in the team knew, who his successor would be or how long he would stay. However, I knew that the 'old guard', those who had been with the company for ages and still clung to the traditional mindset of pure quantity management instead of embracing Lean philosophy, would remain there. This was my fifth year in this company. I had initiated changes only to watch them undone as soon as I took on a different role. TPM reverted to 'repair as needed', and a 'Voice of the Customer' – the customer of Industrial Engineering being production – was no longer conducted. Even the gear Supermarket had to make way for a used machine because it was the quickest way to free up space. Layout planning reverted to a patchwork pattern, as it had been for many years.

Should I fight windmills or start something new? The answer was immediately clear to me. That's precisely why I had chosen this company in the first place. There was no need to leave in order to start something new. This company was big enough. That's why the plunge into product management seemed so appealing to me. I aimed to take responsibility for planning and leading events in various European plants to improve products. Perhaps, I could even extend this task to manufacturing processes and continue to leverage my Lean knowledge.

Christina, the HR Manager at HDA had already supported me well when I took on my Black Belt role for HDA. She agreed to inform her boss in Brussels and sent both of us an invitation to a conference call. Well, the European HR Manager and I were already acquainted – it was Ann-Marie, my former 'student' from the Green Belt course in southern Germany. Here she was, the help we had promised each other during Belt training. The conversation was brief, and she assured me of her full support as well. Some interviews would naturally follow. There was no way around it. With this position, one became a responsible business partner for development, procurement, production, quality management, sales, and marketing.

Ann-Marie organized the discussions with my potential boss and two other Vice Presidents of the European region for January. An exciting time lay ahead for me and my wife once again. The speed at which I was progressing through changes in this company was very unfamiliar to us. However, it was also this unfamiliarity, this novelty, that made the months and years seem like they were on fast forward.

What else happened

We had already visited the island of La Palma in November. Once again, we found ourselves on the street with the small branching gravel path, where houses stood secluded. Again, we didn't venture down. The hill and the whole street were beautiful enough as they were.

Just before our year-end vacation, a Christmas party was held at the small castle in the Bergisches Land. Some seats were assigned, others were not. My name tag was on a table where colleagues from Brussels sat, whom I didn't know – two vice presidents for sales and marketing. We talked about products, Lean methods, cost savings, what their own goals were, as well as mine, and the tasks I had undertaken so far. The evening was varied, and we got along well.

A few days later, it was finally time! The long-awaited year-end vacation. This time we spent the days off with our longtime friends here in Berlin. These friends have been with us our whole lives, and we were very grateful that this was still the case during this commuting phase. We did quite a lot with them on weekends, not as much as before 2005, yet it endured. It's special to have such a close and reliable circle of friends. With twelve friends, it also meant twelve birthdays a year. A colorful mix of joyful gatherings that deepened our friendships. It's the small, but significant things in life that make it so precious.

My Lean-Transformation

A well-known star chef from southern Germany would say, "Whoever complains is to blame!" After completing the Lean Six Sigma Black Belt training, I had immediately got involved in two international projects and had been selected as the Lean Leader in the Bergisches Land, a process that seemed unimaginable to me three years earlier. This had allowed me to gather further valuable experiences in this field. Leading a Lean workshop at the plant's staff meeting had been a particular highlight. Although there were some initial concerns, "I'll read what I want!", the importance of Lean at the leadership level was underscored by a clear message from our common superior.

I was profoundly impressed by the fact that in the Bergisches Land, we had achieved the inversion of the pyramid in some areas during projects. Employees had ideas, and managers implemented them or assisted them in carrying out kaizens. It's one thing to read about this somewhere, but it's much more impressive to experience it firsthand in a project, how resistance slowly turns into support. You witness for yourself that it works. 'Only where you've walked by foot have you truly been'. Since then, I have repeatedly used this concept as a tool to generate new problem-solving ideas and to gain the trust of employees.

2010

Value Analysis and Value Engineering (VA/VE) delve deeply into the worth of a product from the customer's perspective. Can our product efficiently meet the customer's requirements? To enhance the value of a product for the customer, it is essential not only to understand its functionality, but also to analyze the product's value stream all the way to the customer. This intersection between VA/VE and Value Stream Analysis (VSA) is crucial. In many companies, VA/VE is carried out by designers and product management, while value stream analysis is left to the lean experts and the manufacturing team. However, a holistic approach that integrates both aspects is generally more effective and sustainable. However, unfortunately such integration is not common practice.

The Plant in the Bergisches Land

In the very first week of the new year, I had my first telephone interview. To ease into things, the conversation was with my potential new boss, Robert. It went as expected, smoothly, as we were already acquainted from two previous projects. We spoke about my experiences with VA/VE and also discussed my work designing fixtures in my previous position in Berlin. This alleviated his concerns about my lack of design experience.

Next, I had a conversation with Arjen from Brussels. We had spoken extensively at the Christmas party and got along very well. Arjen was a very direct Dutchman. He picked up the phone, greeted me, and asked, "Didn't we have a long conversation at the Christmas party at the castle a few weeks ago?" I confirmed, and he said that we could cut this conversation short then. He supported my hiring and simply asked when I could start. Just two hours later, the next interview followed with the second Vice President. Naturally, it was Roy, the other Vice President at my table during the Christmas party. This conversation also lasted only five minutes. Essentially, he wanted to know when I could begin, as there was pressure from the market to reduce costs. Ann-Marie had orchestrated everything very skillfully. She left nothing to chance. It was also a success for her to recruit an employee from a plant to take on an international role. This is always a success story for HR, whether in a plant or in the region.

Arjen and Roy quickly wrote to Ann-Marie and Robert. Christina prepared the contract for me, and we signed it by the end of January. On April 1st, I transitioned from HDA to the ÄÄtch Group within the parent company. I had redeemed my ticket after just one year, and a new chapter in my professional life began for both myself and my wife. Being an ESA Manager primarily meant traveling to other plants in Europe, working there, and getting to know the countries and their people. How would this affect our commuter lifestyle? It promised to continue being an interesting time for us.

My former boss at HDA, who was also taking on a new international position, gave me some good advice as a farewell. He recommended that I initially stay away from HDA, visiting and supporting other plants first to build relationships there — relationships similar to those already established at HDA. This advice was gratefully accepted. Nothing would please me more,

I thought privately. The eight plants that I was to oversee were located in France (Lens and Roubaix), Italy (Bornago and Trieste), Slovakia (Brezno), Slovenia (Ljubljana), and lastly, HDA with its two locations.

With the new position, I had now reached Level 4 and had the word 'Global' on my business card. The new Plant Manager at HDA, a young and very nice person, once said to me, "When you have the word 'Global' on your business card, you've made it!" Although I was not entirely in agreement, there was a grain of truth in this. In addition to a salary increase, an office of my own was also provided. Initially, I declined the offer of a company car. Given the frequent plane travel and the need for a rental car at each destination, it seemed more practical. The company car would mostly sit idle, and I would have to pay taxes on the monetary value. That didn't seem sensible to me.

Brezno, Slovakia

Starting in February, I began working in my new role a bit ahead of schedule. That month, a VA/VE event took place at the plant in Slovakia, where I was to learn the process. My journey took me from Berlin-Tegel with Air Berlin to Vienna, where it was cold and snowy. A driver was waiting for me there, and he took me to Banská Bystrica in Slovakia in three hours. During the drive, it snowed continuously, the temperatures dropped every 20 kilometers, finally reaching a freezing -13°C. Surprisingly, despite the harsh conditions, there were no traffic jams, as evening traffic in Slovakia was quite light.

Banská Bystrica[viii], with around 80,000 inhabitants, is the sixth-largest city in Slovakia and the cultural and economic center of central Slovakia. The sights in the city center are part of the protected urban area. The central square, 'Námestie SNP' (Square of the Slovak National Uprising), is a very beautiful place, as is the popular pedestrian zone, which exudes a special charm. Banská Bystrica is envied by other cities for this atmosphere. On the 'Námestie Štefana Moyzesa' square, some ancient houses once formed the city castle.

After arriving at the hotel, we met for dinner at a restaurant, where we finally introduced ourselves in person, sat together with a beer, and had an extensive exchange. The VA/VE team had travelled from the USA in a group of three, which was surely a significant reason for wanting a representative in Europe. It was an extremely pleasant team; they truly welcomed me warmly. I already knew many of them from conference calls I had been participating in since January. We agreed to meet for breakfast at 7.00 am the next morning. When we entered the breakfast room the next day and looked out the window, we couldn't believe our eyes. The snowfall had not ceased, and the white blanket had reached over 50 centimeters in height. The temperature had dropped further to -17°C.

We set off in a car to our plant in Brezno, about 30 kilometers away. Driving on the highway and country roads, we could hear the scraping of the vehicle's underside on the icy snow. Several times, we had to avoid higher snow drifts on the highway. Finally, after a 90-minute drive, we reached the plant, with the snowfall continuing until noon.

The carefully prepared event began, and I had the opportunity to learn the company's well-documented process firsthand. Observing the event – both from an observer's position and as a participant – was enjoyable and provided me with many insights. I could see how the process worked, what information and documents were used at each step, and which tools were employed. I also noticed how the participants reacted, acted, and what challenges they faced. Especially amusing and varied were the descriptions of product functions and the creative part of idea generation. The task was to describe the function of a part or assembly with a noun and a verb. During an exercise for better understanding, participants were asked what function a newspaper has. A participant from northern France finally answered, "Wrapping fish." While this might not be the primary function, it was a real secondary function of a newspaper in his region.

In the second part of the event, the ideas were detailed, evaluated regarding material and labor costs, and documented on an A4 sheet. It was a T-chart because it looked like a T; the basic data like quantities, costs, weight, and master data of the part were listed at the top, and the idea was described in short words. On the left side was the current state, separated by a crossbar in the middle, and on the right side was the new state. The whole thing was illustrated with pictures or drawing excerpts. At the end of the eventful week, a final report from the team was always presented to the plant and also to the rest of the ÄÄtch world. We compiled the results and then presented them in a conference call, showcasing our findings through a screen presentation to the entire organization worldwide. The US team and a manager from England handled the entire presentation. The employees who had worked on the proposals during the week only listened. Did they not want to present? I asked my US colleagues, and they said that the English skills were not sufficient for a presentation to a global audience. A first idea began to germinate in me...

By Friday afternoon, everyone had left. In the following week, I began scheduling appointments with other plants for potential future events. While the products to be worked on were predetermined for us this year, the region itself should conduct analyzes with product management and submit proposals for the coming year. The crucial criteria for the selection and prioritization of products were the time of design, margin development, historical quantities over the preceding years, possible consolidations of product lines, and more.

Bornago, Italy

The plant in Bornago was located near Milan. I could fly directly there from Berlin-Tegel with Air Berlin. After picking up my luggage in Malpensa, I collected a rental car and drove for about an hour in the evening, covering nearly 80 kilometers to the hotel, which was just 4 kilometers from the plant. The accommodation was named 'Hotel Angi'. It was run by a very friendly family. The owners, Angelo and Gina, inspired the hotel's name. Their children, Estella and Dante, were both in their forties. Dante was an excellent and regionally renowned chef. The hotel was in the village of Bussero, which lay in the Gorgonzola region. Gorgonzola is not just a region. It is also a city where the famous Italian blue cheese with its unique flavor is produced.

Made from cow's milk, the cheese is distinguished by its characteristic blue veins, giving it a distinctive texture and intense taste. The entire Gorgonzola region is known for its role in Italian cheese production and its rich culinary tradition. Hotel Angi and Dante as the chef fit perfectly into this culinary tradition.

Before hosting my first event, a new purchasing manager for Europe was hired; Gilbert, a Belgian. There was an onboarding event for him. I met all the important purchasing personnel from all European plants at once, and vice versa. Naturally, we all booked at Angi. After dinner, we gathered at the bar. There were five of us, and Gilbert suggested a game, 'Two Truths and a Lie'. In this game, each person takes turns saying three statements about themselves. Two of these statements are true, and one is a lie. The other participants then have to guess which statement is the lie. It's a fun way to learn more about your colleagues while also being creative. It was a funny evening, and we discovered that Gilbert had a pilot's license and had restored and flown an old propeller plane from the 1940s with his father. As a buyer, you need to be good at bluffing. Otherwise, you end up paying too much for materials. Only one person identified this statement as true.

I, being a technician, had a different mindset. Still, two of the four participants believed my lie, a good result for an engineer. I claimed not only to be a Lean Six Sigma Black Belt but also a Judo Black Belt and to have completed a 30-minute decathlon. Two colleagues guessed correctly about my truths. I was a so-called preemie, weighing just 2.4 kilos at birth. Although I started decathlon training at 39, achieved good results and had indeed completed a half-hour decathlon. Some found this unbelievable.

The return journey on Friday evening proved far more compli-
cated than the arrival, particularly the part from the plant to the
Milan-Malpensa airport. During rush hour, Milan is submerged
in traffic chaos. For the same 80-kilometer stretch, one had to
plan between three and four hours. Including returning the
rental car, checking in, and going through security, this could
sometimes take up to six hours. As I always booked the last
flight at 8.30 pm to Tegel and wanted to check in ninety minutes
prior, I left the plant no later than 1.00 pm. The problem was
that you could never precisely predict how long it would actually
take. So, I either arrived just in time or spent a few hours in the
airport lounge. At least I was well taken care of, and away from
the hustle and bustle of the airport.

For visits where we would prepare the event, I always booked
the small Hotel Angi with the Massoni family. In the plant itself,
I now knew a few people from previous meetings. Besides the
purchasers, there were Gabriele and Sara. I knew them from
the OpEx assessments. The three of us, along with some others,
were the assessors in Europe and travelled through the plants
two years ago to evaluate the progress of the Lean transformation. Gabriele now acted as the Lean Leader in Bornago and
Sara as the Quality Manager. Both helped me prepare for my
debut on the VA/VE stage. From the purchasing department,
Nino was assigned to assist me. The preparatory tasks included
assembling the team, inviting participants, organizing rooms,
providing bills of materials and drawings, as well as manufacturing plans as working documents, and planning an evening event.
Additionally, it was necessary to inform the rest of the ÄÄtch
group about the progress. In Italy, team events often had
names like 'Pizza', 'Bowling', or 'Bowling and Pizza'. My first
event was very successful, thanks to the great support from the

Italian colleagues. Contrary to the usual practice, we decided to conduct the event predominantly in the local language rather than in English. This allowed for much deeper and more intensive discussions within the Italian teams than would have been possible in English. If you've ever eaten at a local restaurant in Italy while on vacation, you'll know exactly what I mean.

The team kept me regularly updated on the progress in English and rewarded me with numerous creative ideas. I introduced two additional small changes for the final report. While the team worked on the ideas in Italian during the week, I prepared the final presentation in English. This allowed me to relieve the groups of administrative tasks during the event. For the presentation, I took on the introduction and the general part of the VA/VE analysis. I explained the process, described the product, and presented the results in numbers.

Afterward, each team member from the Italian site had the opportunity to present one of their ideas themselves. Naturally, I asked beforehand who would like to present in front of the global audience. It wasn't everyone's cup of tea, but those who wanted to had, seldom had the chance to speak in front of a worldwide teleconference audience. They found it enriching, and it added a dynamism to the report that the rest of the world found refreshing. This should be the standard practice going forward. Another important aspect was 'develop people first'. Many were excited to explain their proposals and to be introduced by name beforehand.

The proposals were only part of the process. The other essential aspect was to implement these ideas quickly and successfully, focusing on cost reduction. I monitored all projects and had weekly meetings with the plants to offer support, discuss progress, and plan the next steps. Our global team also met weekly via teleconference. These meetings focused on the progress of significant projects nearing completion, upcoming events in the plants, and the value of the idea pipeline.

This pipeline consisted of proposals that had not yet been implemented. Its value served as an indicator of whether we could achieve future productivity goals. The overarching goal was clearly defined: to consistently achieve 120% of the targeted productivity for the year through innovative proposals. However, our region was at a modest 88%. Initially, this might not sound dramatic, but with an annual goal of €12.6 million we were missing a hefty €4.5 million. This was a considerable gap, and Robert faced a real challenge. Filling this pipeline became my task. The plan was to host an event every six weeks. Previously, there had been a maximum of two events per year in Europe. This plan worked; each month, the level of the idea pipeline improved. We could choose the changes we wanted to make and did so.

Roubaix, France

One of the next VA/VE events took me to the plant in Roubaix, France. The location was only about 320 kilometers from the Bergisches Land, approximately a three-and-a-half-hour drive. I could drive there with a rental car. Still, getting past Antwerp was a challenge. Between 11.00 pm and 4.00 am, there was no traffic jam. Yet, I was never there during those hours, so the journey always went quite slowly for me. During the drive, I kept thinking about the film 'Welcome to the Scht'is'. I was heading straight into that region and hoped that my colleagues there would be different from those in the movie; they were, and how!

Roubaix is part of the Métropole Européenne de Lille (Eurometropole Lille), a metropolitan region in northern France. It lies immediately northeast of Lille and is one of the municipalities within this metropolitan region. In a certa n sense, one could consider Roubaix as a sort of suburb or part of the extended urban area of Lille. There are also some historical buildings in Roubaix, such as the Église Saint-Martin. This is a Gothic church built in the 15th century. It is one of the oldest religious buildings in Roubaix and attests to the historical significance of the city. Another outstanding cultural highlight in Roubaix is the La Piscine Museum, housed in a former swimming pool hall. The museum boasts an impressive collection of artworks, textiles, and industrial artifacts.

The plant in Roubaix was acquired by the ÄÄtch Group in 2001. It was a smaller plant, and not as structured as other ÄÄtch Group plants. There, a young, open-minded team awaited me. We worked on a product to reduce costs and thereby increase order intake. This was almost always the goal in VA/VE. Working with this team was particularly enjoyable. The Plant Manager had also organized an evening event: no bowling, no pizza but rather laser shooting in a three-story house with mazes. We received laser guns and sensor vests that recorded the hits. The summer temperatures made for a sweaty experience. The company boss had previously been in the Foreign Legion. His specialty was probably 'urban combat', and so he won the game by far.

Afterwards, we went to a restaurant for dinner. I learned there that there was another young man I had not met before. Raphaël was an ADP who was currently gaining experience in various plants before returning to Roubaix to take on a managerial role in development. In two weeks, he would be attending an ADP meeting in Tomado, USA. That fits, I thought. I would be there for my staff meeting at the same time and hoped to meet him on our company's extensive campus in Tomado.

Before the final report of our event, I asked the team to enter the ideas into the global pipeline during the event. This was another innovation in the process. As a result, the values were immediately visible in the report, which pleased the listeners and Robert very much. Another aspect also occupied me. In cost reduction, it was partly about increasing the company's margin, yet also about being able to lower prices. This was the key to selling more products. I discussed this with the Sales Manager and Production. We agreed that at such events, we had to focus not only on costs but also on the manufacturing process. Without improvements in this area, increased production rates would not be achievable, and the effect of the improvements would be nullified. Thus, I slowly prepared the field for Lean Manufacturing, with Roubaix as my pilot. Lean was the strategy to improve processes towards higher output.

Tomado, USA

Now the time had come for the staff meeting in Tomado, USA. The ÄÄtch Group campus sprawled across an area of about 1.5 by 2 kilometers on a peninsula by the shores of Lake Erie. Lake

Erie is one of the five Great Lakes in North America and lies on the border between the United States and Canada. It is the fourth largest of the Great Lakes both in terms of surface area and volume. The lake covers an area of about 25,700 square kilometers and has a maximum depth of around 64 meters. Besides providing water for the local population and industry, the lake is also a popular destination for recreational activities such as boating and water sports.

Lake Erie is also known for its diverse wildlife, especially its fish stocks. The lake offers a wealth of fish species like perch, pike, bass, carp, and catfish, making it a popular spot for anglers. The coastline stretches for several hundred kilometers, offering numerous beaches and picturesque coastal towns. Many of my colleagues lived and worked near the lake, as the peninsula belonged to the ÄÄtch Group. From the Gatekeeper to the main building's parking lot, the drive took four minutes, winding through a mix of parks and wooded shores. Occasionally, you could see large and small buildings.

The campus provided numerous sports and recreational facilities for employees, as well as barbecue areas for both small and large gatherings. The work atmosphere seemed extremely relaxed, and the employees thoroughly appreciated it. A notable event that underscored this positive atmosphere was a fundraising event featuring an unusual activity: duck-diving.

Given the popularity of baseball in the USA, hitting a target was creatively adapted. Instead of simply throwing at a target, three throws cost $10. A successful hit triggered a mechanism that swung the seat of a chair away, causing the person sitting on it to fall into a pool of cool water. The person on the chair was none other than the Vice President of Global Procurement. Despite her good looks and willingness to volunteer, she was not spared. After falling into the water three times, the cold was clearly visible on her face and body. Nevertheless, she bravely endured, and the throwers did not relent until the entertaining lunch break was over. To ensure no one went hungry, two grills were also in operation. In the end, a substantial amount of money was raised. The company generously matched the collected amount, and Francis, the Vice President, was grateful for hot coffee and plenty of towels.

For the meeting, figures, forecasts, and a list of upcoming events for the remaining and following fiscal year were prepared. Before departure, a coordination conversation took place with my dotted-line manager. Jean, our Vice President for Europe and a Lean advocate, supported the idea that the desire for increased order intake must go hand in hand with enhancing site capacity. Only if both were linked would it lead to success. He went a step further, suggesting that addressing site capacity from US VA/VE should also include driving the productivity of manufacturing costs in Europe alongside material cost savings. Additionally, a presentation was prepared highlighting the connection between material cost savings, market volume effects, and manufacturing processes.

At the staff meeting in Tomado, my presentation received mixed reactions. Some tended to simply assign the problem to manufacturing — 'We just improve the product!' — a mentality I did not find cooperative. Others understood the connection and saw the necessity of thinking about site capacity together. If we developed ideas to increase customer orders by 30%, it would fail without accompanying measures. However, they were unable to develop such ideas; they called for support from manufacturing. This was understandable. Development engineers usually lack knowledge of how manufacturing can be improved, let alone which tools are required to develop ideas.

A particularly notable colleague kept shaking his head throughout my presentation. I couldn't understand how he could be against these ideas. During the break, I asked Venkatesh about his concerns, and he replied, "I have no concerns; it's a great concept you're proposing." Well, he was from India, and in their culture, this type of head-shaking is a gesture of agreement. We both became friends and continued to see each other for a long time within the company. After consulting with the Vice President of Operations in Europe and his boss, my boss Robert agreed with my idea. Now I had a special role in this group. I had the knowledge of how to optimize a product and manufacturing. No one else on the team had that. From now on, besides VA/VE, it was also about process analyzes, improvements, and productivity increases in manufacturing. The side effect was that my savings target was increased from $12.5 to $19.5 million.

On the sidelines of the staff meeting, I also met Andrea, the General Manager of Roubaix in France and FMIT (Firma di Meccanica Industriale Trieste), another small plant in northern Italy. He had just come from lunch with the ADP Raphaël. We introduced ourselves to each other in the courtyard in front of the canteen; a really young and open-minded man. We briefly discussed which products would be suitable for events and then arranged to meet next month in Roubaix. There we would set the priorities and details. The goal development for the following year was planned for this period, and our ideas had to be incorporated there.

Europe

Preparing for events became a routine for me. Together with the factories, I developed a standardised approach, allowing us to increase the pace to one event per month across Europe throughout the year. We addressed both ideas for material cost reduction and ways to eliminate capacity bottlenecks in manufacturing. Ultimately, the goal was always to sell more of the improved product on the market. In the summer, Jean invited me to his staff meeting in Brussels, where I met the entire European management team. We were a group of seven relatively young people who supported him and acted as a team. Together, we travelled to the factories and, with the local leadership teams, developed goals, measures, and budgets for the upcoming fiscal year, as well as event plans. Thanks to my knowledge of Lean, I was able to communicate effectively with Michael, the OpEx Leader for ESA. We worked closely together and undertook joint trips to various locations. This collaboration provided me with significant support in my goal to optimize manufacturing through Lean-oriented measures, and I learned a lot from his approach.

Our first goal development meeting took place in Lens, another plant in northern France. This plant manufactured units for transporting media—either up to oil platforms or wind turbines, or down into mine shafts. Together with the local team, we created strategies and goals for the following year for the plant's various functions. Workplace safety, quality, material management, productivity, and delivery reliability were the core topics. To develop these strategies, we used a tool called the Strategy A3, in combination with the Catchball process. An A3 is literally a sheet of A3-sized paper and is a fundamental element in Lean Manufacturing. I'll explain it in more deta l and touch on the interaction of A3s across different hierarchy levels

- The A3 embodies a Japanese philosophy: if your strategy doesn't fit on an A3 sheet, it might mean it's too complex or extensive. In such cases, it might be advisable to narrow the scope and develop an additional A3. 'Keep it Simple and Stupid', or KISS, is the rule that applies here, helping to clarify goals and priorities and making implementation more efficient. An A3 also requires prioritizing and focusing on key elements. This process can lead to the elimination of less important details and activities, often resulting in a more effective strategy. An A3 has nine interconnected blocks. It doesn't mean these blocks must be printed on a single sheet of paper or written on a computer:

1. The method and the description of the current situation, essentially the reason for the activities
2. Goal setting for the end of the year in specific parameters
3. Gap, the discrepancy between the current state and the goal
4. Analysis of the gap, using a fishbone diagram or matrix
5. Main solution approaches
6. Rapid experiments to verify the impact of the approaches before implementation
7. Detailed action plan: what, when, who

8. Tracking the development of the metrics from box 3
9. Feedback after a year on how the A3 performed. What went well, what didn't, and why?

Logical connection of these elements is crucial.

As previously mentioned, five A3s were created in each plant for quality, safety, delivery reliability, material inventory, and productivity. Often, the same resources are required for different measures. To resolve this competition within the team, there is the Catchball process.

> The idea behind the Catchball process is that the responsible individuals for the different A3 reports interact, provide feedback, and ensure that resources are optimally allocated to the various goals of different functions. This fosters balanced and holistic improvement. The term Catchball highlights the iterative nature of this process, where ideas and information are thrown back and forth between the parties to achieve a common alignment of efforts.

Of course, I also created an A3 for my strategic goals with the various plants. My colleagues did the same, and together we conducted a Catchball process among ourselves, moderated by Jean. To coordinate with the plants, I travelled to these locations several times throughout the year 2011.

The alignment of plant goals and my goals was of utmost importance. My goal had to reflect the sum of the productivity goals of the plants in Euros. The overall goals of the seven European directors formed the goals of our boss Jean, the Vice

President. The goals of the Vice Presidents from Europe, Asia, and America, in turn, contributed to the global Vice President's goal. This process of goal cascading was characterized by alignment and mutual complementarity—never competition. Our collaboration throughout the year was built on this solid foundation. In the Lean world of the Toyota Production System, this process is known as Hoshin Kanri or Goal Deployment.

Hoshin Kanri Explained Briefly

Hoshin Kanri[ix], known as 'Compass Needle Management', is a Japanese management method designed to assist companies in implementing their strategies. It is also referred to as 'Policy Deployment', 'Goal Deployment', 'Management by Policy', or 'Strategy Deployment'. This approach stands as one of the most crucial methods within Lean Management. The core idea behind this methodology is to align the entire organization and all its activities towards a common vision. In the initial step, a guideline or 'True North' (Hoshin) is established to define the relevant objectives and priorities of the company. Subsequently, these objectives are deployed across all levels of the organization. This deployment involves deriving specific actions and strategies for each department and employee based on the defined goals. By adopting this holistic approach, both effectiveness and efficiency are enhanced. When utilizing the Hoshin Kanri method, it is essential to employ the Hoshin Kanri Matrix, also known as the X-Matrix. This tool enables every individual to understand the connection between the r tasks and the company's strategic objectives. When team members lack clear goals or fail to comprehend how their work aligns with strategic company objectives, they often spend unnecessary time on activities. To ensure cohesive direction within the entire team, tasks must be directly linked to these goals.

Trieste, Italy

Another one of these trips led us to FMIT, the small facility in northern Italy where filter systems, cooling units, and water separators for the ÄÄtch Group products were manufactured. I could reach this facility by taking an Air Berlin flight from Düsseldorf or Tegel to Venice, followed by a 2-hour drive on the highway. Although the Trieste Airport was closer, the connection from Germany was initially not as convenient. Following Andrea's recommendation, we chose not to book our hotel in Trieste near the airport, but instead opted for the peninsula of Grado, a seaside resort on the Adriatic, just 30 kilometers from the facility.

Grado is an island in the Adriatic Sea and belongs to the Friuli-Venezia Giulia region in northeastern Italy. Its history dates back to Roman times. Later, Grado became part of the Byzantine Empire and a significant center of Byzantine trade and culture. Grado is also known for its ecclesiastical history. The Basilica of Santa Maria delle Grazie, built in the 6th century, is a remarkable example of Byzantine architecture in Italy. The city was once an episcopal see and is historically associated with the Patriarchate of Aquileia. The Basilica of Aquileia stands there, one of the most important early Christian churches in Europe. Built in the 4th century, it is a designated UNESCO World Heritage Site. Grado's rich history is reflected in its architecture, culture, and way of life. Visitors can explore historical land-marks while enjoying the relaxed atmosphere of a seaside re-sort, which Grado has been since the 19th century. The island's natural thermal springs contributed to its popularity. All this provided us with very relaxed evenings in a cultural setting and fostered a good team atmosphere, which was crucial during our many travels.

The situation at FMIT was unique, and so the development of the strategy did not proceed as smoothly as in other facilities. Lorenzo, the former company founder, and his team still held responsible positions there. The ÄÄtch Group had acquired FMIT in 2003, and he was subsequently appointed as the Gen-eral Manager. Andrea, who had introduced me to Raphaël in Tomado, was his boss. It was probably this contractual arrange-ment that allowed Lorenzo to remain in such a position. We en-countered resistance from some executives within the team during many ideas and discussions. They had their own ideas about how the company should be run, and they believed that traditional methods should be used to set strategies. The mind-set of a large corporation with 68,000 employees had not yet sunk in for them. Jean had a tough time that week, but never-theless, by the end of the week, we had jointly created all the necessary A3s for all functions and supplemented them with our own.

However, the rest of the team at FMIT was great, similar to Rou-baix, with many young, open-minded employees already in lead-ership positions. Pierro was the Operations Manager. He was the son of the second former company founder and completely different from the rest of the management team; open to every-thing new, and interested in Lean. His father had done the only sensible thing. With the money from the sale in hand, he retired and lived happily with his wife. His property bordered on the company's in the rear area. Occasionally, he would drop by, yet only when he wanted something, not to meddle! The company not only impressed with its good products, but also with a turnover rate that was almost zero. Once someone was permanently employed there, they stayed there. They could be sure of that, as long as they didn't oppose the boss too much. So, nobody did.

Scheduling the first event proved to be a challenge for me. Months passed before I finally got the opportunity to visit the facility alone and present the process of such events using examples. However, we also set ourselves the goal of jointly selecting a product for a VA/VE event. Both Lorenzo, his development team, and the team in Bergisches Land had similarities: they showed little openness to change. The consensus at both sites was, "Why should we change our products when they are already among the best and most cost-effective?"

FMIT and Roubaix, on the other hand, had a similar decision-making structure. In France, the short approval processes without involving the ÄÄtch Group offered a clear advantage. Jan Marten and his team made joint and swift decisions. However, this structure proved to be a significant disadvantage here in Trieste. Quick decisions were simply not feasible with the FMIT management team. Even mundane matters such as procuring new tools for production led to discussions lasting for days, if not weeks, in the lengthy management meetings. However, somehow, we managed to jointly select a product for analysis; of course, without any commitment to a timeframe for execution. After all, you can't always get everything immediately!

The planning of my events was done in close collaboration with the respective facilities. The preparation took a total of four weeks, two of which were spent at the facility itself and two weeks running parallel with the preparation at the next facility. I was on the road almost every week – from Milan to Vienna to Paris. In between, I also spent several days in Bergisches Land. The reason was the travel expenses. At that time, these were still submitted manually. However, the facility had no idea for a VA/VE event either. They argued as well that they always developed the most cost-effective option and would rather work on new products than engage in VA/VE. The HDA had always been somewhat stubborn – I was glad about that and now had an idea why my ex-boss had advised me to distance myself from the site at the beginning.

Lean and VA/VE

My first year as the Europe Manager was coming to an end, and it had been quite successful. Travelling had taken on a new dimension. It was no longer limited to flights from Tegel to Düsseldorf and back. Now, the airports of Vienna, Milan, Venice, and Paris were regularly on my itinerary. Visiting other sites even had a small advantage. In the facilities, they didn't have the entire week to prepare for an event with me. After all, they had their actual tasks to attend to. When I suggested arriving in the preparation weeks on Monday noon, they immediately agreed. This allowed me to stay at home more often from Sunday to Monday. Sundays no longer ended for us in the early afternoon!

In the young team at the European level, we had a great atmosphere. Jean, our Vice President, was very Lean-oriented. We learned a lot from him, less about individual tools, more about the process of annual planning with congruent goals. He often stood by his opinion against that of the parent company. Would that work out well? He was the third person in this position in the first five years. My direct boss, Robert, was also satisfied. He had stepped out of the firing line as the idea pipeline was well-filled and the implementation of suggestions had gained speed. Later, he assured me that he definitely didn't regret bringing a manufacturing engineer into the role of a VA/VE manager.

Not only did I have a successful start in my new role, but I also brought my knowledge in Lean into this position. Without considering the problems in manufacturing, the best VA/VE ideas might achieve the desired cost-effect, yet not necessarily or completely the desired increase in production volume. That's why we integrated small value stream analyzes into the events. These emphasized the close customer connection of our events. Furthermore, the knowledge was expanded and successfully passed on to others. The image of the function rounded out, and there was confidence that, over time, the transition into a coaching role would become more and more natural for me. A role I had dreamed of at the beginning of my journey, but was never sure I would ever be able to assume.

What else happened

In April, shortly after I started my new job, we explored a new island in the Atlantic: Fuerteventura. The island impressed with breathtaking beaches, few green areas, but plenty of wind and well-developed bike paths, where professional teams trained in winter. Our stay was extremely relaxing – leisurely days at the beach, hikes in the surroundings of our house, and small excursions shaped our time. On April 15th, during one of our outings, we read in the newspaper that the volcano Eyjafjallajökull in Iceland had erupted the previous evening at 10.00 pm. As we hadn't seen it on TV the night before, the news surprised us. The eruption caused significant disruptions in air traffic in Europe as a result of the ash cloud that entered the atmosphere. The colors of the sky at sunset were impressive. Unfortunately, there was a risk that these particles could damage aircraft engines. Flight operations were suspended in Europe, and we had no idea if we would return in time. I called Robert in the USA; he was understanding. Three days before our return flight, the flight ban was lifted. Fortunately, we were able to fly back on time.

We spent Christmas once again in Berlin. We had already visited the island of La Palma in October and had a good rest. Now, after several years, we wanted to do something together with friends for New Year's Eve. So, we went to a nice location in the very north of Berlin, where we joined a Party with Music in a restaurant.

2011

Value Stream Analysis – If there's a product for a customer, there's also a value stream. It's the art of recognizing and shaping it. At the start of product manufacturing, you must 'input' money into the process, and at the end, you deliver their product to the customer and receive their money. Wouldn't it be great if you could get to the customer's money faster, if you had to invest less, and perhaps could get more out of it? The value stream gives clues on where to start to achieve exactly that.

The Beginning of the Year

The year 2011 began in Berlin with cold temperatures and a blanket of snow. My first planned events were approaching, and the goal for the year was ambitious: to achieve nearly €20 million in productivity savings. Now it was also my task to support the manufacturing area and achieve savings with them; a significant challenge. However, the idea pipeline of the plants was always well-filled. In addition to the VA/VE events, we had started to hold special idea-gathering days at the sites.

Gabriele from Bornago was particularly creative in this regard. His suggestion to drive through the plant with a small 'moderation cart' and ask the employees for their ideas was innovative. We had everything with us, even a rolling flip chart, so that the employees didn't have to leave their workstations. This gave them the opportunity to show us directly in the workshop what they meant – especially important for those who couldn't express themselves as precisely in writing. The 'Go Gemba' concept worked wonderfully in this context. This idea was well-received in the operation, and we implemented it similarly as a 'best practice' in other plants. And so, a new way emerged to obtain creative and valuable ideas for improvements, without having to conduct a week-long event immediately.

Of course, the idea of creative events to increase productivity generally received approval from the Global Product Management Team. However, there was also pushback. Some believed that we should focus on our main tasks instead of constantly diluting the standards of the events with new ideas. The fact that the situation in Europe was different as a result of my background than in America, India, and China didn't quite fit into their picture.

Roubaix, France

Regardless of these concerns, I aimed to conduct value stream analyzes or at least identify bottlenecks in manufacturing at each subsequent event. Particularly in Roubaix, I worked closely with the young team; the young managers were curious. The support of Jan Marten, the new General Manager, and Raphaël was extremely helpful in this regard. The latter rose to become the Engineering Manager over the course of the second year, a remarkable ascent. Well, that was also the goal of the ADP process. The plant was somewhat like the small village in Gaul, which steadfastly followed its own path. As long as they didn't need funds that required approval, they had a lot of freedom.

This was because everyone reported to Jan Marten, and he was a proponent of decision-making, unlike some individuals at FMIT in Italy.

The events at this plant always had a very special atmosphere, not least because of our team activ ties. This year, for example, we ventured into an outdoor go-kart tour – a welcome change from the usual events. However, in Roubaix, there were always unusual events anyway. My goal with this plant now went beyond VA/VE and value stream; I wanted to embed the Lean philosophy throughout the organization. My vision was that not only manufacturing, yet also procurement, design, as well as occupational safety and finance would collectively follow the Lean mindset. Gradually, I assumed a different role, at least for this small plant. Here, the employees not only participated, but they appreciated it. The plant was not in the focus of the Americans and was not on the agenda of the new OpEx Leader for Europe. My nice colleague Michael had unfortunately left the company. Honestly, they weren't actively seeking additional support from these functions either. They observed how much effort was invested in Lean initiatives in other plants, often with instruments that were not relevant to them. A quote from Bob Marley goes, "On a paved road, you can't find the right way."[x] The OpEx leaders always followed the paved road. They had to and they came with a program, a training plan, and a list of tools and boards. That would have overwhelmed this plant. In my case, the approach was different. I accompanied them on their unpaved path and explained to them which Lean tools were available to better shape this path. They chose what best suited their needs and where they could achieve success because successes motivate others to want more of this 'substance'. If it could be introduced independently of other processes, we implemented it. If not, I explained what adjustments were necessary for it to work. Although it certainly took a little longer, it had an advantage. You implement exactly what the plant really wants. That's more sustainable. We weren't bothered by Rüdiger, the new OpEx Leader for Europe. He was far away, on a paved road.

The next event for product improvement was imminent. Jan Marten and the team set the goals very high themselves.

- 15% shorter lead times,
- 10% lower costs, and a
- 25% improved adaptation to customer requirements should help us gain 20% more market share. Assuming we meet the cost goals – how could we then represent the 20% higher market share in manufacturing without additional investments? Together with the team, I discussed how we could achieve these ambitious goals in their plant.

The keywords were:

- Avoid waste,
- Eliminate bottlenecks, and
- Reduce lead time.

The process sounds straightforward, yet it requires utilizing the right tools and then continuously advancing it. There's this peculiar saying about gaining weight, 'you don't gain weight between Christmas and New Year but between New Year and Christmas'. Similarly, in the case of an event, 'you don't save during the event week, but in the year after'. The team was curious and then posed the crucial question; what do we need to apply to achieve this? The great thing about this team was their demand for the right instruments. I acted as their coach, and they always wanted to know which tools we would need. It had a bit of an inverted hierarchy pyramid feel to it. So, I explained to them the sequence that promised sustainable success:

- We need a change agent who takes on the role in the plant of conducting analyzes and organizing events; Raphaël assumed this role
- We need a Sensei to explain things to them; that was my part
- We had to have a process that we wanted to improve, preferably comprehensive for the site; that was our VA/VE topic, with the goal of achieving a 20% increase in market share
- We needed to know and anticipate customer requirements; Jan Marten took care of this with sales
- We needed a value stream to identify bottlenecks, lead times, and waste; that was still missing
- Then we needed ideas to solve the identified problems. The priorities arose from the value stream analysis, and the ideas were still missing

The team agreed to the approach, and we made preparations for a value stream mapping. I began by demonstrating to them how to depict the value stream – what information they required, how it was represented, and how we would proceed. The answer to the last question was surprising for most, not just in Roubaix. You don't go forward, you go backward. The recording starts with shipping, then you go upstream in the material flow until you reach the warehouse with the raw materials. The approach starts with the end customer, as their needs and requirements should be at the center of entrepreneurial action. Reverse analysis ensures that the entire value chain is oriented towards customer satisfaction. Going upstream makes it easier to see where something comes from and when flows merge. Going downstream, you don't easily see which flows run in parallel. By going backward through the production and supply chain, potential bottlenecks, waste, or efficiency problems can be identified. This allows for targeted improvements and increased efficiency. During the following weeks between my visits, they supplemented the picture and information. Of course, I helped them with each visit. It was a new tool for them, and we had fun working with it.

The value stream analysis became an integral part of our VA/VE events. Strictly speaking, it was part of the preparation. This allowed us to focus the attention of a specific group on developing ideas for this topic block during the event. As described earlier, the essence of value stream analysis is to shorten processing times to be shorter than the takt time of the customer. Any deviations are bottlenecks that need to be eliminated.

We identified workstations with high cycle times beforehand, and began at the event to develop ideas to eliminate these bottlenecks. We decided to introduce a Supermarket for customer products. After removal, only minimal configuration work was required for the products. This reduced the cycle time below the takt time. This also led to a significant reduction in the perceived delivery time by the customer. With a corresponding Kanban system, we could effectively replenish the Supermarket.

At the conclusion of the event, everyone was excited (well, almost everyone). There was one exception: an OpEx coach in Europe, although he didn't care for or, better said, wasn't supposed to care for this plant, insisted that only he could conduct a value stream analysis. The saying, 'there can be only one!' may apply to 'Highlanders', but in the world of OpEx, Lean, and Value Stream coaches, that is not applicable. We decided to just continue as we had the support of our superiors.

The implementation of the ideas began immediately after the event week. While Engineering worked on the product changes and Procurement incorporated the changes in the material area, I developed a Kanban game. We simulated the processes for the specific product range every thirty minutes. In the early days of my Lean journey, I had simulated such processes in Berlin and later in the Bergisches Land for my own assurance. As a result, in the case of Roubaix, I was able to develop the game quite quickly. The game boards corresponded to the boxes of the Value Stream analysis. The rules were essentially the parameters contained therein, such as batch size, cycle time, and more. Our products were cut-out pieces of paper, appropriately labelled, as were the Kanban cards, just in a different color – Excel made this possible. One person set the time, and the others moved their products and Kanban cards from box to box, into the warehouse and back out, and finally onto the trucks.

When surrounded by sceptics, you shouldn't have any flaws in the system, and should be prepared for scenarios that are borderline. Although there was initial scepticism, the employees played along with great dedication. They tried to intentionally push the system to its limits, not to reject it, but rather to find solutions on how to make it stable and resilient, even in extreme situations. Eventually, they were convinced that this would become a success story. It became clear that certain measures based on the Supermarket principle would lead to significantly shorter lead times, thus reduced delivery times for the customer.

Below is a somewhat more detailed explanation of the Supermarket principle and its effects.

> The Supermarket principle[xi] is a central concept in lean manufacturing. It aims to streamline material flows and reduce waste. Supermarkets are material buffers between workstations in areas where continuous material flow is not possible. In the Supermarket, specified minimum and maximum quantities are kept for the subsequent process step. If the minimum quantity is undershot, a Kanban signal triggers the production of new parts in the upstream process. This principle is comparable to the logistics in an ordinary supermarket. Only after the removal of certain stock items are the shelves replenished. The rule is: only produce what is needed at the time it is needed.

The quantity of material in the Supermarket and in the entire circulation is determined and limited by the number of Kanban cards. When material is removed, the Kanban card is placed in a box or directly on a board. A certain number of Kanban cards is considered the starting point or signal for replenishment or reproduction. This ensures that only the quantities that have been withdrawn are replenished. The principle naturally also works for finished products or almost finished products. Here, Sales can withdraw according to agreed rules, and Production produces accordingly. It replenishes the warehouse again. Therefore, it is often called the full replenishment principle.

The Supermarket principle is also called the 'pull principle' and not only reduces inventories but also significantly contributes to the reduction of waste. It minimizes the need to store excess materials that are not immediately required. This has a cascade of positive effects: less material means less space required for storage areas, fewer shelves, reduced shelf inspection effort, reduced effort for relocating and searching for material, fewer forklift operations, and accordingly lower costs, as well as fewer risks of accidents. It is not without reason that excessive inventory levels are a significant problem in a company. Once progress is made here, the overall situation improves. It is therefore not surprising that the material turnover rate in a company serves as an indicator of the level of lean principles achieved.

The Supermarket principle also promotes greater flexibility, as production processes can adapt more quickly to changing demand or production requirements. Furthermore, it improves transparency in material flow and enables teams to identify and address bottlenecks and weaknesses in real-time. Quality is also positively influenced. The less material is in circulation, the less is affected in the event of a serial defect.

In summary, it can be said that the Supermarket principle enables more efficient, waste-free production that is aligned with actual needs. By controlling and optimizing material flow, it promotes the agility and competitiveness of companies relying on lean manufacturing principles.

Raleigh, USA

The upcoming August staff meeting this year didn't take place in Tomado. We gathered in Raleigh on the East Coast in North Carolina. Even the top managers of the Technical Department were present. While preparing facts, figures, forecasts, and plans, I also devised something special for my own benefit. In the company, there was a mentoring program where a manager, who stands at least two hierarchical levels above, supports an employee in their professional development. However, with the constantly changing supervisors in Europe, it felt difficult to me to orient towards any one person or receive continuous feedback for further development. Early in the morning before the staff meeting, I arranged meetings with the Head of the Business Unit (Level 1) and the Global Operation Vice President (the fourth in six years) to discuss my ideas with them. I also inquired with the Head of the Business Unit if there was anyone he could recommend as a mentor. He knew someone who had also coached him: Luke McPherson, our OpEx Vice President and also a Lean and 3P specialist.

I quickly reached out to him. We discussed my goals and what my achievements had been so far. He agreed to the mentoring, and I was very glad about it. Our regular phone calls in the following years and the time we spent together during his visits were extremely enriching and led to many valuable tips for me. It significantly influenced my career path, as would later become evident. Luke was actually the co-author of a book on 3P techniques – a toolbox that meant nothing to me back then. I was glad that I slowly grasped Lean and could strategically use the tools from this toolbox.

The Staff Meeting proceeded in an unusual setting but in familiar ways, well, maybe not entirely. There was still a poignant moment. Shortly after the lunch break, the screens of our laptops on the tables shook. Some desktop computers had malfunctioned, and other colleagues held their laptops in hand, standing incredulously and excitedly in the aisle. The poignant moment lasted only about thirty seconds, however, everyone felt it.

On August 23, 2011, at 1.51 pm, an earthquake occurred in Virginia, which was felt in North Carolina and other adjacent states. It had a magnitude of about 5.8 on the Richter scale and was one of the stronger earthquakes in the region. Thirty seconds were very short for an earthquake of this magnitude. While the epicenter was in Mineral, Virginia, the tremors were felt in parts of Ohio and other states. This event caused noticeable tremors and piqued the interest of many people in the region, as earthquakes in this area are rather rare. It was also called the Virginia Earthquake of 2011. Fortunately, nothing serious happened.

The next day was our team event. We went on a whitewater kayaking trip two hours away from Raleigh, naturally in Virginia, where the earthquake had occurred the day before. I sat in a tandem canoe with a nice colleague. It was a rather calm whitewater, considering there were complete beginners, and nothing was supposed to happen. As we turned around a rock, we saw a black snake quite close to our paddles on the rock. It was a cobra on a rock, causing some excitement. Robert urged us to leave quickly, and we did.

At the restaurant after the event, he revealed to us that he would be leaving the company and the department would be dissolved. The VA/VE managers were to report to the Head of Engineering of the largest plant from then on. I was an exception, as my expertise was in manufacturing and not in design. I was to report to the Vice President of Operations for Europe. We already knew each other quite well. My dotted line to Jean became a full line. This ran smoothly for a few weeks until in September, the Global VP of Operations announced that Jean would also be going his own way, and Frederick would take over his position. Another change in management – my decision regarding the mentoring had been spot on. Frederick was a Frenchman from Charmes, who often commuted between his house in Nice and the plants. Our good relationship benefited from this shared commuting experience and my rudimentary French skills. In six years, he was the fourth Vice President for Europe; certainly not a job for me.

Trieste, Italy

Miracles are rare, but they can and do happen again and again. In 2011, I actually managed to schedule an appointment for my first event in Trieste at FMIT. The product had already been selected through tough and lengthy discussions. It was slowly facing market pressure, with declining orders and continuously decreasing margins. The customer demanded a greater functional gain from the product, ideally at a consistent price. Our preparations were meticulous, because nothing could be left to chance here. My goal was to be able to come back, and this would only be possible with success.

Before the event took place, Frederick, my new boss, also held his staff meeting at this wonderful location between the Adriatic Sea and the Alps. As part of this meeting, we, like last year, developed strategies and goals for the following year with the local team for the various functions of the plant. Occupational safety, quality, materials management, productivity, and delivery reliability were the core themes. This process was a constant in the company. Even Jean, his predecessor, had conducted the annual planning of the plants and the region in this way. If the people didn't stay, at least the important processes did. It went a bit smoother than the previous year. Lorenzo and his team apparently understood that these strategies were not meant to cause harm. In the end, the site had to approve all projects so still had everything under its' direct control.

Of course, such events also included team activities. In the afternoon, we visited a large winery in the Friuli-Venezia Giulia region. The Brda winery is located in the wine region of the same name, which extends on both the Slovenian and Italian sides of the border, very close to Trieste. The landscape is characterized by gentle hills and vineyards, and there are some wineries that have their cellars in the hills, partly on both sides of the border. As the region was historically part of the Habsburg Empire and later part of Yugoslavia, some wineries have developed on both sides of the border over the decades and are also connected, so to speak, in small-scale cross-border trade.

The wines were stored in large underground cellars in the mountain. Above these cellar vaults, there were properties made of natural stone. We were also able to participate in a wine tasting. Our Occupational Safety Manager was not very happy about it. Yet the game wasn't called 'make a wish', but rather 'this is how it is!'

Now back to my first event at FMIT in Trieste. VA/VE events were actually always a success because the idea generators were also the ones who were allowed to implement the most. As a moderator, you just had to tap into the ideas in people's heads. The real challenge, however, was turning these suggestions into reality. As a result of the very specific circumstances, this was now even easier in Trieste than in the large plants. The development team reported directly to the General Manager, who, after a long process of consideration, now wanted to see as many functional improvements and cost reductions as possible. Initially, his rejecting argument was that their products were already perfect and there was no need for VA/VE ideas. Now, these VA/VE ideas were given high priority – an encouraging step. 'Well, there you go', I thought, and had a small sense of achievement

My Hotels

In selecting my hotels, I deviated slightly from the company standard. Not that they were more expensive than the standard partners; they were actually always cheaper. It just required a bit more effort for our travel service in Antwerp to book them. Month after month, I alternated between stays in Lens, Roubaix, Bornago, Brezno, and occasionally in Trieste. It was important to me not only to appear as a guest, but to be welcomed as a valued regular. My choice was always the small, privately run accommodations. The island of Grado in the Adriatic had a special place in my heart. It was a recommendation from Andrea that we had followed the previous year, and one I continued to uphold. Initially, I tried out different hotels there until I finally discovered the right one. Breakfast on the rooftop terrace offered a charming view of the sea, and evenings were spent in a cozy trattoria near the waterfront. Sometimes I even managed to go for a swim in the evenings, or simply walk for miles through the tidal flats, or jog on the beach before heading to the sauna reserved for me at the hotel.

It wasn't just on Grado that I found a special haven. I also placed great importance on the choice of accommodation in other places. In Bussero near Bornago, my first chose was always the Hotel Angi. A lovely family ran this hotel, and the entire family worked hand in hand. The team always reserved my favorite, Room 101, slightly larger than the others and right next to the family's quarters on the ground floor. This room was always available for me, and the service was outstanding. The cuisine was on the verge of earning a Michelin star. Dante, the son and chef of the house, was incredib y inventive. I had wonderful evenings there with many colleagues. I won't deny that it was also good to be able to submit these bills as expenses. Leo the Labrador always greeted me warmly. Sometimes, in the evenings, he would lie down next to my feet and enjoy being petted while the family had dinner. I also enjoyed the special atmosphere of the Hotel Plaza in Banská Bystrica in Slovakia. Although it was slightly larger than the Angi, there was no constant turnover of staff here either. Like at the Angi, a special room was reserved for me with the number 104, and the existing sauna (as well as the fully equipped fitness room), acded to the feeling of well-being. I reserved them as needed from the car that always picked me up from the airport in Vienna; a service I truly

169

enjoyed. Our company had avoided having its employees drive rental cars in Slovakia. Upon each of my arrivals, I was greeted with a warm 'Welcome at Home' – truly a pleasant feeling. At Christmas time, there was at least one red Air Berlin heart on all the Christmas trees in the hotels.

The hospitality in Lens and Roubaix was of an incredibly familial quality. In both places, the stay was at so-called chambre d'hôte establishments – charming farms that also bred horses. At the farm near Lens, evenings were spent with the family at the table with wine or beer, speaking exclusively French, and learning a lot from it. At the other farm in Roubaix, breakfast and dinner were brought directly to my room. The apartment was quite long, about 20 meters, and was located above the stables of the show horses, which also enjoyed their stay on this farm. In the mornings, I had to pass by the stalls after breakfast. If the horses hadn't yet had their breakfast, they would sometimes nudge me as I walked by.

My days were filled with unique experiences. I witnessed the births of foals that grew to know me from when they were small, and I admired impressive show jumping horses of the French team, some of which stood up to 1.80 meters tall. One afternoon, I helped to catch a particularly curious and adventurous foal that had managed to escape, running around the courtyard. In the summer, I participated in rehearsals and concerts held in picturesque barns, especially during the Fête de la Musique on June 21st in France.

Set amidst a green environment, I found an atmosphere of well-being here that made each of my trips an extremely pleasant experience. My way of working allowed me to find a balance between work and wonderful experiences that is difficult for many people to achieve. In this balance, I found perfection; I worked intensely and efficiently without neglecting the joys of life.

My Lean-Transformation

In my own Lean transformation, I felt incredibly comfortable. My mentor was a highly respected individual; after all, he had written a book on 3P himself. I made a mental note to eventually read it, to understand what 3P really was. He supported me through occasional coaching calls. The plants around Europe and India demanded tools from me; I learned about them and then tried them out in the factories. For me, it still held true, 'Only where you have walked by foot have you truly been'.

The goals were achieved, and the factories recognized that I had become a competent point of contact not only for VA/VE issues but also for Lean matters. The full-time OpEx leader focused solely on Brezno and the HDA, while the smaller factories had to wait for other support. That was my niche. Now I found myself in close proximity to my desired role as a coach, just as Ron has been in the Bergisches Land a few years previously. After all, I was already 54 years old, the same age as Ron had been then.

End of the Year

The ambitious goal of almost €20 million in savings for material and manufacturing productivity had been achieved, and I was already looking forward to the bonus payment next March. This was perceived with goodwill and also with a certain surprise in Brussels. Now, when the headquarters in Tomado also wanted to see savings in general administration, it felt like all eyes were on me. There was a question in Brussels of whether I could also take on this task – improvements in the administrative area, namely SG&A productivity (Sales, General, and Administration). This idea carried some delicacy, because Sales and Marketing were reluctant to allow insights into their cards and costs. Nevertheless, there was no choice for me, so I took on this task for the coming year. At the same time, they expanded my regional responsibility to include India, the Middle East, and Africa (EMEIA). I now had the immense responsibility of supporting ten factories, with a savings target of €30 million. All the players at this table were seasoned poker players and showed exactly the same face and behavior when it came to savings in their areas.

This year was relatively stable, with no major personnel changes in my direct environment. An exception was the replacement of the Global Vice President - Operation – Bob, Roger's successor, was now Allister. In six years, there had now been five vice presidents, though this had a negligible effect on me. Besides, Ron was now my steadfast mentor, while other managers came and went like the tides. As a team, we worked diligently on our goals, and my event activities reached a new peak in number and intensity. The HDA increasingly faded into the background, exactly as my former boss had recommended. During this time, I almost exclusively turned to other sites.

Wherever I came from during the year, I saw the summer lilacs blooming along the railway tracks in the summer. It was already the seventh time. Should we even continue counting? If I were to retire at the age of 66, we would reach a total of nineteen lilac blooms. The number didn't sit well with us, but there was no prospect of ending the commute.

2012

> Problem solving is of paramount importance, as continuous improvement is one of the primary components of Lean thinking. We understand that problems are most likely to be identified at the scene of the action, the Gemba. Only when I solve a problem do I achieve improvement. However, there are different types of problems: 'Just Do Its,' where extensive analysis is not required; fundamental problems that require a change to a completely different level; and problems resulting from deviations from the normal state. For each type of problem, there is the right tool. Choosing the appropriate tool is not an art, but an extremely important and serious task.

The Beginning of the Year

The turn of the year took us to La Palma. However, on this visit we were disappointed with our accommodation for the very first time. Cleanliness, location, and facilities did not meet our expectations. It was simply dismal, and we longed to find a familiar standard with each stay. After three days, we decided to call Ira - the woman with whom we had stayed several times before and always been satisfied. Fortunately, guests had cancelled their reservation with her, and her bungalow was available. This was a true Christmas gift. Our joy at reuniting was great. In the evenings, we sat together several times and had lively conversations. During these discussions, we even brought up the idea of whether she would possibly sell the annex or the bungalow – someday. Eventually, we broached the topic of price and discussed how to sensibly divide the property. This would be a way for us to find a familiar standard with each stay.

Ultimately, we decided against purchasing the bungalow. One reason for this was the road about 150 meters below. Previously, we couldn't hear it, but now construction work had begun to remove stones, gradually increasing traffic noise. Despite the disruption of these first three days, the vacation was very relaxing and educational. We realized that finding a house according to our wishes was not so easy. Our relationship with Ira was in no way tarnished by this. She also had concerns. She didn't want to sell the cow she milked. For her, as an immigrant from Russia, it was her retirement provision after she separated from her husband. Ira's ex-husband owned the other half of the property, which also had three houses, and he also had a wife, and daughter. They all got along, but were separate in terms of both family and finances.

A new year also dawned in the company. After Robert left the previous year, I found myself under Jean's leadership initially. When Jean then said goodbye, finally Frederick became my Manager. Besides I had a good rapport with Emanuel, our President. Secretly, my hope was that the year 2012 would be somewhat calmer in terms of personnel turnover. It began with a slightly different surprise: The colleagues who opposed my idea of expanding VA/VE to the manufacturing sector last year now received a President's Award: The topic - what a surprise! - was the expansion of VA/VE events to the manufacturing sector and a holistic view of the process. Now the idea came from the 'right' people, and they proclaimed that this process should now be used by everyone in this form, and not otherwise. This was a little frustrating to me. Nevertheless, I immediately recognized improvement potential in their version of our idea. They had standardized everything, from the size of the sticky notes and the whiteboard to the ranking of ideas based on savings potential.

All the plants in the USA were large, English was spoken at all sites, and it was one country. If you drive forty kilometers west of Düsseldorf in Germany, you quickly reach the Netherlands, another ninety minutes and you are in Belgium, and another ninety minutes later you are in France. Four different cultures in just four hours. The plants in Europe and India varied greatly in size. This was a result of the company integrations by the ÄÄtch Group. While rejoicing over an idea worth €50,000 in the Bergisches Land, Germany, was commonplace, this amount was simply unrealistic in France. In a small plant in France, there is jubilation when an idea worth €5,000 can be implemented. The ratios were even more extreme compared to India, of course. Thus, the American mindset of 'big, bigger, America' led to frustration at the smaller sites. Why should a colleague in India develop an idea worth a thousand Euros if it ended up being the lowest priority on the list? I didn't strictly adhere to the rules and adjusted the values to the size of the plant. I was also allowed to use the sticky notes that were available and deviated from the US standard.

Ahmedabad, India

Ahmedabad, with its 8.4 million inhabitants, ranks as the seventh-largest city in India. It is situated in the western part of the country, along the Sabarmati River, in the state of Gujarat. The climate in Ahmedabad is hot and dry during the summer months. The monsoon season spans from June to August. Between November and January, temperatures are somewhat cooler, with daytime temperatures dipping below 30°C and nighttime temperatures hovering around 10°C.

The city is also renowned as the birthplace of Mahatma Gandhi. It has evolved into a significant trading hub for textiles and cotton. Several magnificent landmarks define Ahmedabad. For me, the two most impressive ones were the Sidi Saiyyed Mosque, built between 1572 and 1573, and the Mahatma Gandhi Museum situated along the banks of the Sabarmati River.

The first invitation for such an event, named the 'Productivity Summit', in our region was planned for February in India. A comprehensive team gathered on-site, and our expectations were high. The team in Ahmedabad had invested much work and time in preparing for this event, and they were deeply passionate about it. Naturally, the little notes and whiteboards did not adhere to American standards in terms of dimensions. Similarly, the ratio between labor and material costs differed fundamentally between America and India. What a surprise! These standards do not determine the success of an event; it is the ideas that matter. I must emphasize that this event was fantastic. Even smaller little notes couldn't change that fact. Employees from production, engineering, procurement, and sales were actively involved. Essentially, everything proceeded as we had been practicing in Europe for over a year. Well, almost. In Europe, we focused on a specific area and product range. The 'new' American approach considered the entire plant and almost all products. They aimed to shine with big numbers. 'Great show!' Still, was this approach effective and sustainable?

We filled the idea pipeline to the brim. Yet, somehow, this approach didn't feel quite right. It didn't align with the principles of Lean Manufacturing. Now we had a mountain of ideas that needed to be prioritized. Many ideas fell by the wayside because as soon as the market situation, demand, or product changed, they lost their value. This entire process reminded me, drawing a comparison from manufacturing, of large batch sizes and high inventories. Both ultimately lead to waste and high administrative overhead. The comparison with excessive material inventories and the resulting waste chain also applies to ideas!

The impressions I gathered in India were overwhelming, particularly regarding clothing. On the outbound journey, my suitcase probably lost its way in Munich or Abu Dhabi and went off track. Besides reporting the loss at 4.30 am in India with 25 other passengers, the following days were very exciting. I had to acquire some Indian clothing, which was quite an adventure. It was Sunday, and we went to a bazaar. Many things were extremely colorful and glittery. However, I could still negotiate prices; in fact, you couldn't buy anything without bargaining! I looked quite native at times, but was relieved when my suitcase finally arrived at the hotel on Tuesday evening.

Back in Europe, I continued my events and weekly conference calls with the ten plants and the administration in Brussels. When it was finally Delhi's turn, the small plant initially reported its key figures. Everything was somewhat smaller compared to Ahmedabad, and Ahmedabad, in turn, was already smaller than Bornago. However, in the end, they asked me to conduct an event in Delhi, just like the one in Ahmedabad the previous week. I was impressed by their willingness to invest so much time and effort. They wanted to be respected and treated with as much attention as the other plants. This was again a niche for me to jump into.

Bornago, Italy

In May, a planned event took place in Bornago. We were brainstorming ideas for a large device, with all participants equipped with laptops. During our meeting on the ground floor, we suddenly heard loud voices, almost screams. People started rushing out of the building as it began to tremble, even on the ground floor. A series of severe earthquakes had rocked the Emilia-Romagna region in northern Italy, near Parma, on May 20th. The magnitude of these quakes was about 6.1 on the Richter scale. Although they lasted only a few seconds, they caused significant damage to buildings, infrastructure, and industry in the area. 27 people lost their lives as a result.

Fortunately, the factory remained unscathed, and only a few glasses and bottles were broken in my beloved Hotel Angi. No one was injured in the area around Bussero, and that was the most important thing in this situation. It was my second earthquake in ten months of business travel. I truly experienced moving moments in my profession.

Delhi, India

The request from Delhi for a major event was discussed with Frederick. As a sign of equality and respect, we agreed. We planned everything meticulously and organized both the trip and the event. This time, I didn't invite anyone from the USA. I worked closely with colleagues from Delhi and Ahmedabad. During the event, they were proud of every idea presented, akin to the Spaniards. In the end, we developed an impressive yet manageable idea pipeline for the site and achieved some truly good process improvements. Although the outcome barely affected the overall productivity of the ÄÄtch Group sector, this event allowed me to forge a close relationship with an entire plant. The employees in Delhi dedicated themselves to the implementation. They safely achieved their goals the following year, and we talked about this event for a long time. It made them feel like part of a grand orchestra.

However, even more impressive was what I experienced during this event. Our CEO visited the plant with his team, so all meeting rooms were occupied. I had to go to the hotel in Delhi for my conference call with the plants. My room on the tenth floor of the Radisson Blu Hotel offered an impressive view of the 32-million metropolis. You could see the skyline and also the slums evenly distributed throughout the neighborhood, dominating the outskirts. A haze hung over everything, casting a yellowish tint on the sunlight like a filter. Although I was using a headset, I suddenly heard noises in the room during the call. I located the source of the clattering. It turned out the hangers in the closet were loose and hitting the door. Immediately afterward, I went to the window and was shocked to see the pool directly below. Sometimes, after a few moments, I could even look down to the ground floor window facade of the building. The building swayed in a range of more than a meter in both directions. Nothing was damaged. I called reception, yet they hadn't noticed anything on the ground floor. Nevertheless, they checked the internet and confirmed there had been an earthquake further away.

On August 11, 2012, a severe earthquake occurred in the border region between Iran and Iraq. With a magnitude of about 6.4, this earthquake caused significant damage and claimed several hundred lives in both countries. The tremors were felt as far as India. The Radisson Blu was constructed very securely; it swayed but nothing broke. In these experiences, movement, in this case, of tectonic plates, is not beneficial. On the contrary, it has devastating effects. This was now the third earthquake I had experienced in twelve months, and it was the most severe with the greatest damage. Privately, I hoped these events would finally come to an end for me.

Lens, France

Lens is a city in the Hauts-de-France region of northern France, with an interesting history intertwined with industrial development and the impacts of both world wars. Lens was once a significant center for mining in northeastern France. The coal industry played a crucial role in the economic development of the region. The city was shaped by the industrial revolution and mining. In December 2012, the Louvre-Lens was opened on a former mining site. It is a branch of the museum in Paris. This modern museum presents an impressive collection of artworks from the Louvre in Paris.

At the end of last year, Frederick called me again. The Vice President of Product Management from the USA had contacted him.

It was about developing and standardizing a new product. The application area was on oil platforms, in open-pit mining, and large wind turbines. Large quantities of media were transported to the sites with these products. Similar products, manufactured by other companies, as well as by another plant of the ÄÄtch Group in North America, were available on the market. This was the direct result of the expansion strategy of the ÄÄtch Group. One variant was developed and produced in Bellingham, near the Canadian border, whereas the other products originated in Harnes, a suburb of Lens in northern France, and were originally developed for mining.

In earlier times, the region around Lens was firmly in the grip of mining. The high-performance unit supplied miners with water, air, and other media in the tunnels. However, as in the Ruhr area and Saarland, the mining industry in this region faced a similar fate – it declined. In view of this, the product was modified for use in pressure and suction operation, as well as for other media. This reminds me again of how important movement is. Of course, the competition was not asleep either. The product managers faced the challenging task of increasing market share while reducing costs. The employees in Bellingham were just as convinced of their product as their colleagues in Harnes were of theirs.

It was decided to conduct a teardown analysis with the two products of the ÄÄtch Group and a competitor's product. Organizing and implementing this was to be my task. I was familiar with this type of analysis, but had never conducted one before. Some colleagues from the USA helped me with the preparations, which would take about three months.

First, let me explain the teardown analysis:

- The teardown analysis is a method for completely disassembling and analyzing a product down to its smallest components. It is used to examine design, materials, and manufacturing processes to identify weaknesses and optimization potentials. The insights gained contribute to product improvement and cost reduction.

Here are the steps we took in analyzing the high-performance unit 'Medi-Trans':

- Preparation and Documentation: We ensured that all necessary tools, equipment, and safety measures were in place. We took photos and notes to document the process. We reviewed repair and service manuals, identified the exact tool requirements, and the required area. During the teardown, no time was spent searching for items, as times were also assessed. All drawings, parts lists, and maintenance schedules were provided to the team as handouts
- Removal of Coverings: These were measured and weighed so that later the various products could be compared with measurable values
- Analysis of the Motor and Drive System: The electric motor driving the pump was closely examined. We checked its performance, capacity, construction, and made notes on the electrical connections and cable routes
- Examination of Impellers and Blades: We dismantled the pump and examined the condition of the parts for wear, cracks, or other damage

- Inspection of the Gearbox: The gearbox was opened to inspect the gear configuration, the condition of the gears, and the bearings
- Evaluation of Control Electronics: The control electronics responsible for operating the pump were examined to identify damaged components
- Verification of Safety Features: We ensured that all safety devices and emergency switches met legal requirements and functioned correctly
- Analysis of Connectors: All connectors uniting the various components of the pump were checked to ensure they were properly tightened and in good condition.
- Assessment of Wear and Ageing: We estimated the wear and ageing of all pump parts and checked if maintenance was required
- Summary and Reporting: After completing the teardown analysis, we compiled a report containing all the key findings, issues, and potential improvements. This report was intended to serve as the basis for the redevelopment of a standardized, uniform product for all regions

Of course, we would not be able to conduct the teardowns and analyzes during this event week. The disassembly had to be done beforehand. In Harnes, we were provided with an annex building for the analysis. After tidying up, we were able to set up three rows of tables, each six meters long, one row for each product. The tables were covered with white cardboard. Pascal, the service technician in Harnes, dismantled the three products and cleaned everything. The tables were divided into assemblies. In each row, you could find the equivalent assembly of the other product in the same position. This allowed for a quick comparison of the components and identification of differences. We provided drawings and parts lists. This was the basis for the actual event. There was only one downside. The room was not heated, and it was winter. In Harnes, the nights were sometimes very cold – the thermometer in the car showed -7°C. A few gas heaters and hot tea helped us in this situation.

For the event at the end of January, we invited 26 participants, including engineers, assemblers, service personnel, product managers, and Lean specialists. The service technicians came from both Bellingham and Harnes. As the various products were mainly sold in the regions of the respective plants, the employees were mostly familiar with 'their' device. Especially Ephraim, the service technician from Bellingham, impressed us. He was an absolute expert, living in the USA, and a Canadian with indigenous roots. He travelled to the most remote parts of the world, including Siberia, to perform repairs. And he was fair and open to new or different ideas, which could not be said of his colleagues in the design department in Bellingham, but partly also of the developers in Harnes.

The three products were analyzed by mixed teams from Bellingham and Harnes. When it came to an initial evaluation, Ephraim asked me to speak alone with his colleagues from Bellingham first. He found many differences between the American and European solutions. However, based on his field experience, he often found the European solutions more advantageous. That was tough news for the designers from Bellingham. So, we designed a new pump that consisted of the best solutions from the French, the Bellingham product, and an external solution. This innovative pump station had fewer individual parts, a lighter weight, and of course, was more cost-effective. It was produced at both locations, Bellingham and Harnes, and successfully re-placed two obsolete products. This transition also brought clear benefits for procurement, as the quantities were significantly higher due to the standardization of one product. With this step, we could reduce the complexity of the products. We had made a good start. The entire product portfolio in this segment was to be streamlined in this way.

The final presentation took place as planned on Friday that same week, in the cold premises. In my usual role, I reported on the overall process, while the team members presented the spe-cific solutions. I also spoke with Crystie, the Vice President who had initiated the entire project. She had a mischievous twinkle in her eye. She told me that despite her cold feet, everything had gone well. And she had cold feet several times – the first time was when she found out during the preparations for the analysis that I had never done something like this before; but in the end, she was very pleased because the result was more than satisfactory for her.

My Lean-Transformation

This year brought a remarkable innovation: the introduction of the 9-Step Problem-Solving Model. This structured method of-fers an extremely effective approach to successfully addressing deviations from the normal state and returning them to the nor-mal level. The approach promotes a systematic approach to problem-solving and supports sustainable solution finding.

Here's a brief explanation of the 9 steps, which were documented on an A3 sheet:

1. Step 1: the process starts with the clear identification of the problem. What was the goal, what is the current state, what is the gap?
2. Step 2: involves a multi-stage Pareto analysis of the problem. The largest bar is broken down into its components.
3. Step 3: goal setting aims to eliminate the last largest bar. What exactly needs to be done by when to achieve this?
4. Step 4: we use the proven method of children asking them 'why' until they come up with the truth. It's the '5-Why Analysis' to uncover the root causes of the problem. Here, we examine the why behind the why in many consecutive steps. This analysis leads us to the most promising solution approaches
5. Step 5: solutions are evaluated by stating 'Because we introduced this solution, the why' before it was eliminated. This determines the validity of the solutions
6. Step 6: Additionally, we create a list of possible solutions to be tested in advance
7. Step 7: The last three boxes involve the detailed development of an action plan
8. Step 8: carefully measurement and comparison of the results achieved with the previously established goals in Box 3
9. Step 9: provides feedback throughout the entire process

Training all Change Agents in the plants to become 9-Step Trainers was a crucial step. They should be able to train additional employees in this tool in the plants as needed. What would I do in my small plants? There were no OpEx Leaders or Change Agents available. Should I wait until one of the European OpEx colleagues has time to hold courses in France or Italy? That would slow down the pace of our projects and was not a valid option for me. My desire went beyond just using the tool – I also wanted to be trained as a trainer. The OpEx Leader had some concerns; however, my decision was firm, as my boss also supported me on this issue. It was about ensuring that small plants did not get stuck in the waiting loop of the OpEx department. In case of problems that occurred during an event or a project in one of the plants, I could conduct training and train my colleagues in the problem-solving process.

Throughout the year, I initially participated in training weeks myself and also taught a group of people from various administrative functions for two weeks. The training took place in Bolton, UK. The name reminded me of the 'Bolton Wanderers', a former Premier League club from the suburbs of Manchester. That's where my Black Belt colleague Rick experienced his football career when the club was still playing in the third English league. Surprisingly, the training venue was near the stadium. Moreover, the hotel was even part of the stadium and located under the stands. During dinner and breakfast, you could see into the arena. Even though there was no game at the time, it was a great feeling. Just the thought that 28,000 spectators would stand on the steep stands at the edge of the field and create a lot of noise gave me a slight thrill. An inspiring feeling that reminded me of long-forgotten footballing times.

The lawn of the 'Wanderers' was simply perfect. Now, it was such that the grandstand roof provided shade to part of the lawn during the day, as the sun doesn't shine so high in England. Another part, however, was in the sun for a few hours a day. This 'immense' imbalance in lighting conditions was balanced out by the club in the evenings. The 'shady side' received several hours of UV lighting via wagons that drove over the shaded areas. I had never seen that before. Evidently, someone had successfully practiced 'problem-solving' there.

My journey also took me via London with a stopover and change to Manchester. Through Facebook, I had re-established contact with my cousin Brian after many years, who lived with his wife Fennah near London's airport. Spontaneously, I suggested that we meet during a planned four-hour layover at Heathrow Airport to see each other again after 45 years. Said and done – we used the ninety minutes we had left and exchanged memories. On the way to check-in again, I mentioned in the elevator that I was a Black Belt, and promptly received the business card of a head-hunter, who was standing next to us and offered me a job. However, I politely declined, as I was very happy with my current company.

The training in Bolton lasted for three days, followed by another one two weeks later. After successfully completing my own 9-step project, I became a 9-Step Trainer myself. Yet this journey brought not only professional development, but also a happy reunion with my cousin and his wife. We have been in contact ever since. It was undoubtedly fortunate to have made this journey to UK.

End of the Year

It's true, this year has indeed been quite 'moving' for me, not just because of the earthquakes. It also deeply touched me that so many lives were lost. Fortunately, the places where I was and where our factories are located were not affected. Everyone remained unharmed here. We once again achieved our productivity goals, so I could expect a solid bonus payment for this fiscal year as well. However, there was a slight catch. We actually exceeded productivity because the unit numbers were above plan. However, we were told that fluctuations in unit numbers don't necessarily indicate productivity. I could understand that. Becoming a trainer with the 9-step program further empowered me, making me more independent. Systematic problem-solving was crucial for the success of our projects. I was able to offer increasingly comprehensive consultations in the small factories, and they gratefully accepted it, venturing down unconventional paths with me.

Along the routes to and from the airports, I once again saw the delicate blooms of the butterfly bush – for the eighth time. With Air Berlin, I initially achieved golden status and then established myself as a platinum member, which brought me many comforts. Pre-boarding without invitation, VIP status, a glass of champagne before departure, and complimentary meals on international flights – for an airline without a European business class, it was truly enjoyable.

As 2012 came to a close, we spent some time in La Palma at Finca El Horizonte in Las Manchas. The cottages were almost like hobbit houses, one had to stoop to enter. The location was simply breathtaking. Situated at 500 meters altitude outside Las Manchas, we had an indescribable view of the Atlantic. In the valley, we could hear goat bells, and occasionally a dog barked. Jogging in this area was more akin to athletic training. Nonetheless, I managed to run to the tennis court and back, and once even completed an eleven-kilometer circuit over Todoque, past Ira's house, where we had stayed several times before. I had tackled such inclines when I used to compete, and it certainly helped me in some running disciplines back then.

We had already begun looking at properties with real estate agents, but so far, nothing suitable had been found. Perhaps next time, as we still have time. Meanwhile, our relaxation was assured, and we also enjoyed the evenings in the two small cottages and on the terrace in between.

2013

Pareto forever ... 80/20 ... 80% of problems are driven by 20% of the causes. However, even these 20% can be quite diverse. That's why sustainable problem-solving approaches, like the 9-Step Problem-Solving method, generate a cascade of Paretos. This effectively narrows down the various main causes, and sometimes even provides a solution during the Pareto analysis itself. By creating multiple Pareto levels, you can precisely target the biggest problems. It's like focusing a laser on a well-defined target and eliminating it. Progress might not always be swift, but it is certainly sustainable!

The Beginning of the Year

In the picturesque cottage named 'El Horizonte', we enjoyed relaxed days in the new year. We spent New Year's Eve in a different setting, staying at the Hotel Sol La Palma and celebrating with a lively party in the festive ballroom with guests and locals. A DJ played dance music that night. The traditional ritual of eating twelve grapes at the turn of the year, with one wish for each grape at each chime, proved to be an amusing challenge. This was a 'Just-do-it' problem that didn't require a 9-Step approach. Shortly after midnight, a single firework was launched in Puerto Naos as the New Year's celebration; impressively relaxed and unpretentious. The next morning, after a sumptuous hotel breakfast, we took a refreshing New Year's swim in the 22°C Atlantic surf at 11.30 am before driving the four kilometers back to the house. However, the vacation sadly was coming to an end.

A few days later, we were back in Berlin. We would have loved to stay longer. I prepared for my upcoming business trips, and the year began professionally just as the old one had ended; with preparations, events, and conference calls.

New Evaluation Methods

The productivity goals for this year were set at just over $30 million in savings—the most ambitious target I had ever been given. I knew we all had to work hard to achieve it. VA/VE and productivity events were one way to get there. However, without a stable order intake and smoothly running production in the plants, it would be nearly impossible. The discussions with the Finance Department in Brussels became more intense. We had creative ideas, and they had to prove whether the increased productivity could be specifically attributed in the P&L or whether it was an improvement in profit margin as a result of a changed pricing structure. The saying 'Charity begins at home' holds true. In this case, we were not their home when it came to productivity. The various vice presidents for sales and marketing were at home, sitting in Brussels, proudly presenting their sales successes through margin increases.

Despite this, the events went very well over the course of the year. The realization of ideas was on schedule, and when you used the planned production volume as a multiplier, we were on track. Yet, we consistently lost our productivity at the end of each month. I opened discussions in the plants with the question: Why are we not meeting our productivity targets? The moderation cards were filled with a variety of reasons, ranging from 'rejection of ideas by development' to 'the originally planned quantities are not being met' and 'controlling reports negative productivity'. "Wait a minute! What?" I asked for clarification. Yes, it turned out that because of the drop in orders in the plants, there was insufficient utilization. This led to unabsorbed costs. Unfortunately, they were not reported as special costs by controlling, but as negative productivity. In the Pareto analysis, this factor was at the top in every plant.

There was a very bad mood between Finance and Production. This was because when business had been booming the year before, and we could report productivity, we were told then that increases in volume and the product mix did not generate productivity. It was calculated out as a volume effect. Now we were seriously told that declining quantities and the changed mix were, of course, 'negative productivity', not a volume effect like the year before, and that's why we hadn't met our targets.

The logic behind these arguments still escapes me. To be honest, I was quite upset back then and even had a heated verbal exchange with the Finance Director in Brussels. At that moment, I feared I might have to change my job again. However, it turned out, that an Italian can handle loud arguments, or he simply recognized the illogical reasoning of the Finance Department. In my case, there were no consequences for me, yet the said Finance Director left the team after just four months.

All the great ideas from the teams were implemented and led to significant savings. Finally at the end of the month, the Finance Department looked at the P&L, created a reconciliation from last year to the current year, and what remained at the end was considered real productivity. Productivity had evolved into a calculated sum of other numbers, to bridge the financial gap between the previous year and the current year. It was no longer the leading metric. This naturally led to demotivation among the teams in the plants I oversaw.

This also brought a new dynamic into play. The plants began to think about how they could eliminate this major bar in the Pareto analysis. They started to manufacture more in-house and purchase fewer services and materials. This improved cost coverage, and we had fewer corrections. The year might not be perfect, yet it was a step in the right direction. The more a factory can 'breathe', the more flexible it is, of course. However, this was also a double-edged sword. Often, purchasing costs were lower than the total costs of in-house production. A Swabian European manager had formulated a solution to this dilemma years before in his 'native language'. He suggested comparing only variable costs with purchasing costs and excluding the fixed cost block. For him, these were the 'e-costs'. The 'e' came from 'Di seen eh doa!' (They're here anyway!). After all, these costs were supposed to be absorbed by a higher share of in-house production.

Brussels, Belgium

On account of the new rules and methods for increasing productivity, as well as the requirement to achieve savings in the SG&A area this year, my path increasingly led me to Brussels. This city is truly a traffic disaster. The word 'parking' seems to immediately put dollar signs in people's eyes. Our European headquarters, like those of a hundred other companies, was located near

Zaventem Airport. When driving there, one had to plan for at least 25 additional minutes just to find a parking spot. There were indeed parking spaces in the building's underground garage, but not nearly enough for all employees. During my initial visits, I always found a parking spot somewhere in the vicinity and then made my way into the building in the rain—it always rains in Brussels. Once inside, I exchanged a few words with the ladies at the reception and handed out my Air Berlin heart candies, which always delighted Liesbeth and Mareike.

Once a year, I even brought flowers for the reception. Naturally, I always announced my visits in advance via email. This allowed the two to prepare my visitor badge in time and, if necessary, organize a meeting room. I had also once asked if any employee with a parking spot might be traveling when I arrived at the headquarters. "Bien sûr." was the answer. So that's what we always did. And I regularly had a parking spot in the underground garage, which was rare among visitors.

One day, when Liesbeth couldn't reach me, she sent a fax to Caroline, the Executive Assistant in Bergisches Land, who also supported me with travel arrangements. "Hello Caroline, Max can take Emanuel's parking spot tomorrow [he was our CEO]. He is in Dublin for a sales meeting." When the CEO of HDA happened to read the fax, he was very irritated. He immediately asked Caroline, " Caroline, why does Max get Emanuel's parking spot from Liesbeth, while I always have to stand outside in the rain?" Caroline, by the way, also got her heart candies when I was in Bergisches Land. She later revealed to me that she already had a reply ready, which she did not voice, "Because Max flies with Air Berlin and not with another German airline." He probably wouldn't have understood that. So, she simply said, "I have no idea." What our professor instilled in us at the beginning of our careers has always stayed with me—attentiveness towards receptionists and gatekeepers can be invaluable.

Structural Changes

Throughout September, a certain unrest spread among the management level as a rumor made the rounds: the newly created regional presidents and the entire hierarchy below them, established three years ago, were to be eliminated. Over the preceding years, the regions had gained increasing decision-making power, which displeased the headquarters in the USA. In Tomado, there was concern about losing influence, and the investors were worried. The resulting insecurity led to a sort of paralysis. The fear of making a mistake overshadowed everything. However, I was convinced that the last few months of the year would not determine whether someone would stay or go — the weight of the preceding years would be decisive.

September finally brought clarity. While I was in Lens preparing for an event, a global company meeting was held via video conference. The announcement of a reorganization effective January 1, 2014, followed. Emanuel, our President for Europe and India, was immediately relieved of his duties. The Lens plant, where I was currently located, was reassigned to another sector of the group and no longer fell under my responsibility. The level below the President was partially dissolved, and my superior Frederick's position was to be newly filled. At my level — there were seven directors in Europe — four left the company immediately and one a few weeks later. Eva, the Quality Manager from Slovakia, and I survived this restructuring.

Despite this, I felt uncertain. I didn't know who my new boss would be or what tasks would come my way. The stress also manifested physically: a shingles outbreak made me suffer and I was unable to travel for ten days. In December, I sought advice from my mentor and the HR manager in Tomado. Both assured me that I had nothing to worry about. My new boss was to be Ethan, the current Vice President of Operations from America. He was originally from Scotland and would be returning to Europe with his family. Sharing this information with colleagues, especially those from the USA, they wished me good luck with my new boss. To the Americans, he seemed a bit eccentric. I already suspected why; Americans and Scots really don't have much in common. However, Ethan did not contact me in the following weeks, so I picked up the phone and called him.

We had a ten-minute conversation about various topics. He also confirmed that I was not in danger and should simply continue working as before. He said, " I had been following with great interest what you were doing with the plants in Europe over the preceding two years and would have liked to have someone like you in America, but that role didn't exist there." Apparently, he already had an idea of what he wanted to do with me. He asked if I was also responsible for India, which I affirmed. Ethan then responded that he didn't want that. It was too dangerous. A friend of his had been hospitalized during a business trip there over a minor issue. In the end, it kept getting worse, and he lost a foot as a result of an infection. He didn't want to expose me to this danger, so my focus would be working in Europe. Very caring, I thought, and decided to take a vacation with my wife on La Palma.

My Lean-Transformation

In my Lean development process, the preceding year did not bring any new insights. However, in retrospect, such a phase sometimes seems essential. It is comparable to training in sports. When you constantly learn new exercises and techniques, it becomes difficult to consolidate and refine what has already been learned. Therefore, this year was a year of refinement for me. The fact that I was still in the process and didn't have to worry was already a significant success. Evidently, I had woken up on time in the morning and was quick enough to get started and catch a gazelle. I had survived so far.

End of the Year

This time, despite professional uncertainties, we had already looked at two properties on our favorite island on the Internet. We arrived six days before Christmas, and as always, radiant summer weather awaited us on La Palma. In Las Manchas, we settled into our quarters this time; a small house on a spacious property, where the owner lived with her family. Three lively little dogs brought additional joy. On the second day, we drove to the island's unofficial capital, Los Llanos, and visited the realtor whose listings we had found online. He had time spontaneously, and we set off to see the proposed properties.

The first was near the Hobbit House El Horizonte, where we had stayed the previous year, but that was directly on the road. It turned out to be too small and not quite enough for us. The second property, however, had a dreamy garden, and the house exuded a certain charm. Unfortunately, it showed clear signs of needing renovation, and the location on a steep road didn't seem ideal either. During our visit, we repeatedly heard the roar of an engine every five minutes as a car accelerated up the nearby mountain road. Obviously, this was not the right place for us either.

At that moment, the realtor remarked that he knew exactly what we were looking for and could show us another house. We drove uphill to Tacande and turned into a steep road that already seemed familiar to us. We had stayed here several times before, and it was only a few meters to the paved path we had always wanted to walk down, but never did. The realtor turned on the blinker and said, "We need to turn here; the house is a bit secluded in a cul-de-sac." We slowly followed the short path downhill, parked, and stood in front of a duplex with a breathtaking view over the valley down to the ocean. The entire property was co-owned, although the areas had been individually used so far. The house was not too big, nor was the property, and the terrace offered a stupendous view. The other half of the duplex was occasionally rented out, the owners living a few kilometers away in a separate and very large house. It seemed almost perfect. We expressed our interest and indicated that we would make a decision by December 28th.

Over the holidays, we had a wealth of considerations to make. How many times had we been here? How much were we willing to invest? Was the location really as good as it seemed? Was there something we had overlooked? What were the neighbors like? Was there still room to negotiate the price? These questions occupied us during these reflective days. On Boxing Day, we made our decision. We tried to negotiate the price a bit and expressed our desire for another viewing, as well as the installation of a stove with four ceramic hobs and an oven, instead of the two-burner gas stove. The realtor took our requests and consulted with the seller.

To our delight, all our wishes were granted. Regarding the neighbors, the realtor informed us that they were all German or Swiss families of retirement age; we would be the youngest. With this certainty, we decided to sign a preliminary contract and make the down payment after our return to Berlin. We spent the remaining time on the island with extensive hikes, swimming in the sea, and another New Year's Eve celebration at the Hotel Sol La Palma, including the twelve wish-filled grapes in the last twelve seconds of the year. We stayed there for another night. As we stood on the balcony with a glass of champagne on New Year's Eve, celebrating our decision, a shooting star promptly passed by in the sky. It felt as if nothing could go wrong. During our return trip, we kept looking at the pictures we had taken of the house, property, and the impressive view. Finally, we knew what lay at the end of that mysterious paved path. Moreover, now we could always be there, enjoying our comfort standard, the climate, and the view on this wonderful island, which was actually a volcanic island.

3P, or the Production Preparation Process, is a fascinating and immensely powerful tool—a comprehensive toolbox, if you will. It allows for the scalable simulation, detailed analysis, and improvement of both simple and complex processes from the outset. Deeply rooted in Lean thinking, this process is characterized by an exceptionally systematic approach, incorporating 'Kaizens within Kaizens'—continuous improvements within the improvement process itself. The unique aspect of this method is that everything is created at a 1:10 scale using inexpensive materials like cardboard, paper, or wood. No steel is invested until all improvement loops have been successfully completed.

Uncertain Beginning of the Year

After returning to Berlin, we initially had several tasks to complete regarding the house purchase. We needed to arrange insurance, establish or deepen contacts with potential managers on the island – all of this kept us intensely occupied. Meanwhile, the job uncertainty continued to nag at me. The words of the HR Manager and my potential future boss echoed in my thoughts, and I decided to keep working. I set myself a timeframe of three months. Numerous events were on the horizon; in Roubaix, I continued to guide the team on the path of Lean transformation, and my monthly conference calls became the focus of my work. I was constantly travelling and was rarely found in the Bergisches Land. This also had to do with the newly hired Plant Manager. My plan was to work with the team on productivity and supermarket topics, but he curtly said, "You're not doing anything with my team here, and we need your office for something else!" Without further prompting, I left the plant and didn't return to that unwelcoming environment for many months. Caroline missed the chocolate hearts.

Always on the move, I heard that sometime in the summer, visitors from the USA were at the HDA plant, and the meeting rooms were occupied. It was customary to ask if they could use the large conference table in the Plant Manager's office, and the usual response was, "Of course, my office is at your disposal!" The guests did ask, and they were allowed to use it. In the evening, the two had more work to do — Americans often work late while traveling to stay in touch with colleagues back home. The Plant Manager said he was leaving, and they mentioned they'd like to continue using the office. He replied, "Feel free." Then he left the room and locked the office with the two guests inside. The 'prisoners' had to call the gatekeeper to be freed. This was one of the Plant Manager's last strange actions. A new one was sought again — this would be the ninth since 2005, the year I started in the Bergisches Land. The search lasted until late autumn.

Weeks and months passed. During this time, many colleagues left the company, while others were satisfied with the new roles they had taken on. However, my new boss remained strangely absent. Meanwhile, I learned that a close contact of mine, the Global Vice President for Engineering, would come to the Bergisches Land. We knew each other from several meetings, and I had organized a four-day tour through five plants for his closest employee across Europe. They wanted to explain how VA/VE was implemented in the company and were speechless about what we had already accomplished in this area. We were miles ahead of them.

My self-imposed three-month deadline had expired, and some colleagues who had already taken on new positions strongly advised me to look for a role within the company as a 'Plan B'. I decided to ask Lionel for a meeting, explained the situation with Ethan, and prepared a detailed concept for standardized procedures for new and modified designs. Improving this process had become my heartfelt wish in recent years, leading many VA/VE events and relying on the design department to implement ideas.

On the day of the meeting, I reserved a conference room for Lionel and myself. Before presenting the concept, we exchanged background information. He explained that the company had a code of conduct stating that approval from the current boss and colleagues was required if someone wanted to change departments or received an offer. He assured me that he would express his interest in me as he had a suitable position in his area. This way, there wouldn't be a conflict with Ethan, which I appreciated. I found this approach to be very fair.

The presentation of the concept went very positively. He told me that some of the ideas were already being discussed in Engineering and that the overall concept had his full approval. He then forwarded the request to his colleagues and my new, unfortunately somewhat reserved, boss. The responses arrived within a very short time. There were three, "Okay for me" replies. The fourth response ended the process. My new boss immediately reported that he had planned me for another position. With that, the matter was settled, and Lionel thanked me

for the presented concept ideas. He could now implement
them with his team. One year on, it seemed that the modification
processes in development had become more structured
and faster.

Return of Security

On April 30th, I booked all my flights until autumn for my trips
to Düsseldorf, Milan, Paris, and Vienna from home. Around 8.00
pm, my phone rang, and it was Ethan. He was at the annual
staff meeting in Tomado, where strategies and initiatives were
being discussed. In India, a new plant was planned, supported
by 3P techniques. 3P stands for 'Production Preparation Process'
and involves 1:10 scale simulations to identify errors early
and conduct Kaizens during a simulation. It's a Lean Management
method focused on efficiently planning production processes
and work environments. 3P aims to develop new production
or work processes from scratch, eliminating any waste
that may occur in the operations. I found this highly interesting,
and he asked if it would be feasible for me to fly to India for a
week every three weeks. There, a Shingijutsu consultant would
provide me with an on-the-job training in 3P, teaching me the
whole toolbox.

Shingijutsu Consulting is a highly renowned Japanese consulting
firm specializing in the 'Production Preparation Process' (3P).
The company was founded by former Toyota employees who
were directly trained by Taiichi Ohno, the founder of the Toyota
Production System. This was something unique, training from
an eminent Japanese consultant. At the end of the year, I was

to take on the role of 3P Coach for Europe. This decision would also mean that I would once again have to give up my previous tasks. Productivity would become the responsibility of the plants, while VA/VE would be restructured in collaboration with Engineering and Procurement.

Of course, I agreed, nevertheless I reminded him of our earlier conversation where he had advised against my trips to India because they were too dangerous. He laughed and assured me that the company would take all measures in case of an emergency, even using the CEO's corporate jet to bring me back. He was very serious, as Ethan was well connected up to the top leadership level, including our CEO. I then inquired about the start date of this training. He suggested it could start in three weeks. Now, it was a matter of quickly receiving the invitation letter from India, applying for an Indian visa — Express Visa is the code to unlock this chest — and making other preparations. Fortunately, the necessary vaccinations were already completed, as I had been to Ahmedabad and Delhi the previous year. The next morning, I cancelled all bookings with Air Berlin (they were still within the 24-hour free cancellation period).

The Handover

There was hardly any time to train my colleagues who would be conducting VA/VE in the future. I informed the plants and quickly planned two VA/VE events; the plants understood the urgency and supported me. These events would serve a dual purpose as training sessions. These special events took place in Roubaix and Trieste. Future coaches from other European plants also attended, taking turns as moderators. During the events, I ensured to stay in the background, providing support to the budding moderators. This allowed the team to get to know each other and begin building a mutual support network. At the same time, I deepened my knowledge of 3P, which was linked to my new role. Finally, I read the novella Luke had written on the subject. He was considered a 3P expert in the company and worldwide, and he had connections with the Shingijutsu consultants. All preparations and handovers went according to plan and, with each passing day, my anticipation for what was to come grew.

The Finca

Before heading to India, we flew to La Palma in mid-May for the notary appointment to finalize the house purchase. The sellers kindly allowed us to stay in the house before the official sale, while they stayed with friends nearby. This was our first time meeting them. They were selling their beloved home after over twenty years to move closer to their children in the Hannover region, who ran a restaurant. Their emotional connection to the house was evident during their final moments on the terrace.

We were unaware that in Spain, it's customary to bring the payment or a certified check to the notary appointment. Consequently, we had to reschedule for the following week. We quickly arranged the transfer of the purchase amount, and everything proceeded smoothly afterward. We also signed a management contract with a woman who owned the house we had stayed in the previous December. She was an experienced property manager with a network of craftsmen, invaluable on this island. Some repairs were required. During that week, we used the renovated kitchen and introduced ourselves to the neighbors, finding a very friendly and welcoming community.

In July, we planned to return to La Palma for our silver wedding anniversary, intending to carry out renovations, make altera- tions, and purchase some new furniture. And yes, La Palma even has an IKEA! However, you can only browse there; the stock is in Tenerife, but deliveries are made within two to four days. We celebrated our anniversary with a lavish dinner at a small beach called Los Guirres, then headed up to the finca to enjoy the sunset with a glass of champagne.

Ahmedabad, India

Finally, the time had come. I had an appointment in India where the Japanese consultant, his interpreter, and my colleague Joe from America would be present. We met on-site and stayed in the same hotel. Prior to this trip, I had immersed myself in Japa- nese and Indian cultures and read my mentor Luke's book on 3P multiple times. This novel conveyed techniques and steps viv- idly, embedded in a story, which left me feeling well-prepared for this journey and my renewed learning phase. I already knew some people from the plant from various staff meetings and the productivity event last year. The reception was warm from all sides, and we quickly got started.

We headed into the old manufacturing hall, a hot and noisy en- vironment. At the edge of the hall awaited a room approxi- mately twelve by fifteen meters. What I saw there deeply impressed me. Contrary to all safety regulations, we had to remove our safety shoes before entering. Oil and chips on the ground were an absolute 'No-Go' in this room. The floor was covered with cardboard, representing the area of the new plant at a scale of 1:10. As the project had been running for a few weeks, there were already many small models of machines, products, parts, cranes, and workbenches, as well as people. Everything could be moved aside, and we could sit down to simulate individual processes as a team, while sipping peppermint tea. Manufacturing employees explained what they would do in what sequence, what they needed for it, and where it should ideally be placed. If a crane was required, another team member would craft it out of cardboard. Double-walled cardboard, glue guns, sharp knives, scissors, and rulers were our tools. Depending on the complexity, the object was ready in ten to thirty minutes and could be 'deployed'. I don't know what was more impressive: the fact that we simulated everything, the level of detail, the output, or how many improvements we could make in the model without spending any money. Everything was impressive to me.

The 3P simulation begins with analyzing the product portfolio. It examines which product families exist, whether they have similar scopes, times, and process steps, and the production quantities. Based on this information, the number of required stations and the cycle time are determined, leading to a preliminary layout for the cell, line, or plant.

For the most common product type, a fishbone diagram is created. Parts from the drawings are cut out and glued onto a wall chart along with the corresponding lines of the bill of materials. A thread shows the path where this part will be processed further. The time sequences are also evaluated at this point. Participants from all functions are involved: occupational safety, quality, development, purchasing, work preparation, logistics, warehouse management, Lean experts, the employees themselves, and the 3P moderator. Each step of the process is carefully analyzed to identify potential problems or risks. Color-coded sticky notes are placed over critical points in the fishbone diagram identified as potential problem sources, along with corresponding comments. These notes are numbered and used to create a Kaizen list, which is then prioritized. Throughout the project, the listed measures for continuous improvement are implemented.

The questions covered various aspects:

What steps are performed first? How heavy is the part to be processed? How is it presented to the worker? Are special fixtures or devices required? How long does it take to pick up or insert the part? Where are tools and aids placed? Are connections or operating resources required? How long does the assembly take? All these questions led to detailed planning of the workstation. At the same time, a shadow board with the necessary tools and aids was designed – all initially on paper. The collected information was used to document the workflow with estimated times in a preliminary standard worksheet. Thus, we had a detailed work plan with times and all information before the plant even existed. I found that simply ingenious. As the entire process takes place without having the material, it is also called 'air guitar playing'.

With the first draft of the fishbone diagram complete, we moved on to the next phase: 'Squeeze the Fish'. This process is akin to SMED (Single Minute Exchange of Die) and involves preparing as many steps as possible outside the main production line. The more we can integrate into pre-assemblies, the fewer stations the main line needs, and the shorter the product's throughput time becomes. The ideal outcome is a fish that is shorter in length than in width.

Setting up supermarkets after pre-assemblies before the assembly line can significantly reduce waste. Process steps are then assigned to workstations to achieve balanced workloads, visualized in a bar chart per station known as a 'Yamazumi'. Yamazumi, a term from Lean management, translates to 'stacked bar chart' and displays the workload distribution across workstations.

The goal of the Yamazumi diagram is to balance the workload and ensure the takt time—the rhythm the production process must follow to meet customer demand—is adhered to. Ideally, the bars in this diagram should be of equal height and none should exceed the takt time. This balance indicates that work is evenly distributed, supporting takt time adherence and preventing bottlenecks. Additionally, pre-assembly workloads are included as additional bars, which should be shorter than those in the main assembly line, creating a pull effect and enhancing efficiency.

The pull effect ensures that the next pre-assembly unit is only produced when the assembly line has used and installed the previous one. With pre-assemblies preparing most of the work, the main assembly has fewer tasks, making production smoother and faster. This means the fish is 'compressed'!

Achieving this often requires several rounds of Kaizen and changes.

The initial layout draft is represented and simulated at a 1:10 scale. All participants from various functions, including safety, quality, development, purchasing, logistics, warehousing, Lean experts, employees, and the 3P moderator, simulate each process step in the optimized layout and note any changes. The Kaizen list is updated with each iteration.

With each round of simulation without actual material – playing 'air guitar' – more details and issues are revealed. The 'Kaizen-in-Kaizen' philosophy addresses these. At the end of such a cycle, the team has all the necessary information to create a standard work sheet covering the entire assembly process. Remarkably, we had yet to spend a single cent on equipment, relying only on cardboard and paper. Changes at this stage are easy and inexpensive to implement. This approach, devoid of physical workstations or parts, was fascinating, as Mr. Spock would say. Even the replaced cardboard models formed a 'Dollar Mountain', a reminder of the savings achieved by simulating first.

Simulating workflows in the 1:10 floor model was a captivating process. We placed white paper on the cardboard and built the layout. Employee and material paths were visualized in spaghetti diagrams, color-coded for idle paths, material paths, and paths with tools and aids. The distance covered by employees was calculated based on this scale. In other plants, we later refined this approach using colored threads to measure distances.

Through multiple rounds of 'Trystorming', the layout evolved into a final picture. Materials were better placed, tools optimized, and paths shortened. An amusing anecdote from a Slovak plant involved three marathon runners among six employees at an optimized workstation. After reducing their daily paths by four kilometers thanks to 3P and spaghetti diagrams, they joked about needing to train more in the evenings. The assembly paths had indeed become part of their daily step count.

Amidst the project, there were challenges. In India, as in any plant, we encountered resistance, notably from those we called 'Cave Dwellers', who resisted change. Their attitude seemed to involve completing tasks but not prioritizing them. This led to several heated discussions between us and the Shingijutsu consultant, with the translator from Goa deftly translating from Japanese to Hindi and English. Tensions rose, and it almost seemed like our consultant might leave, which would have been disastrous as Shingijutsu Consulting is known for its uncompromising nature. Despite this, our consultant was genuinely kind, especially when things went according to his plan.

My work ethic proved valuable in this collaboration. I always completed my tasks on time, and when I took responsibility for the team, I did so diligently. Even if the result wasn't perfect, our consultant appreciated the effort – because the worst thing would have been to leave tasks undone. Stagnation means no progress, and without progress, no experience can be gained.

Culinary Delights in India

My culinary experience of India was noteworthy. The factory cafeteria served local dishes, and I noticed an interesting quirk: the food was served in two separate lines. My contact explained that one line offered spicy meals, whereas the other featured dishes of extreme heat, which he strongly advised against trying. Interestingly, not all Indian employees opted for the spicier line.

Curry is a staple spice in India, and I wanted to bring some curry spice mixes home. My colleagues informed me that store-bought mixes often lacked the quality they were accustomed to. In India, it is a tradition for families to make their own curry once a year. They offered to get me all the ingredients as a set so it was possible for me to take it home in my luggage. They also provided me with recipes to try. Fortunately, all the ingredients were dry and could be transported in my carry-on luggage.

Upon arriving in Berlin, customs asked me to open my small suitcase. They found a lot of green herbs and were curious: bay leaves, cumin, cardamom, chili, black peppercorns, turmeric, fennel seeds, cloves, and more – but no illegal substances! At home, I experimented with various recipes, and since then, we have our own family curry. A Thuringian bratwurst from the grill, with ketchup and our curry, is something you can't buy anywhere! I sent photos of my culinary creativity to my Indian colleagues, and they were delighted. On my next trip, I had to bring a sample for their expert opinion, and they gave the green light to our homemade curry.

In the state of Gujarat, public alcohol consumption was prohibited. Even though it was allowed to buy something in the hotel shop with a passport, the prices were exorbitant. So, during our stay in Ahmedabad, we found ourselves thirsty in the desert; surrounded by water and lemonade, yet without the pleasure of something stronger. One evening in the hotel, the translator suggested we have our dinner in his hotel room, as we still had some meetings to discuss. We ordered food from the restaurant and had it delivered to his room. The Shingi and I joined him. The translator was from Goa, a state in southern India heavily influenced by tourism. There, it was simply impossible to ban the sale of alcohol; he had a bottle of single-malt whisky with him. The three of us enjoyed a very pleasant dinner with two glasses without ice. And, of course, we discussed some business points. It was, after all, a working meeting.

Celebrating Festivals in India

Throughout the summer, simulations were conducted, and I experienced the Indian high summer for the first time. The heat was simply unparalleled, reaching 48°C with extreme humidity just before the monsoon rains. In August, the Ganapati festival, also known as Ganesh Chaturthi or Ganeshotsav, was approaching. This significant Hindu festival celebrates the birth of Lord Ganesha, the elephant-headed god of wisdom and fortune. The festival spans several days, typically occurring between August and September, marked by colorful processions, rituals, and prayers.

Preparations for the festival include crafting Ganesha statues from clay, often in impressive sizes and creative designs. These statues are placed in homes and communities and are worshipped by devotees. During the festival, people offer coconuts, sweets, fruits, and flowers, praying for protection, prosperity, and success.

The highlights of Ganesh Chaturthi are the vibrant processions, where Ganesha statues are carried through the streets to the accompaniment of music, dance, and applause. Devotees lead the statues to rivers or bodies of water, where they are ritually immersed, symbolizing the deity's return to his divine abode. This act signifies unity with the divine.

Ganesh Chaturthi is not only a religious festival, it is also a time of community, celebration, and cultural events. It brings together people from diverse backgrounds and faiths to share the joy and spirituality of the festival.

In August, the monsoon rains also arrived in India. In Ahmedabad, a city of 8.4 million people, it seemed as if the entire population was out on the streets that day. Decorated and singing, accompanied by their elaborately painted statues, they all headed to the Sabarmati River. The streets, already usually congested, were even more crowded, yet traffic somehow always seems to flow in India. On this day, however, it flowed much less. The trip from the hotel to work took a full hour instead of the usual twenty minutes, and the return journey became a two-hour test of patience. The streets of Ahmedabad turned into flooded rivers, and traffic stalled. People danced in the monsoon rain on the beds of trucks carrying their figures to the river, and sometimes a record twelve people rode in the sputtering three- to four-seat tuk-tuks. It was an impressive experience for me.

Wrapping Up the Project

With a tight schedule, we continued our simulations. Construction of the new plant had already begun, which required us to meet specific deadlines for information and decisions. The engineers required precise details for planning connections and determining whether overhead cranes or mobile, foundation less portals were necessary. Fortunately, we stayed on schedule and even began 3P preparations for the plant's second phase.

As autumn approached, an idea took root in me. Starting in 2015, it would be my task to introduce 3P to the European plants. I had already scheduled introductory events for October and November. However, a particular challenge awaited in the plant in Bornago near Milan, where Gabriele, eager for change, faced continued resistance from some colleagues. Gabriele and I had been pioneers in Lean and OpEx for seven years, making us the last two Lean practitioners who had witnessed and participated in all the company's initiatives. Gabriele kept a sort of history book of all the initiatives orchestrated by Tomado, which we often perused for amusement.

In consultation with Ethan, I proposed that Gabriele accompany me on my final trip of 2014 to India, to gain a multiplier for future activities in Italy. My proposal was well received and quickly approved by plant management. I prepared Gabriele for what he would see there. We coordinated our travel plans and

met in festive December in Ahmedabad. Traveling separately –
he from Milan, and my trip began in Berlin – we reunited at our
hotel and went to the plant the next morning. The impressions
overwhelmed him, just as they had me in early summer. He absorbed all the information he saw, almost like Harry Potter
opening a toolbox to find a house with seven rooms and fourteen cabinets full of tools offering unimagined possibilities!

Throughout the year, my Indian colleagues gave me the opportunity to experience the richness of their festivals and consistently invited me to join in the celebrations. This time, I brought
Christmas treats, some clipped pine branches from my garden,
and pictures of European Christmas markets on my laptop.
They were thrilled by the glittering world and sparkling splen-
dor, which also played a special role in their culture. The fact
that it was a Christian holiday did not bother them at all. After
all, our large plant housed people of various faiths, and India,
the world's second most populous country, has about 25 million
Christians.

This week, we planned other activities as well. It marked not
only the end of my work year, but also the near-completion of
the project. Gabriele probably wouldn't return to India anytime
soon; nor would I. Time for shopping! He needed gifts for his
family, and I for my wife. Our suitcases were half-empty on arrival, giving us ample space for various purchases. A hotel taxi
with a chauffeur was ready to navigate us through the evening
streets of Ahmedabad. In a shop, I bought a beautiful patchwork quilt with cushion covers and some fragrant spices. Gabriele was drawn to natural pearls. The stock was limited, and
the shop owner explained he was moving away from trading
pearls to work on his karma. Whoever bought all the pearls at

once would get a very generous discount. After a brief online search, we found the price unbeatable. Gabriele decided to purchase all the pearls for his family.

We strolled through a few more shops in different districts, where I purchased dark blue silk and ten meters of a fascinating pattern. To cap off the evening, we visited a reputable jeweler. Our goal was to buy emeralds, and we spent the last two hours of the day in his shop. Amid an impressive selection of thousands of emeralds, we chose some wonderful specimens. These magnificent stones varied in size and could later be fashioned into necklaces, rings, and earrings. Particularly impressive was the jeweler's meticulous care and precision. After making our selections and completing the purchase, the shop staff conducted a thorough inventory check to ensure everything was in order. Only when all numbers matched were we and the staff allowed to leave the store with our treasures. Our bags were full; however, our wallets were lighter. Christmas could come.

Throughout this year, I had taken many long flights. The trips to India also gave me the option of working from home. Traveling to India meant departing Berlin on Saturday afternoons and arriving in India on Sunday mornings at 5.00 am. The return journey was similar – leaving Ahmedabad at 4.00 am on Saturday and arriving in Berlin by midday. Despite all the challenges, delays, and occasional wandering luggage, each visit was simply fantastic. The luggage situation though proved somewhat cumbersome. I contacted the hotel to ask if they could wash my clothes between stays and keep my suitcase there. From then on, this worked out perfectly, freeing me from the airlines' problems. What's more, entry became much smoother as I no longer had to wait for my luggage and could proceed directly to customs. This little convenience afforded me not only more time, it was also a bit more comfort in an otherwise demanding travel routine.

My preferred airline was, of course, Air Berlin in cooperation with Etihad via Abu Dhabi. Once, the son of our neighbor on La Palma, who was a Swiss captain for Air Berlin, flew me from Berlin to Zurich. From Zurich, I continued to Abu Dhabi. Thanks to my platinum membership, I enjoyed all the perks, including lounge access. Often, I used miles for upgrades or simply paid for the comfort directly. I was particularly fascinated on my first arrival in Ahmedabad, locating my driver from the Gateway Hotel at 4.30 am. Between 2.00 and 4.00 am, around ten planes landed from all over the world, yet there were only 4 to 6 immigration counters, resulting in long lines. The baggage claim took about an hour.

Just after customs, there was an exit consisting of two rows. About ten meters behind, families and drivers waited. There were around a thousand people, yet I never had to search long, as the sign with the EG logo and my name was always conspicuous in the first row. In the car, chilled water always awaited me. After all, at 35°C in the early morning, water was the most precious commodity.

The Plant in the Bergisches Land

Amid all these exciting developments, there was a special episode at HDA. The Plant Manager, who once told me I should have nothing to do with his team and had locked two guests in his office, was dismissed in the summer. Finding a suitable successor proved challenging. In October, I called my friend and former college mate Hans to wish him a happy birthday. I spontaneously asked if he would be interested in the Plant Manager position in the Bergisches Land. Hans had rich experience in the automotive sector and was well-versed in Lean principles. Much of what I had learned from a visit to one of his plants years ago was thanks to him. I had secretly hoped for this answer, but his quick and clear agreement surprised me positively.

After this call, I immediately informed Ethan. His enthusiasm for the idea was palpable, and he asked me for the necessary documents. I contacted Hans again, and he submitted everything via email. A conversation between him and Ethan – who would also be his superior – followed. The conversation went very well, overcoming the first hurdle. Within just ten days, three phone interviews and a visit by Hans to the Bergisches Land took place, all of which were very successful. By mid-November, it was clear: Hans was the new Plant Manager of HDA. However, he lived in Lower Saxony at the time.

Well, my apartment was mostly empty, and I would often be at other plants in the future. So, my proposal was, that he could rent my furnished apartment, and I would clear out my personal belongings. He accepted this offer, and in return for the rent, he received a 'subsidy' from the company added to his salary. Besides the referral bonus for this decision, there would be additional monthly income – a very pleasant solution. After many years, we were once again working side by side for the same company, as we did at the beginning of our careers. Whether we would also retire together remained open. But an exciting journey had brought us together again.

My Lean Transformation

Undoubtedly, this year was the most eventful and exciting for me. It's hard to capture all the experiences and insights in a few words. The Japanese consultant formally assessed me at the end of the year; through intense training and regular use of 3P tools, which are all Lean tools, I had now become a true Lean Sensei. During my intensive 3P training in India under the guidance of the Japanese Sensei, I experienced the most captivating moments in Lean Manufacturing. After this experience, I had knowledge and insights that many of my colleagues, even if they were Lean specialists, did not possess.

I now had my hands full because I held the 3P toolbox with all its tools. Was I at my goal? No, not yet. Because now, with this new toolbox and knowledge, it was just beginning. I was very excited about the new year and grateful to have such a supportive boss and advocate. Forgotten was the rough and doubt-filled start with Ethan. Plants could no longer make significant investments and modifications without first conducting a 3P project together. With almost five years in my position as 'Productivity Leader EMEIA' (Europe, Middle East, India, Africa), I could authentically represent this philosophy in various plants. My events garnered more interest than ever before. Finally, I was the coach I had hoped to be at the beginning of my journey in the Bergisches Land when Ron, the English Plant Manager from Brezno, mentored us at HDA. What started as an uncertain year turned into a breathtaking development for me. The only question that occasionally came up was how long this tool would be used in the ÄÄtch group. Would it be just another line in Gabriele's historical record after a year?

End of the Year

This year was marked by professional challenges and personal milestones. Frequent flights from Berlin gave me rare glimpses of nature's beauty, such as the blooming summer lilac. The summer was especially significant as we established our own home on La Palma and celebrated our 25th wedding anniversary there. Even in winter, we spent time on the island, bringing culinary delights from Berlin and enjoying life with our neighbors. Evenings on the terrace, with a glass of red wine in hand, allowed us to reflect on the year and its memories.

The changing seasons mirrored the continuous growth in both my professional and personal life. The blooming butterfly lilac became a symbol of these changes and progress. Our time on La Palma was particularly valuable, where we built a close community with our neighbors and shared special moments, cooking and celebrating together.

In quiet moments, I often reflected on the year, especially the unforgettable experiences in India. Conversations with our neighbor, who had been to India decades ago, brought those memories vividly back. Each sunset we watched from the terrace was a peaceful end to a busy day and a symbol of the fulfilling experiences of the preceding year.

Spaghetti Diagram, or How Yarn Took Over Our Work. A Spaghetti Diagram is a straightforward yet potent visualization technique employed in Lean initiatives and process improvement projects. It helps to illustrate the actual movement paths of people, machines, or materials within a specific process.

In our factory layout drafts, we used yarn to trace the material's pathways instead of merely drawing lines with pens. After taking a photograph, we unraveled the yarn and applied the scale to calculate the distances travelled.

This approach not only offered a clear visual representation but also provided precise measurements, significantly enhancing our process analysis and improvements.

The Beginning of the Year

Returning to Berlin, we were quickly back to our routine of commuting and flights. My 'Training on the Job' in Ahmedabad was completed, and the project continued without Shingijutsu-Consulting's involvement. By the end of the preceding year, I had already informed all plants about the principles of 3P, conducted a training program, and begun assessing the current state with the teams. My supervisor Ethan supported my efforts by announcing that future investments would only be approved after undergoing a 3P project, creating a sense of urgency.

Roubaix, France

An intriguing development occurred in Roubaix, where a major redesign of production was planned. The project was nearly finished and awaited final approval in the USA. However, it now required my swift intervention. Initially, my colleagues in Roubaix were sceptical, as the anticipated immediate approval was delayed. However, they knew my drive for implementing changes.

During this time, I recalled a serious yet amusing anecdote my boss had shared. It involved a Shingijutsu consultant leading an improvement of material flow in a plant. Each manager was given specific tasks, accompanied by the clear message that nothing was impossible. Some were to find ideas to reduce inventory, others to improve visualization, and the Logistics Manager was challenged to reduce the number of forklifts by 50%.

The layout was such that the processing hall was adjacent to the painting hall, where parts had to be transported. To protect workers from unpleasant odors, there was a long, massive wall with a single passage at the hall's end. The direct line to the destination was only about 20 meters, yet the actual travel distance was 150 meters. The Logistics Manager was repeatedly urged to find creative ways for parts to travel the short distance directly to the next processing station, yet he stubbornly refused to question the wall or consider installing a gate.

Finally, during the third meeting in the hall, the Logistics Manager again declared, "The wall cannot be torn down or opened!" Silence fell. The Shingijutsu consultant then spotted a forklift, got on it, raised the forks to about 1.5 meters, and charged full speed at the wall. The forks pierced the wall and got stuck. The consultant said, "See? The wall can be opened!" He then left the company, and Shingijutsu-Consulting ended its collaboration with the firm permanently. They would never again contract with the consulting group. This episode highlighted how rigidity and unwillingness to change can doom a Lean initiative.

The similarity to the situation in Roubaix was striking. There were similar bottlenecks in material flow at this production site. The assembly and painting of blowers took place in one hall, but for transport to the neighboring hall, where they were stored in a FiFo inventory for shipping, forklifts could only travel in one direction for safety reasons. This significantly extended the distances.

The colleagues in Roubaix were unaware of the Shingijutsu anecdote. I shared it with them before we began our tour of the production. Their reactions were a mix of laughter and amazement. When we reached the spot where parts were picked up for transport by the forklift, I stopped the group. "How far is the destination for the forklift driver?" was my question. They replied, "About 50 meters one way, then 50 meters back, and another 10 meters across – a total of about 110 meters." Then I asked how far the destination was in a direct line. The answer surprised them, "About 10 meters, on the other side of the wall."

At that moment, I saw the first participants in the tour looking at each other, their eyes widening, and they began to murmur, "Let's leave the forklift here and think about how we can create a direct passage for the parts." I heard them say. This was the moment they internalized the essence of 3P thinking –

questioning assumptions, recognizing inefficient processes, and finding creative solutions.

The breakthrough, in the truest sense of the word, came when the wall between the production areas was opened four weeks later, creating a passage. This opening symbolized not only a physical change, yet it was also the team's acceptance of 3P as a powerful tool. We worked through the entire project, developed a completely new layout, identified three additional 3P projects, and decided on immediate implementations. The entire team supported this new approach. Raphael, now the Production Manager, was a great asset.

This plant had been my transformation project for some time. With 3P, the process accelerated significantly, resulting in a major leap forward. The barriers of inefficient processes and old habits were literally torn down, making way for new ways of thinking and acting. This marked the beginning of an exciting transformation journey, changing not just the physical production processes but also the mindset of the entire workforce.

Building Trust and Friendship

The discussions and events that propelled the plant forward created a strong bond between the management in Roubaix and me, evolving into genuine friendship. We trusted and appreciated each other, even sharing jokes. During my frequent visits to Roubaix, I noticed the sirens wailing every first Wednesday of the month at noon. Initially, I thought it signaled a fire or forest fire. Curious, I asked the team about it. They jokingly said, "We test the sirens monthly to ensure we can warn the population if the Germans come back." While said in jest, the monthly siren tests in France have historical roots dating back to the World Wars, originally developed as protective measures against potential attacks and now serving as warnings for general dangers.

Every time I heard the sirens later, I'd say, "Too late, I'm already here!" This always caused hearty laughter, and soon after, we would head to Le General for lunch, as it was noon.

Bornago, Italy

In each of the facilities, a 3P project was now underway. The goal was not to passively accept fate, but to actively shape the future. In Bornago, we were granted a space that we used for simulating an assembly process, akin to what we had done previously in India. Gabriele's enthusiasm, which had accompanied me last December, also ignited others in the team. Assuming the role of Lean Leader and 3P Coach for the site, he guided us through simulations of various scenarios devised the previous autumn. When I asked for wool for the event, I initially received puzzled looks. Nonetheless, we turned it into an engaging experience, finding ways to shorten transport routes. Colorful threads of wool became our constant companions, visualizing movements within the process. These threads were used to create a spaghetti diagram for material flow in the plant.

Following initial analysis, we identified transport routes and promptly devised a new layout for the facility, once again employing the wool threads. This approach allowed us to reduce planned routes in the new layout by 25%. In Bornago, a literal breakthrough was made between assembly and testing, allowing 2000 kilograms of gearboxes to be pulled into the adjacent hall using a powered hand trolley, bypassing forklifts and detours. The Shingi anecdote appeared to motivate people, demonstrating their readiness for profound change and their departure from outdated thinking patterns.

Brezno, Slovakia

The largest 3P project on European soil took place in Brezno, Slovakia. This facility stood as Europe's flagship in Lean Manufacturing, having made significant strides in process flow, visual signals, and other Lean elements. The production lines were synchronized and ran very efficiently. In a vacant section of the hall, we constructed a scale model of the most productive line at a 1:10 ratio. The goal was to integrate additional products into this line, thereby reducing customer cycle time and throughput times. We also aimed to further increase the pre-assembly component. This ambitious project brought us great joy in our work.

Before proceeding, however, there was the matter of personnel. Who would be the 3P Coach? The Lean Leader was not an option, fully engaged in a Value Stream Transformation for the plant. The Plant Manager had an idea. There was an employee who had coordinated the introduction of modified parts into serial production. "Hmm," I thought, "what qualifies him for Lean and 3P, and for assembly processes?" He spoke decent English, undoubtedly a major advantage; he also took private lessons in

Banská Bystrica and had a technical education. Furthermore, he had worked extensively with wood privately, renovating and making habitable an old family house. Through his role as Change Coordinator, he knew the people in the warehouse, logistics, and assembly at the plant. He was also familiar with assembly processes.

After our introduction, the choice was clear to me. He candidly listed what he lacked, yet there was chemistry between us. Martin had grown up in a somewhat totalitarian state, which also turned out to be an advantage. His boss told him, "We want to introduce 3P, which is a correct and important thing. Let them explain everything to you, but please don't be subservient." And that was how it went. He asked questions, I explained the connections. Then came an 'Ano', which is 'Yes', and it was done. When he finished, he wanted to know what the next instrument we wanted to use was. Like Raphaël in Roubaix, he was curious and demanding, but still much more malleable. Joe, my colleague in the USA, had significant reservations, although we selected him as our 3P Coordinator.

During this period, he developed excellently. Internal meetings were conducted in Slovak, as he knew exactly what and how to explain and demand something. This proved to be an extremely effective process. We shifted some work steps to pre-assembly, optimized operations at the assembly stations, and used the Yamazumi Chart to balance the workload across all stations. This enabled us to integrate additional products into the line. This development significantly bolstered the team's confidence in the process.

Previously, critical questions had arisen. After all, the plant had been undergoing a Value Stream Transformation for nearly two years, and most found it difficult to imagine that significant improvements to the line were still possible. Rüdiger, the Regional OpEx Leader, insisted that we should not obstruct the value stream analysis activities and doubted our success. However, this critique did not deter us. The results of the 3P activities spoke for themselves and for us. Hannah, the OpEx Leader at the plant, was also surprised by what we had achieved. She asked to join us whenever she had time. Clearly, she wanted to learn some of what we were doing. Through my regular contacts with colleagues, I learned that we were not alone in our 3P project. At the same time, similar lines were being meticulously constructed and analyzed at Toddville in the USA and in China. This realization touched me, yet also made me cautious.

Tomado, USA

At the end of March, I received my first invitation to the Annual Management Meeting in Tomado. This invitation was a tremendous recognition for me, as it was uncommon for someone in my position to be invited to the top management's leadership meeting. In early May, I travelled to the USA with my former college friend Hans, who was now the Plant Manager at HDA. During the preceding Operations Meeting, I had the opportunity to present ongoing 3P projects, their status, and next steps. Alongside plant managers, my boss and the Global Operations Vice President were also present. The plants emphasized the importance and value of implementing jointly developed visions. They then presented their plans for the upcoming year, which included actions for implementing the 3P projects. The Hoshin Kanri process was still ongoing. It was a lively discussion in a pleasant atmosphere.

We both had an extremely enjoyable time there. With ten years already spent in the company, I knew many people in this circle. During this trip, I introduced Hans to these individuals. Evenings after dinner were filled with games and conversations. Some games were rather nonsensical, like Cornhole — throwing corn-filled bags onto a slightly inclined board with a hole ten meters away. Points were scored if the bag landed on the board or went into the hole. We stood together, sipped wine, and engaged in lively conversation. This opportunity allowed us to address various matters — a remarkable experience of what could be achieved through official channels. We also spent several hours in the area of our campus reserved for 3P projects.

The activities there were impressive in scale. Joe and his team even had their own carpentry and model shop — a luxury unimaginable for us in Europe. Models from Toddville, Brezno, and Cangzhou were simulated and placed side by side. I noticed that products from Brezno were integrated into models from Toddville and Cangzhou. In Brezno itself, the challenge was to integrate their own products more efficiently into production lines and eliminate an assembly line. In addition to the scaled 1:10 layouts, each plant had boards displaying basic data and crucial information. The board for Brezno identified 'HDA' as the source for high-quality gearboxes. This specific product line could only be manufactured by HDA, supplying all sites worldwide. Conversely, the boards for Toddville and Cangzhou listed Cangzhou as the primary source, with Toddville as a secondary supplier. That struck me as quite odd.

233

These products constituted a significant portion of profits for the plant in the Bergisches Land – the bread-and-butter products. The connections were clear. Parts of Brezno's production would now go to China and America, and HDA would no longer serve as the supplier for Cangzhou and Toddville. From budget discussions, we knew that the European market accounted for only 20% of Brezno's revenue. This immediately raised the question of whether a plant with an 80% revenue reduction could even be sustained. The same consideration applied to the HDA site. Much of its production went to this internal customer. Without the 'bread and butter' products, there would be a significant hole in fixed cost coverage. We both understood that all of this was unequivocal evidence of an impending dramatic change in the company. However, it was not possible for me to immediately share my thoughts with others.

During that week, Hans and I also met my former boss, Robert. He had since established himself in a company specializing in aircraft seat manufacturing. As Senior Engineer in Engineering, he now steered the company's course in producing aircraft seats. Our meeting provided an opportunity to reminisce about our shared past. Our conversations spanned countless topics, illuminating our shared experiences. During these discussions, he confided in me about his initial hesitation in hiring a manufacturing engineer for the position of VA/VE Manager in Europe, rather than the usual choice of a design engineer. Nevertheless, he was ultimately pleased with that decision. All the principles I had once explained to him about Lean management, visualizations, and productivity had become integral to his daily work in the aviation conglomerate. Our shared experiences enabled him to make a successful start in his new role.

However, by the end of that conference, I faced a serious problem. My prostate was swollen. This issue forced me to visit the restroom at increasingly shorter intervals, yet with no satisfactory results, and the situation worsened by the hour. Particularly on our last excursion to Toddville, the challenge became impossible to ignore. While Hans enjoyed the standard tour for newcomers, I longed for a visit focusing on Total Productive Maintenance (TPM) and pushed my problems aside as much as possible. I knew there was a restroom at every corner of the factory from previous years.

While they proudly presented their latest optimization programs, I revealed the superficial nature of these approaches. A musty smell pervaded the factory floor, saturated with rancid cutting fluid. This was a clear sign that cleanliness was only superficial. I walked a few steps behind the machines with them. There, accumulations of old shavings soaked in cutting fluid revealed their extensive surfaces, spreading the unpleasant smell. My question about the healthiness of inhaling such air received no positive answer. When I asked about the sustainability of their TPM program, given the air was saturated with bacteria and the workshop smell was hardly bearable, they realized their cleaning efforts were far from sufficient.

During that time, I could hardly let thirty minutes pass without needing to visit the restroom again. The agony persisted during the return journey to Tomado. In the evening, we met with Amal and Aditi, who brought their sweet child named Aira along. The evening was filled with pleasant camaraderie in a fine restaurant, unfortunately it brought me no relief. Night fell, and the pain reached an unbearable intensity. At two in the morning, I staggered to the hotel reception and called for an ambulance. After agonizingly long 25 minutes, help finally arrived. My words were barely coherent. In the clinic, they provided me with painkillers that brought some relief. However, their effect gradually waned. Around 3.30 in the morning, it was my turn for the MRI scan, followed by the placement of a catheter. This measure brought noticeable relief as 1.1 liters of urine flowed from my bladder, which was on the verge of bursting. My condition slowly improved from unconsciousness. Back at the hotel, breakfast was already being served, and upon hearing of my situation from the reception, Hans rushed to me immediately.

A few hours later, we were on the return flight with United and Air Berlin to Germany. The catheter was to remain for the next four days. the medication prescribed by the clinic were aimed at reducing swelling. Thus, I flew on to Vienna to attend a preparatory meeting in Brezno. My hope was, that this unwelcome companion could be removed there in Slovakia and that all would be well again. Indeed, it was removed, yet my discomfort persisted. Within 24 hours, it was necessary for me to return to the hospital, where another catheter was inserted before I finally flew to Berlin. An appointment with the urologist awaited me there, and I went straight to it.

After only ten days, the operation followed, ending with relief — everything was benign, without any signs of cancer. Recovery was mostly smooth, but not entirely. I had spent about three weeks with the catheter, leaving clear marks. The urethra was chafed, scarred, and once again blocked urine flow. It was inevitable to have immediate surgery in the hospital's emergency room. Fortunately, this intervention proceeded smoothly.

When I returned to the working world, it was already mid-August.

Re-entry

I re-entered daily life with vigor, diving straight into action. Across all plants except in the Bergisches Land, concrete 3P projects were in full swing. Simultaneously, the implementation of Lean activities progressed smoothly, especially in Roubaix. There, everyone was highly motivated, led by the management team. We aimed for a complete mixed-model line with batch size 1 and hand-guided assembly carts, alongside entirely mobile facility setups – all equipped with wheels, capable of reconfiguration within minutes. This ambitious endeavor stood as our collective flagship project, poised to effectuate site transformation.

My time was divided, spending one week each month in Roubaix, Bornago, Brezno, and FMIT on the Adriatic. These quaint, individual lodgings I'd booked for years now felt like a second home. With my apartment in the Bergisches Land already occupied by Hans, during my rare visits there, I opted for a hotel. During this period, I spent only a few days at the plant.

As a result of my protracted medical history, the summer almost passed me by this year. Once I had weathered it all, we flew to the Azores for the third time. The island of Terceira offered us an oasis of tranquility where we could recharge our energies, immerse ourselves in the beauty of the landscape and wildlife. We encountered whales and dolphins, closer than we had ever been before. We hiked through verdant forests and explored caverns adorned with stalactites. However, as always, we spent our Christmas holiday on La Palma, hiking, relaxing on the beach, swimming, and savoring life to the fullest — particularly on the quiet, empty shores. It felt comforting to have such a retreat. We ushered in the New Year at the Hotel Romantica in Barlovento, a serene location in the north of the island. This region is characterized by a more humid climate, resulting in lush green landscapes with dense forests. Camellias bloomed profusely along the roadsides, almost like weeds — an enchanting sight!

2016

'Manage Daily Improvements (MDI)' encourages every manager, supervisor, and in advanced Lean organizations, every employee to make daily improvements. The key question is 'what have you improved today'? To identify opportunities for improvement, one must 'Go Gemba', meaning to go to the actual place where work is done and observe the process. The current state is visualized on the MDI board, including an hourly plan for the day. Deviations from the plan should be highlighted in red, while goal achievements should be marked in green. Any deviations should be explained, offering insights into areas with improvement potential. Take action, if your team hasn't already done so!

The Beginning of the Year

On New Year's Day, we went for a morning hike in the lush north, checked out, and headed to Puerto Tazacorte for a New Year's dip at the beach. Time and again, we cooled off in the sea, swimming freely. In the afternoon, at 'El Trebol' restaurant, we savored Pescado del Dia with a glass of white wine. Afterwards, we returned to the beach. While listening to the soothing waves, the silence was pierced by the ringing of my phone. Glancing at the display, I recognized the familiar number and name – it was my boss, Ethan. His call during vacation hinted at something crucial. After the usual greetings, he inquired about my well-being and disclosed that he was in the USA for a strategic discussion. The news he had to deliver concerned a plant closure decided by the parent company.

My thoughts immediately turned to the facility in the Bergisches Land. However, before I could voice it, Ethan clarified that it wasn't that plant but rather Brezno. This decision puzzled me – why Brezno, the site making significant strides in Lean Management? The puzzle pieces I gathered in Tomado now painted a grim reality. Ethan urgently stressed the confidentiality of this information. He explained that I might notice slight deviations in orders related to the 3P project. Back in Tomado, I had sensed that this 3P initiative aimed more at standardization for knowledge transfer; now I knew.

It was a moment of mourning for me. I gradually realized my mission in Brezno had been to prepare the plant for closure. More significantly, it seemed the company had sent me to India to create a 3P specialist for Europe – not only to implement 3P in Europe, but also to steer the process in Brezno. Early deployment of US personnel would have revealed the true mission. Through simulation and standardization, products could easily transition to other locations. Motivating local colleagues and guiding the successful restructuring became my task, all while keeping the impending development strictly confidential. This aspect of the 3P project could never be openly discussed.

Brezno, Slovakia

This year, on account of the project, I frequented Brezno often. Oddly enough, working with the team remained enjoyable, despite my personal concerns. We tackled another production line this year, integrating a product still in development. Our aim for this line was to significantly reduce cycle times and synchronize operations at each station down to the minute. 'Yamazumi' became a favorite term among my Slovak colleagues. Additionally, we supported development through 3P with a one-to-one mock-up for the new package, jointly developed between Tomado and Brezno.

A one-to-one mock-up in the context of product development is a full-scale physical model or prototype designed to visualize the planned product, assess its appearance, footprint, and component accessibility for operators. Moreover, the mock-up simulates service accessibility, ensuring maintenance and repairs can be efficiently conducted. Crafted from wood, plastic, or cardboard, such mock-ups swiftly illustrate new package designs, evaluating design elements, functionality, and user experience realistically before actual development and production commence. These mock-ups are often used in individual meetings between developers, designers, and stakeholders to gather feedback, make adjustments, and convey a precise understanding of the final product.

Amidst this exciting process, the presence of our American colleagues was unmistakable. They were now allowed to visit as we were constructing a new product as a 3P mock-up. Toddville was also set to manufacture this product. Driven by curiosity and a desire for insights into our operations, they aimed to capture images. While documenting the mock-up and its production line would have been acceptable, they also ventured unchecked into the assembly hall.

Naturally, their behavior caused unrest among the workforce, prompting us to intervene. They were clandestinely documenting processes of products slated to be taken over by them later.

The US colleagues were incensed by our actions and brought in their boss. They complained of the plant's lack of cooperation, failing to grasp their own role as the bull in the China shop. Ultimately, their conduct backfired. The Global Vice President decided they were not permitted to photograph other workstations. The only accomplishment of the Toddville gentlemen was that, henceforth, they received virtually no support from Brezno during the project's remainder. Congratulations, a spectacular own goal!

Unfortunately, the unrest and heated debates that ensued were irreparable. From that point on, the Slovak colleagues clearly saw where this project was headed. At the time, Slovakia's job market was highly favorable for employees, resulting in resignations from some of our best workers who immediately sought new opportunities. As they say, the best leave first. Special thanks to the Toddville team, whose undiplomatic approach and lack of sensitivity shook the project's previous equilibrium.

By week's end, I joined Jaroslav, the Plant Manager, the Production Manager Zoltán, and Martin, my 3P Coach, for dinner. We enjoyed a good steak and one or two beers. Both are excellent choices in Banská Bystrica. Colleagues from Roubaix, who attended events there, were also impressed by the steak's quality and preparation. After toasting, Jaroslav informed me that Zoltán would be leaving the ÄÄtch Group. The search for a new Production Manager was already concluded. I looked at them with widened eyes, and Jaroslav added that I would have less 3P support as Martin was now the new Production Manager. Knowing where things were headed, reduced 3P support didn't bother me. I was genuinely happy for Martin. From Change Notification Coordinator to 3P Coach to Production Manager in just under two years – what a journey for him! He beamed at me, the only one truly smiling, as the three of us knew the reality, even if left unspoken.

Tomado, USA

During the annual leadership meeting in Tomado, I informed Tyler, the Sector President, that I was supporting an ÄÄtch Group site in France not currently under OpEx department focus. His initial reaction was mixed. He favored the idea that only facilities in the midst of value stream transformations should receive support. This selective approach aimed to incentivize employees to move to the supported plants.

I regarded him with a hint of dissatisfaction and explained that, while this might work between Toddville and Southern Pines, I already had concerns about Campbellsville, Ohio. Few would want to move there as it's a dry town in the Midwest, a fact Tyler, a wine enthusiast, immediately understood. Furthermore, I emphasized that no Frenchman would relocate to Germany, just to work at an ÄÄtch Group facility undergoing transformation support. The same applied to Italians, who would be unwilling to live and work in France.

Eventually, he agreed with my approach and arguments to support the small plant in France, announcing his intention to visit personally. The board also echoed this sentiment a few weeks later, concerned about the slow integration progress of the facility in Northern France. The board confronted their team, questioning why the Roubaix plant's integration wasn't progressing faster. At acquisition, it resembled a 'garage', and there were suspicions that little had changed. Concerns mounted that the ÄÄtch Group could become a laughing stock in America if the French plant were sold, implying mismanagement of acquired companies. Consequently, it was decided that one of the senior executives should visit Roubaix every quarter to initiate Lean initiatives aligned with ÄÄtch Group standards.

Roubaix, France

Through nearly two years of continuous coaching, we had prepared diligently. Several well-maintained MDI boards tracked hourly progress at selected machines and in various areas. Unlike the transformation process plants where Group Leaders handled this task, technicians and operators updated records themselves. A continuous improvement problem-solving process was established, and we conducted daily Gemba walks and numerous other initiatives. Unintentionally, my experience at HDA greatly aided in implementing these measures. Whatever I introduced to the team in Roubaix, I did it differently than it had been done at HDA.

Two months later, Tyler visited. What he witnessed deeply impressed him. The fact that this 'garage' now resembled a fully functional plant and operated with an extremely pragmatic approach to 3P and Lean, without a Lean Leader, was noteworthy. Standing before an MDI board, discussing the process with him, a technician approached Tyler directly, causing him to widen his eyes momentarily, but the situation clarified itself. The technician had to update the board at the top of the hour. It was his job, and he cared little whether a Sector President stood before him at that moment. Tyler was thoroughly impressed; he had never seen this in any plant before.

At the end, there was the usual brief meeting where he shared his impressions and typically offered advice on what needed to change. The boss's summary of the visit could be described as follows, "Although we initially thought of it as a backyard garage, you've successfully initiated the Lean transformation path without help from Tomado, and you're somewhere towards the upper middle of transformational plants. If you need resources for the next steps, they are available. Just keep going, because if you continue like this, you'll be very high in the company rankings next year." Later, Ethan told us that this praise from the Sector President was nearly unmatched. It was genuinely heartfelt, as Ethan was a close friend of Tyler's. This year-end recognition was a wonderful reward for the team.

Brussels, Belgium

In the spring, Ethan planned to inspect the Ahmedabad plant two months before its one-year anniversary. His flight route took him from Brussels through London to India in the morning. However, he fell ill over the weekend and cancelled the trip at short notice. As it turned out, this was fortunate. On the morning of March 22, 2016, precisely at 7.58 am, explosions rocked Brussels Airport. These attacks, also at a metro station in the city, claimed 32 lives and left over 300 injured. He later declared this a twist of fate. If he had been in the bustling check-in hall at that time, he would have surely been directly affected by the tragedy.

Another colleague subsequently made the trip to India via Frankfurt. Unfortunately, this visit to the newly built plant revealed it now resembled a five-year-old facility rather than the one-year-old it was. Ethan asked me to travel there to assess standards with the team and, most importantly, to outline necessary actions to restore the shine of the new construction. Thus, I spent a total of two stays in Ahmedabad, during which we revitalized the newly constructed building externally and in operational areas, giving it structure and restoring its former newness.

Bornago, Italy

Upon my return, Ethan and I had our regular and always pleasant semi-annual discussion. It was during this conversation that I learned about the search for a Value Stream Coach for the Bornago plant. They already had a preference for the position, and they wanted me. We both discussed the potential consequences. He expressed confidence that I could do it, although it didn't sound very convincing. Then he got to the point. Ethan was certain that as a Multi-Site Manager, I would be much more effective, and wouldn't be satisfied working in just one plant. This statement relieved me as my perception was very similar. I loved traveling across Europe, coaching and supporting plants, returning after four weeks to discuss results and next steps. Staying in one place wouldn't have satisfied me, and in fact, he didn't want that either. He wanted to deploy me where I was most urgently needed.

During my stay in Bornago, the Head of Product Management and the Plant Manager asked me to join them for a scheduled meeting after lunch. There, they offered me the Value Stream Coach position and informed me that we would have a conference call with America immediately afterward to discuss further details. They were only waiting for my quick 'yes', but to their surprise, it didn't come quickly, or at all. My refusal of the offer left them completely stunned, and they were at a loss for words. During the subsequent conference call from America, the first question was, "Do we have a new Value Stream Coach?" They had to answer in the negative, and their search continued.

The Plant in the Bergisches Land

The HDA's Value Stream Coach would take over this position a quarter later. My boss supported this move. Rüdiger didn't have much backing from HDA's personnel, and I believe the Bergisches Land site was glad to see him move on to his new role in Italy. Somehow, the site hadn't made significant progress, but it did have a great Mission Control Board. Although the position in Bornago was considered 'full-time', Rüdiger couldn't let go of HDA. He still saw himself as the OpEx Leader for all plants, a role that hadn't existed since the 2013 restructuring. By declining Bornago, I lost two supporters there, although many others understood me. Consequently, my 3P activities at this site naturally reduced to zero. It was to be expected; some were a bit offended, and others saw their chance to get me out. "We are now a Value Stream site under transformation. We no longer need 3P. You can do that somewhere else!" Wounded pride in its purest form.

As Molière once said, "When one door closes, another opens." And so, it was. The General Manager of FMIT became more open to new ideas, allowing me to begin implementing 3P there. However, my boss initially asked me to assist in the Bergisches Land. There, where the VS Coach had (almost) left the plant to support Bornago, yet somehow kept reappearing and expecting reports. The transformation of the plant stalled, and there was a significant backlog of orders for profitable products. This, in turn, caused growing dissatisfaction among customers, sales, and headquarters.

I immediately recalled my first Black Belt project, which had a very similar starting point. We reviewed the relevant part of the value stream, updated it, and worked together on fundamentals. We analyzed which parts were available, in what quantities along the supply chain, or at least ordered, and when they would arrive. It's hard to believe, but the plant had no overview of this, and it was a task the VS Coach was incapable of handling.

We manually allocated quantities to orders, and so gained a real understanding of what could be processed and delivered. This was what my boss aimed to achieve. Apart from an appealing board, the entire Lean transformation had yielded little substance so far. It wasn't about optimizing processes down to the minute; it was simply about transparency and supply chain optimization. In fact, through our analysis, we gained an overview of available parts. In a concerted effort, we gradually reduced the backlog of orders. However, this process required time and patience, before its positive effects became noticeable. We decided to conduct another Value Stream Analysis the following spring, and establish adjusted measures.

Somehow, I couldn't help myself. I tried once again to impart Lean thinking to the workshop-level executives. The meeting room was full, and I explained the concepts to them, from standard work and problem identification to their role as 'helpers' for assemblers and machine operators. At this point, one could immediately noticed crossed arms. Fundamentally, some department heads, group leaders, and even the Works Council didn't seem to grasp the seriousness of the situation in the Bergisches Land. I repeatedly heard questions like, "Why do we have to do all this? The others will never be able to produce our products with our quality!"

Eventually, I had enough and asked them when was the last time they received a new product for the site. Silence filled the room until someone finally mentioned that the new high-quality level prototype would soon be coming, and then things would pick up again. I confirmed that HDA would produce the prototype. However, I told them that for series production, the plant in China and Toddville were designated as alternative sites. Again, there was silence. "Have you received any major investments during the last 4 years?" was my question to the team. Again, silence, and no one had an answer. I recommended they educate themselves on what becomes of a site that receives no new products and no investments. Some left the meeting thoughtful, their mindsets slowly shifting, while others saw me as a pessimist, merely trying to impose my Lean ideas.

What else happened

After a hike on our favorite island in autumn, we arrived in the evening at the parking lot of Hotel Sol La Palma. We had booked a massage there. As we made our way to the wellness area, the ringing of my phone broke the silence. It was Ethan. After a few words, he got to the point. The events in Brussels in March had deeply shaken and unsettled him and his family, prompting them to decide to return to the USA—despite their Scottish origins. He would be leaving the ÄÄtch Group, moving to another company, and only traveling within America where his family would feel safer. In the interim, Luke, the Global Vice President of Operations, would take over from October onwards. This was, of course, the good part of the bad news for me, as Luke had been my mentor for many years. He had recommended 3P to me and together with Ethan, had brought me to my current position.

The bad part of the news was evident. I was losing my best boss so far, my advocate who had reached the highest management levels. Additionally, he informed me that the closure of Brezno would be announced in December. If I had any personal matters to settle there, I should do so beforehand, as future trips would be out of the question. Furthermore, he predicted that the ÄÄtch Group still had three years of work for me. However, this would mean that at the age of 62, I would no longer have a job – a bit too early to be out of work. This was something I really had to work on and create a plan for.

Later, I called Luke briefly. He assured me that we would be getting a capable new boss – a young, Lean-oriented manager. He was to come from a company that had been part of the ÄÄtch

Group before becoming an independent corporation listed on the stock exchange. I awaited this development with curiosity. Just before the announcement of the plant closure, in early December, it was time for me to say goodbye to the lovely staff of Hotel Plaza in Banská Bystrica. With colleagues, I could only do so in a limited way, as the end had not yet been announced officially. A subtle sadness hung in the air. I had developed a Change Request Clerk into a 3P Coach and imparted all my knowledge to him. In less than two years, Martin had already risen to become Production Manager and was now poised for his next career step. Our connection remained strong, as I had accompanied him on his journey from desk clerk to manager. He was to be the next Plant Manager. Luckily, I had nothing more to do with the subsequent course of this closure. I had made my contribution with the 3P project, then focused on other issues within the group.

End of the Year

This autumn, we returned once again to our winter retreat on the enchanting Isla Bonita, La Palma. The pleasant Atlantic temperatures in September and the generous sun exposure invited us, as they did every year, to enjoy ourselves. For the seventh time, we climbed to the summit of Pico Beyenado at 1,860 meters, enchanted by the visual beauty of the surroundings and looking forward to a relaxing massage at Hotel Sol La Palma on the beach.

The hiking trail to Pico Beyenado on La Palma winds through impressive natural landscapes and offers varied views. During the ascent, a fascinating view opens up of the majestic Cumbre Vieja with its striking volcanic landscapes. From the summit area, there is a breathtaking panorama over the picturesque valley of Tacande and the charming town of Puerto de Tazacorte, situated directly on the deep blue Atlantic. This hike combines the island's beauty with challenging terrain, and rewards hikers with unforgettable vistas.

2017

> 'Mixed Model Line: The Ideal Spot for a Picnic in Manufacturing'
>
> A 'Mixed Model Line' is a production line meticulously designed to manufacture various products or variants efficiently, typically in batch sizes of one, without requiring changeover processes. It employs methods such as just-in-time delivery, pre-assembled part kits, and modular assembly systems on wheels. Work content at each station is meticulously levelled. This setup optimizes production capacity utilization, while enabling rapid response to market condition changes. Everything can be swiftly moved aside or reassembled within minutes.

The announcement in December about the impending closure of Brezno felt like the final blow of an auctioneer's gavel. Some had already pieced together the scenario as a result of the insensitive approach of the visitors from the USA. Nevertheless, for many of our colleagues, it marked the end of an era. For older employees nearing retirement, it shattered their world just before the holidays. However, others were relatively unconcerned work-wise. The Slovak job market enticed with numerous attractive opportunities, even at renowned companies. Well-trained professionals with OpEx experience were in high demand and well compensated in Slovakia – highly qualified individuals were eager to leave the company early. Zoltán had already departed the previous year. Thus, the ÄÄtch Group faced a dilemma as it needed precisely these highly qualified individuals to successfully manage the relocation. Bonus payments kept employees engaged until the end.

The Plant in the Bergisches Land

The year at the Bergisches Land plant began with great excitement, largely resulting from unfolding events in Slovakia. By late January, our new boss Ünal introduced himself. Hailing from Turkey, he made an extremely personable first impression. Despite having received some background information from the HR Department, Ünal showed keen interest in my responsibilities during our initial discussions. After I detailed my tasks, he began recounting his own career journey within the company, emphasizing his strong affinity for Lean Manufacturing.

Suddenly, Ünal grew serious and revealed a secret that would significantly impact the upcoming year. Four of us, managers operating within Europe, myself included, hailed from HDA. This group comprised Rüdiger, the OpEx Coach, Ralf, the EHS Manager, Georg, the Quality Manager, and myself. The situation at HDA was dire, both in terms of financial metrics and manufacturing conditions. Ranking in the lower third of the company's internal standings was unacceptable for a plant entrenched in a long-standing Lean transformation.

Ünal made it starkly clear, "We have one year to get this site back on track; otherwise, it will be shut down. The lights will go out." In this critical phase, he stressed the need for our full support at HDA to improve the situation. He emphasized, "It cannot be that a site stagnates while the four most competent employees are busy supporting other plants." Aware of our existing contracts, Ünal presented this as a temporary measure under exceptional circumstances.

The value stream transformation had made scant progress thus far. While some initiatives were underway, progress aboard the HDA ship had been sluggish and unsteady. My task was to inject speed into its implementation and course correction. Meanwhile, Ünal would undertake trips to India and Bornago to relieve Rüdiger, the VS coach, Ralf, Georg, and myself. Despite everything, this arrangement seemed fair to me, given its transitional nature.

The EHS Manager adamantly declined the assignment. He reported directly to Mary in the USA, prioritizing safety and environmental concerns across all regional plants, including HDA. After three months, he departed the company.

For the OpEx Manager, this represented another opportunity. Having been involved in driving progress with the team in the Bergisches Land until the previous year, he struggled with a mismatch in chemistry with the team. While highly proficient technically, his lack of process experience led to him not being taken seriously by the manufacturing team. He agreed to provide the required support, needing to hand over a few matters – him in Bornago and me in Ahmedabad. The plan was to prepare and execute a new value stream analysis with his change agent and the team in the first half of the year, a decision finalized with Ethan the previous year. By mid-last year, Rüdiger had already expressed concerns over the vacancy of the second change agent position, despite initiating a job posting a long time ago. Nevertheless, there had been a few applications, with interviews scheduled for the following weeks.

Georg and I fully endorsed the approach. He faced no issues supporting HDA exclusively, much like myself. My trip to India had already been booked and remained unaffected. Before his departure, Ethan had tasked me with ensuring the progress made last year and leading another Kaizen session. Due to turn-over, key knowledge holders had departed, and I was also tasked with training new colleagues during this visit. My new boss and I agreed that my full support for HDA would commence in early March.

Ünal had no concerns that progress in Ahmedabad, Bornago, Roubaix, and Triest would stall without our support. He was more willing to accept this than see no positive development at Bergisches Land. His primary interest clearly lay in this site. This became his and now my primary goal agreement, which was one part of our bonus. We had a deal, although other plants in France, India, and Italy were far from pleased.

There was another change in the HDA personnel. In the spring, the ÄÄtch Group reached a mutual agreement with Hans on a severance package. Ünal personally took charge of the team and operations at HDA. Hans was nearing retirement, whereas I anticipated remaining with the company up to that point. We had managed, albeit narrowly, to share our first and last positions within the same company. My assumption was, that I would continue there until retirement, marking a closure in our professional journeys.

The situation with the value stream analysis at HDA proved to be challenging. Despite the measures taken in the preceding year, no significant improvements in the critical metrics had materialized. Consequently, it was decided to conduct a fresh value stream analysis to pinpoint problem areas more clearly and devise new solutions.

Rüdiger was tasked with preparing this renewed value stream analysis, but encountered significant difficulties in doing so. Up until four weeks before the planned event, he struggled to adequately develop the current value stream with the team. He proposed postponing the event because he refused to base it on the old value stream, while the team rejected his standard approach, which involved full-day meetings for complete re-documentation. The OpEx representatives, as already mentioned, always went the paved way. There had to be formal meetings with him as the moderator and everything had to be worked out anew. In his eyes, other ways were not suitable.

Moreover, Rüdiger and the remaining change agent primarily saw themselves as advisors to the team rather than active, contributing members. They lacked the initiative to independently prepare tasks and refine them in close collaboration with their colleagues in Bergisches Land. During his tenure at HDA, Rüdiger had not engaged deeply with the processes. His mastery lay in OpEx tools, an area where he excelled. However, crafting a framework upon which the team could build was not within his scope. His knowledge was either incomplete or he was overly cautious about making mistakes. Faced with this predicament, Ünal turned to me to take charge of this task.

The situation can indeed be likened to football. Sometimes, a superb team has a world-class coach, yet chemistry fails to spark, leading to the threat of relegation. On the other hand, with a new coach who might not necessarily be better, the team manages to perform at the top. This analogy mirrored our circumstances perfectly. I confess – I had held a responsible position at this plant for several years, where I knew many employees personally and thoroughly. They perceived me as pragmatic and experienced in processes, which undoubtedly helped establish necessary trust.

The art lay in providing the team with a solid, documented process framework that resonated with them. Equally important was ensuring that colleagues on the production floor felt the coach's support not only in terms of tools, but also in their technical endeavors.

Back in 2009, during my first Black Belt project, I meticulously created a detailed value stream for this product line and documented it on my computer. This became my foundation for preparations. Updating my version conscientiously, I laid out a variant on brown paper across the wall. I invited colleagues to drop by whenever convenient, even relocating my office predominantly to this room. It wasn't standard practice, yet this unconventional approach yielded results. Paths are forged by walking them. Colleagues came by, even after hours, grateful that much of the groundwork had been laid out, allowing them to amend and provide updated data. Preparation concluded within fourteen days, ensuring punctual execution of the value stream analysis.

After the value stream analysis, while I was on vacation, I supported the work to the best of my ability. The event's outcomes were a series of multi-day Kaizens termed Rapid Improvement Events (RIEs). These, too, required meticulous preparation. Rüdiger and the change agent insisted on the six-week preparation cycle, the established norm, limiting events to once per month. This pace proved insufficient to achieve desired progress by year-end. It was already May – what could we achieve with only eight events left? We called for more.

Guided by the wisdom of 'don't let perfect be the enemy of good', my proposal to Ünal was, that we streamline preparation, deviating slightly from corporate standards. This decision reduced preparation time to four weeks and accelerated the process. Indeed, we managed to hold two events per month. The arithmetic was simple: Sixteen at 80% is more effective than eight at 100%. By August, I led six RIEs—an achievement in itself.

Initially, resistance during the RIEs was expected from colleagues, both to the events themselves and their pace. I sensed that some employees still hadn't grasped the critical path that the plant was on. Then, almost miraculously, corporate headquarters reshaped reality over the summer, by relocating HDA's main product line to China. This shift profoundly impacted plant capacity, productivity, and overall profitability.

I once again gathered all cell and group leaders, posing the question, 'what becomes of a plant stripped of its flagship products, with minimal investments and no new products?' The only chance lay in making as many changes and improvements as possible that year. Some employees grasped this hidden message, inspiring others in turn; a few remained oblivious.

The events ran like clockwork. During the RIEs, I took on tasks like assembling shelves, stocking boxes with parts, drilling holes in concrete, or wielding a jackhammer. One evening, I painted the floor until midnight for an event, allowing the team to set up shelves the next morning. A colleague from a neighboring department, who had known me for years, observed. He asked, "What must we do to get such support for our area?" My immediate response was, "15% more output and a commitment that everyone pitches in and gets hands-on during the event, just like I do here!"

The following day, we struck a deal within the team to organize another event, even though this department wasn't part of the transformation zone – it dealt with different products. What applied on a larger scale for Roubaix's plant held true for a department in Bergisches Land. The Deputy Works Council Chairman operated in this area, and from my perspective, this turned out to be the best and most intensive event in HDA's history. I drafted various layout designs and discussed them with colleagues, group leaders, and cell managers. Once settled on a layout, we engaged with maintenance and crafted a detailed action plan for the week. I scripted roles for everyone, ensuring clear responsibilities. We anticipated substantial support from maintenance, and indeed, we received it.

Everyone, including employees from other departments and the works council, initially said to us, "You're crazy, you'll never pull this off in five days!" With each day bringing progress, they became more and more impressed by the spirit and the scale of the changes we were implementing. Some bystanders even asked if they could help. Cranes were relocated, machines rearranged, concrete work carried out, small parts shelves reorganized, the floor and the entire facility were painted – we practically turned everything upside down, nothing remained in its place. We worked with jackhammers, cut with circular saws, welded, and drilled anchor holes with diamond drills into the concrete.

One employee, initially sceptical, asked about the secret. My answer was, "In an event, you have to implement things you discuss and decide immediately. If you talk about them again, the process stalls and you achieve little in such an event." The words were well chosen, yet I still saw question marks in his eyes. It wasn't the language he understood. He often wore camouflage-design pants, probably enjoyed playing martial video games, so I said to him, "If you take prisoners in war, you've lost the war!" Suddenly, I saw a nod of understanding from him. The right language apparently matters, even if it doesn't perfectly align with company culture.

Another circumstance that increased my role in the VSA proceedings was Rüdiger finally filling the vacant Change Agent position – at least that's what many thought, including the applicant. The candidate's first name sounded familiar to me because it was quite distinctive, but the surname didn't match. A brief investigation revealed that Rüdiger had hired the same employee whom the company had dismissed years previously, due to his lack of success. That was the year when two out of three Lean coaches had to leave. I temporarily took on his role as Lean Leader back then.

This employee had changed his name because of marriage. When this information spread in the plant, it caused considerable discontent. No one wanted to see him back in the company. His name, as they say, was 'burned'. I informed the management, and they discussed the matter with their superiors. Eventually, the recently signed contract had to be terminated before he started. This cost the company time because the position re-mained vacant again; it cost money because a salary had to be paid; it cost reputation, because such things quickly spread in the job market.

This situation, coupled with the lack of progress in Bornago and the Bergisches Land, led to the OpEx Leader finally being 'al-lowed to go'. It turned out that impressive Mission Control Boards alone were not enough, nor was the dull preparation and execution of Kaizens sufficient, if the metrics did not move in the right direction afterward. Americans may appreciate shows and standards, but if progress stagnates despite the show – in this case, very late recognition. Certainly, the frequent changes of both the European and global Vice Presidents as well as the Global OpEx Leader contributed to this. Each of them wanted to get to know the staff first, and once they did, they were gone again.

Now, there was the opportunity for me to further expand my role in the Bergisches Land. Leading Mission Control meetings, updating the boards, driving the RIEs (Rapid Improvement Events), and leading these events were all part of my responsi-bilities. From all this I really could learn a lot for the future. On the other site Bornago once again lacked a VS Leader.

Roubaix, France

In the summer of the year, Jan Marten, the General Manager of Roubaix, received a visit from Luke, the Global Vice President of Operations. Though pleased with the progress, Luke still felt the pace was unsatisfactory. The immediate question arose; how could they better support Roubaix? The answer came swiftly, "We need Max back, our coach!" Luke inquired why Max was no longer on-site, and Ünal explained he had been working in the Bergisches Land since May. The consequence was clear. Starting September, I had the opportunity to travel to France for a week each month to continue coaching the emerging team. Back in Roubaix, we could finally advance with planning the new line.

During the summer, with Jan Marten and Raphaël on vacation, I continued working on the project with Alain. Alain had constructed the assembly carts from standard profiles and assembled everything in the end. His ingenuity in this area was admirable. To be honest, before coming from Berlin to the Bergisches Land, I was only familiar with the usual process: universal fixtures were designed by an engineer, tendered, and procured with a safety certificate. This process typically took eighteen months or longer and consumed a considerable sum. The equipment was so secure – and thus costly – that it required approval from the managing director. Good German craftsmanship with a safety factor of three.

Alain, a freelance designer working for a French temporary agency, had designed and procured the entire concept in just four months, using exclusively standard profiles. Nearly everyone was on holiday when the delivery arrived. Alain and I assembled the prototype together and then went through the entire simulation protocol, including 'playing air guitar'. During the vacation period, we didn't want to overly burden the Assembler, so we conducted the first two rounds of the simulation ourselves.

In the preceding weeks, Alain had observed the process multiple times and documented many details. He took on the role of Assembler, while I assumed the roles of Industrial Engineer and Lean specialist. Despite having few physical parts, we knew their shape and weight from the drawings and parts lists. Alain had meticulously noted how the Assembler would lift the parts. Ergonomics played a crucial role, both in terms of the parts and the equipment.

Alain said, "I'll start with the housing." I asked, "How will you lift it, what does it weigh, where and how should it be positioned?" He explained that we needed a jib crane and screw eyes, and that the housing weighed 36 kilograms. Where would the screw eyes be stored, or would they come with the part? Ideally, the part should be delivered in the center of the crane's swing radius, as too much force would be required to turn it at the edge. Additionally, it should be positioned on a pallet so that it wouldn't need to be rotated or flipped, ideally at the height of the fixture.

The slowest parts of the assembly process were the crane's upward and downward movements. Well, ergonomics also apply broadly to equipment. Ignoring that slows operations and leads to increased wear. I asked about the exact positions of the eyes. Alain suggested that rather than the Assembler, the provisioning should screw the eyes into the housing, as they would also need to lift it. This was a great idea, as it could shift a minute from the line's workflow and reduce the space required for auxiliary tools. Similarly, we went through the entire 45-minute assembly process and prepared the work area.

Only then did we invite the Assembler. Despite feeling well-prepared, Robert provided us with numerous valuable suggestions for further changes. We were very grateful for his feedback, which we incorporated into the final design of the fixture, workstation, and process. This 'air guitar playing' during the simulation was indeed an effective tool in the 3P process. After Jan Marten and Raphaël returned, the series was ordered with the necessary adjustments. The delivery time for everything was just three months.

Not only Jan and Raphaël, but also Anne and her husband were on vacation. The innkeepers of the farm spent four weeks in Provence and had actually closed the farm. During these four weeks, I had planned two visits to Roubaix. Anne offered me a reduced price. I could stay alone on the farm, use my room, and take care of myself. She revealed a 'secret entrance' to the courtyard of the three-sided farm. The key was in the apartment. The refrigerator was stocked with various items – champagne, wine, juices, jam, butter, and more – so I didn't need to shop much. Essentially, they entrusted me with their part of their farm. Occasionally, someone came to take care of the horses; otherwise, I was alone there. At the end of the week, I placed the money in the drawer where the lodging receipt was also kept. All this showed great trust.

The Plant in the Bergisches Land

The decision for me to return to Roubaix had become easier for Ünal, as the HDA had moved up from the fourth last place to the upper third in the plant ranking. All our events bore fruit in the

Bergisches Land. It was an outcome one wouldn't have dared to dream of at the beginning of the year. However, there were also bitter pills to swallow. My observations in Tomado regarding the new products had proven true. New products were consistently transferred to Toddville and Cangzhou in China. The 'bread and butter' product was shifted to China.

Altogether, this led to underemployment in the Bergisches Land. As personnel adjustments couldn't be made quickly enough, the site's productivity metric plummeted. Lead time, delivery reliability, quality, and workplace safety remained exemplary. Would what we had achieved be sufficient? Or would the HDA suffer the same fate as Brezno? Following the announcement in December 2016, Brezno was closed on December 1, 2017. The 3P project had done its job well. Through all the simulations and standardizations, intense exchanges with other sites enabled the entire production to be relocated within a few months. My colleague and friend Rick also had a successful project.

What else happened

In February, upon my arrival in India – it was just 4.30 in the morning – as usual, I first anticipated an extensive sleep at the hotel, to rest until noon. When I finally woke, I called my wife. She was having breakfast and had already perused the newspaper. In the real estate section, she stumbled upon an extremely captivating offer: a sixty-square-meter apartment in time sharing, for ten weeks from March to May, situated on the topmost of five floors in a charming French holiday resort in Roquebrune, near Menton, just a kilometer from Monaco. A direct footpath to the sea, without a single road in between, and a generous sun terrace overlooking the bay made this offer almost irresistible. Incredibly, the price was so tempting, and the property was being sold by a lady from Berlin, as the result of a tragic death in the family.

My wife promptly wrote an email to the seller expressing our sincere interest in the property. Thanks to my wife, we were first in line, and just a few weeks later, we received the contract, which we signed without hesitation. This winter retreat could even be reached without an airplane. The weather in Provence in March and April already indulged with beautiful spring-like mildness. The Maritime Alps and the coastal hiking trails along the Côte d'Azur virtually invited extended hikes at such temperatures. And the enchanting medieval villages in the Alps transported us back to a time when the world seemed to stand still. We already planned to come here regularly in the coming springs.

It was August when I saw the summer lilacs bloom for the thirteenth time on my train rides to Düsseldorf Airport. How many more times would this happen? Until my retirement it would be six more times? This would still be a long time to go. Meanwhile, managers at HDA were receiving partial retirement contracts. Among them were the Production Manager, the cell leaders, and the Quality Manager, who also worked across Europe. A kind colleague had shared a copy of his contract with me, and the conditions were pretty good. It was a big wish, to get such a contact too! Most of my colleagues would retire between the end of 2019 and 2020. This coincided with Ethan's prediction in the fall of 2016 that the company would still have about three years of work for me; presumably, this applied to others as well. And it aligned with Ünal's statement, "We have a year for the turnaround." Therefore, I decided to inquire in the HR Department whether this opportunity would also be considered for me. Although I didn't have a contract with HDA, I had one with the ÄÄtch Group in the Bergisches Land. The lady from the HR Department looked at me with wide, incredulous eyes and said, "You're at Level 4, that won't work!" Nevertheless, she agreed to check with the boss.

It took a while for this review, and so I finally first received my company car, a fringe benefit I had consistently declined before. Where would it be parked, where could I use it? Now, nearing the end of my career, I accepted this offer. After all, there was the possibility to take over the vehicle at the end of the lease, that is, at the beginning of retirement. A blue Mercedes sedan was now available for my use, both professionally and privately. This luxury offered some compensation for the changes in the aviation sector. Air Berlin had declared bankruptcy. This was a shock for me, as all my flights had previously been with Air Berlin, Niki, or Iberia; about 1,700 flights in twelve years. The hearts I received from the flight attendants were my 'special currency' in hotels and at the Brussels headquarters. During my frequent visits, I always received a warm welcome, as I pampered the teams in the hotels and factories with the little hearts each time. I probably ate the fewest hearts myself; otherwise, my bundle would surely have burst soon.

Whether I travelled with Air Berlin, Etihad, or the Star Alliance, it didn't matter. I was often on the road and had to undergo the company's health check again in July. I was always seen as a role model for fitness and blood pressure. This time, the company doctor noted slightly elevated blood pressure and occasional extra heartbeats. Unfortunately, neither of these situations adhered to the saying 'more is better'. Therefore, he referred me to a cardiologist, where I had an appointment in early August. The cardiologist conducted a comprehensive examination of the cardiovascular system. In the end, much to my relief, he told me he'd like to have my heart because it was functioning so well. The arrhythmias were benign, as they disappeared under stress during the exercise ECG. However, he was only interested in my heart, not my entire circulatory system.

During the ultrasound, he discovered that one of my carotid arteries was 85% blocked and the other 70%, posing a high risk of stroke. He explained to me that with narrowing vessels and elevated blood pressure, particles could break off from the vessel walls, travel to the brain, and cause a stroke. This was despite my active lifestyle, weighing only 73 kilograms at 1.75 meters tall, and maintaining a healthy diet. The cause lay in a lipid metabolism disorder, leading to plaque buildup even with minimal blood fats. The consequences of such a stroke depended on the size of the dislodged particle: from mini-strokes leaving no lasting impact to a lifetime in a wheelchair or even death. When I asked what could be done, he explained that the narrowed artery could be cleaned through surgery—essentially cutting it open, cleaning it, and sewing it back together. However, the risk of a stroke during or after the surgery was about 7%. Therefore, they would not perform surgery immediately, but rather lower my blood fat levels with medication and take blood thinners to prevent further plaque buildup and keep everything flowing smoothly. I decided to follow this path, continue my physical activities, and undertake travel unrestricted.

A few months later, in December, my trips brought me to Roubaix again. It was just two weeks before our annual stay in La
Palma, which my wife especially deserved. Raphaël and I had a
discussion about a Yamazumi chart for the mixed-model line for
large components. Standing at the whiteboard we aimed to
level the processes using the chart. As I was drawing and writing on the board, my right arm suddenly drooped, and the
words I wanted to say or write became unclear. Sitting down, it
became evident that the feeling in my right-hand fingers had
vanished.

Typing on the keyboard became difficult; the keys were not dis-
cernable to my fingertips and I missed them frequently.
Raphaël had another meeting to attend. He sensed something
was wrong and asked, "Are you ok, Max?" When I managed to
form a coherent sentence and told him, "Oui, pas de problème."
we both felt reassured – probably me more than him. After a
few minutes, a tingling sensation began. I could again grasp a
glass of water, hold it, and drink. With each passing minute, my
condition gradually improved until, from my untrained perspective, it seemed normal by the afternoon. The next day, I drove
back to Düsseldorf as usual, boarded the plane, and was home
by evening. Naturally, I told my wife about it and promised to
discuss it with my doctor in March. For now, we wanted to go
on vacation to our house after such an eventful and demanding
year.

Before our flight to La Palma, I experienced two more significant
professional moments. The first was a dinner with Ünal and
Frank, the EHS leader of HDA. We went to a Turkish restaurant
in Essen and had a truly delightful meal. Ünal, with his Turkish
roots, ordered dishes offside the official menu, enhancing the

experience even more. Before we began with the appetizers, Ünal asked that everything discussed that evening stay within the restaurant walls, particularly what he had to say. Then we started our conversations and the sumptuous dinner. We talked about the many Kaizen weeks this year and what we had achieved, having turned many things for the better. Yes, we also shared some laughs about things that didn't work, as everything stayed in the room.

Ünal elaborated, having participated in two events himself as a team member, shelving items and painting the floor with Frank and me. This had impressed many employees, motivating them to come up with ideas and get hands-on. He expressed his appreciation for our efforts and thanked us again. As a result, we had significantly improved in four out of five OpEx ranking categories, placing us in the top third of all seventy global sites. Ünal then told me that I would likely spend more time at FMIT next year, where a significant step in OpEx was also required. He asked Frank if he knew there was another ÄÄtch Group site in Essen from a different segment, and advised that perhaps he should get in touch with those colleagues.

When we asked about the state of the HDA plant after eleven out of twelve months, Ünal replied, "The loss of some products to China in the summer, leading to a decline in volumes, hit us hard. It wasn't enough to turn things around. We are sinking." This news struck us deeply. We understood its significance, just as we had understood Ünal's words in January when he told us we had a year for the turnaround. The year was almost over, and the ship was now sinking. Although I had seen the signs long before in Tomado and repeatedly explained the consequences to the staff in the Bergisches Land, I felt very saddened at that moment as it had become a reality.

The very same plant where I had started after my move from Berlin, where I had learned so much despite – or perhaps because of – all the resistance at all levels, was now heading inexorably towards the abyss. Nonetheless, we tried to keep the evening positive. We talked about the successful events and the amusing experiences during them. However, it already felt like a retrospective on a closing chapter. We set aside the topic of the future that evening; for the HDA, there was none.

The second experience was a result of my request for an early retirement contract in the summer. The promised review extended into late autumn. Finally, I received a draft contract and was asked for various details about my regular retirement date and my wife's income. Everything matched my expectations. Now, shortly before the start of the Christmas holiday in December, the company provided me with the greatest gift one could wish for; an irrevocable early retirement contract until my retirement.

I only had to work until October 2020. From February 2018, the active phase of early retirement with a slightly reduced salary would start for me, accumulating a credit balance. From November 2020, the passive phase would begin, with the same salary yet with 100% free time. This passive phase would last until my official retirement at the end of July 2023. I immediately signed the papers and made a copy of the contract. This was our Christmas gift to ourselves. Now we were both very happy. My wife had not believed I would get such a contract. I had doubted it for a while too. However, now it was there. Since

2005, I had seen the summer lilac bloom thirteen times; now, there would be three more, but not six anymore.

'Right-sized equipment' refers to having equipment that is perfectly tailored to the needs, without unnecessary extras. The 3P process leads to such right-sized equipment, which in turn reduces the material and space requirements for production. With right-sized equipment, maintenance needs and energy consumption are also reduced. Moreover, equipment that is appropriately sized is easier to operate, design, manufacture, and assemble, thus costing less overall!

The Beginning of the Year

The annual vacation at our house brought the usual soothing relaxation. Hiking, swimming, and a glass of wine on the terrace – accompanied by good food, with or without our friendly neighbors – not only promised untroubled relaxation, but also delivered just that. Yet, at times, some aspects seemed surreal. We listened to Berlin's 88.8 radio station with the weather report, sitting on the sunny terrace during the Christmas season at 24℃, contemplating whether to go hiking or swimming. Moreover, there was the part-time retirement contract, which was set to end our nomadic life in 33 months. That also felt somewhat surreal. The countdown had begun! A commute that had originally been planned for three years would then have turned into fifteen, in which I saw the summer lilac bloom sixteen times. However, this count wouldn't reach nineteen years. Thus, in mid-January, we returned once again, refreshed, to the European mainland – back to reality.

The Plant in the Bergisches Land

Already in the second week, the first event in the Bergisches Land awaited me. Even though I already knew the plant's future after the dinner with Ünal in December, the event had to be conducted with the team professionally. I had done the same in Brezno; anything else would have been irresponsible. The goal of this Kaizen was to improve the small parts manufacturing. In this unit, oil seals and other high-quality parts with tolerances in the thousandths of a millimeter were precisely manufactured for HDA's most profitable products. Due to a variety of measures taken the previous year, where other areas of the value stream were continuously optimized, small parts manufacturing had now become the bottleneck in the process for high-end gearboxes and had thus gained importance.

Now it was time for the Kaizen week to eliminate this new bottleneck. Step by step, we planned to first conduct a 5S, then optimize the workflow with minor equipment modifications, and finally make the work areas more transparent through visual measures, and once again introduce supermarkets that should significantly improve the missing parts situation in the assembly line. Additionally, the machines and the floor were to be painted after cleaning, so that the entire department would shine anew. Our goal was to recognize the cell's condition at a glance – whether everything was in normal condition or whether there were deviations. This intense week presented us with challenges, but as always, we managed, and on Friday, we could hold a successful closing meeting with the team and management.

That Friday, however, the management received very surprising news from the corporate headquarters in Tomado. Unexpectedly, Luke announced a visit for the following Tuesday. This meant only three days' notice, including the weekend. Normally, such visits were planned four weeks in advance to ensure that the relevant employees had time. When we asked about the agenda and topics, we received the response, "Luke has the agenda with him, that's enough." We only got the key points of the visit. At 9.00 am, the management team was to meet with Luke, and at 11.30 am, there was a short-notice company meeting.

A company meeting with Luke had never happened before. This time, everything was different from what had been known in the Bergisches Land, and soon rumors were swirling throughout the plant. Speculations ranged from, "We're getting the money for investments in new machines." To, "The new products are coming to us after all and not going to China and Toddville," and even to, "The plant closure will be announced." Only those who shut themselves off from reality – the dreamers – still believed in financial support and production commitments. If you don't notice the small changes and signals, you can't accept the big ones when they happen later.

Nonetheless, on Monday, we ensured everything was in order. For some, it was the usual routine before such a visit; for others, it was the doomed attempt to prevent the inevitable by cleaning. However, the effort was much less than previously, as the site had already greatly improved in every way over the preceding year, including order and cleanliness. A good foundation had been laid. In the 'hope' faction, it felt like water on the mills.

Tuesday arrived, and the management team gathered in the meeting room, with a view of the entrance and the parking lot. Both were visible directly through the window. At 8.55 am, two taxis arrived, and not only did Luke get out, but also Rick, my colleague as Black Belt. Unknown people got out of the second taxi. Rick's arrival had not been announced and caused consternation among many colleagues. Everyone knew he was an experienced manager in plant closures and had previously relocated and closed the Brezno plant in Slovakia within eleven months. When the employees saw him, some began to cry. These were the people who had consistently denied the reality until that day, and had always been convinced that no one could match their plant in terms of quality. It was clear to everyone that Rick would only come if he had a project. And his projects were called 'relocate and close operations'.

Luke and Rick were also accompanied by security personnel and psychologists. At 9.00 am, all visitors and HDA executives, Ünal and I, were gathered in the conference room. We were then informed about the upcoming plant closure. Of course, we were not allowed to tell the other colleagues until the meeting at 11.30 am. Some took advantage of the psychologists in the 120 seemingly endless minutes until the company meeting. At 11.30 am, the entire workforce gathered in the canteen. In brief words, the decision was communicated to the employees. The meeting ended after twenty minutes, without questions being allowed. This sealed the end of the more than 140-year history of the Haus der Aussicht, or HDA-ÄÄtch. A sad chapter that brought many colleagues to tears. Some of them had already been working for this company for the fourth generation. Now the lights would go out within the next 24 months, by the end of 2019. When Ethan mentioned to me in the fall of 2016 that the company still had three years of work for me, the closure of the site was probably already a done deal. Everything seemed to follow a grand plan and had been set for years. The union protested loudly and vocally; however, it didn't change the fact.

The Project 'Deer'

Every child gets a name, and so did this one. The decision to close the plant in the Bergisches Land and move production to China and the USA was given the project name 'Deer'. In times of uncertainty or danger, a deer typically retreats or flees. Thus, the project name subtly reflected certain aspects of the ÄÄtch Group's condition. It was all speculation, even if there's always a grain of truth in such things. For the preceding two years, there had been talks at the investor level with the Dullas Parks Company about a possible takeover or merger. The restructuring of the plant network, which began with the closure of the Brezno plant by the ÄÄtch Group, was likely part of the framework for these negotiations, essentially the master plan for the merger.

My boss had yet another of his ideas. He suggested that I organize a workshop in Brussels to concretize the handover of production and the corresponding information flow. In the coming weeks, I was heavily involved as a moderator. There were many preparations to be made, both in the Bergisches Land and in the USA, for the significant meeting in Brussels. Processes had to be documented, and future interfaces defined. All this had to be aligned with the processes in America. The matter became even more complex on account of the decision that part of the team in the Bergisches Land would remain at the second site near the small castle. Besides the large production site that was to be closed, there was a second site where OEM products were configured. For instance, trucks were fitted with special gearboxes to perform additional functions. The repair of special gearboxes also took place at this site. The entire OEM business unit was to continue and be logistically integrated into the new workflows. Instead of receiving gearboxes from the plant a few hundred meters away, this business would now get them from the USA and China, with some customer-specific adjustments done on-site.

This was a highly ambitious goal. Information flow and delivery times were set to become a very challenging issue. To prevent customers from facing delivery times of three to four months, minimum stocks had to be built up, later functioning as a Supermarket. It was crazy, but we planned to drastically ramp up production on this product line in the Bergisches Land, while the plant was preparing for closure. Try explaining that to the employees and the Works Council!

For several weeks, we had preparatory meetings with the teams in the USA and from HDA. Eventually, my boss tasked me, as a final support for the plant, with leading the major project kick-off meeting in Brussels. Thirty people from around the world were to set the necessary steps for the new processes. We analyzed weaknesses and set measures to address them. The workshop spanned four days. It may sound strange, but I enjoyed it. The company had already chosen me as a mediator in the past when there were conflicts between the locations, yet this was a larger scale. Some would lose almost everything, others would gain so much, and I had to mold the two camps into one team with newly designed processes. In the end, we had a plan, everyone knew each other and knew whom to contact if questions arose.

What they didn't know was who would remain in the team, who would still have to leave, or who would simply choose to leave for better opportunities elsewhere. The 'Deer' project was now handed over to those leading the local groups. We didn't have to present it to the 'world' in a call, because the world was in Brussels that week. With that, my professional dealings with 'HDA' were concluded though on a personal level, I still had an apartment in the Bergisches Land.

My next assignment was to conduct a value stream analysis in Trieste, where Lorenzo still acted as the guardian of old rules, delaying and blocking many things. This was planned for the autumn, with preparations to start before my vacation, ie, early April. That was the plan.

Sometimes Things turn out differently

We had already planned our first stay in our newly acquired ten-week timeshare on the Côte d'Azur for March and were very much looking forward to it. We finally wanted to explore the picturesque villages and hike in the Maritime Alps. Before that, in early March, my semi-annual check-up with the cardiologist was scheduled. I told him about the recent incidents in France at the whiteboard, and his reaction was remarkable and alarming to me. He seemed very concerned and urged me to cancel everything planned for the coming weeks, including our vacation in France. The incidents in December were minor strokes, and only by luck had I escaped without lasting damage or ended up in a wheelchair.

He immediately contacted two specialist clinics while I was still undergoing the stress ECG. The next day, I found myself in an MRI, and a date for a procedure on my carotid artery was set for ten days later. I was stunned. My wife was very sad that we had to cancel our stay in Roquebrune. Nevertheless, it was clear to both of us that the operation was necessary. The risk of a severe stroke was too great after the incident in France. It was greater than the 7% risk during the operation. I informed Ünal about the developments, kept him updated, and we agreed that preparations for the VSA in Trieste could start in a few weeks. We reluctantly cancelled the planned trip to our new apartment, and I went to the specialist clinic for the procedure. Without going into details, I can say that everything went well. Two days after the operation, I returned home to Berlin by train. Flying was not allowed. I was not travel-fit for four weeks.

For the follow-up in Berlin, I consulted a vascular specialist who urgently recommended treating blocked veins as well. I thought, if you're going to do it, do it right, and so I underwent another operation at the end of June. In July, my wife and I finally relaxed on Sylt and celebrated our thirtieth wedding anniversary. As we travelled to Sylt by train, we saw the summer lilac blooming along some railway embankments. It was the first bloom within the framework of my part-time retirement contract. Now, there would only be two more, we thought and rejoiced.

Trieste, Italy

Now, in May, it was finally time. I could travel again, and the preparations for the event in Trieste began slightly later than planned. The General Manager, who had blocked so many things, was gradually becoming more approachable. One level above him, there was a rotation of personnel, and coalitions were forming, seeking more influence over the site. He could no longer oppose the value stream analysis; he could only delay it. Preparations were interrupted again, as I had the vein surgery and spent the missed vacation with my wife on Sylt.

Of course, a VSA also requires a very concrete objective. The management team struggled to make decisions about visit schedules or new screwdrivers. Now they had to develop and agree on the objective for a value stream analysis, something some of them didn't even want. It was a weeks-long battle with part of the team to reach an agreement on the current state, objectives, the gap, and the necessary training. Everything progressed very slowly, but we finally agreed on a date in October. I immediately sent out a 'Save the Date' to the participants and formally invited them. There were very many responses quickly. Everyone wanted to come to this site, as it was usually not easy to get permission to visit Trieste. It usually required a 'visa' from Lorenzo. It was now up to me to assemble the teams and write a minute-by-minute script for the week. The script had been a 'must-have' for me for years. As a coach, you always need to be two to three steps ahead, in order to present the next steps to the teams.

A person in Trieste had to be assigned for the processes and documentation. Unfortunately, there wasn't yet a change agent there like in Bornago with whom I could prepare things. Angelo worked for Paolo and was essentially the Industrial Engineer on the team. However, he had no experience with Lean or value stream analyzes. This did not make things easier. Preparations had to take place not only during my visits, but also in the time between visits. Angelo was to organize and lead this. He was to assign tasks to colleagues and support them in the implementation. It was quite a demanding task. His standing with his colleagues was unfortunately not the best. He had a tough time and could only manage the task with the help of Paolo, the Production Manager. During my visits, I supported the two of them, and the value stream documentation gradually took shape week by week until it was about fifteen meters long, covering several walls. This was a good sign, as it was documented in great detail.

My script for the week also gradually took shape. I always wrote the schedule for the week backwards. On Friday, the result had to be presented worldwide by 2.00 pm; the Future State, the future appearance of the value stream, had to be finished by 12.00 pm at the latest. By Thursday evening, all ideas had to be evaluated and prioritized. This meant that ideas generation, which began on Wednesday, had to be completed by Thursday noon. By Tuesday evening, the problem areas of the current state had to be sorted and evaluated, and this action started on Tuesday morning. Monday was dedicated to information exchange and explaining the current state by the process-responsible team leaders of the event.

You could discuss individual steps, their duration, and instruments with me, as well as slightly altered time frames for certain processes, but not the milestones in the schedule. Everything was divided into 30-minute blocks with planned breaks and meal deliveries, allowing us to assess and control progress. This mirrored the principle of production progress boards in manufacturing. A smaller control period led to fewer deviations in 'missteps. The 'Frequency and Magnitude' principle could be effectively applied here as well.

It's a bit like large television shows. Some participants can be chosen as the show master, while others are required to participate as specified by the broadcaster. The one who 'had to' participate was Lorenzo, and he was still the biggest sceptic. In the wrong group configuration, he could block progress. So, I formed two teams dedicated to the core processes and one team for general, overarching topics. Lorenzo was placed in the latter. To ensure he didn't dominate this team, or appear in the other teams and stir up discussions, I tasked my boss with occupying Lorenzo with strategic questions and other matters. Ünal was good at this and found the idea amusing, being in the team with Lorenzo and distracting him. He trusted that I would coach the rest of the teams in the right direction.

There was also some organizational news Ünal shared with me. The headquarters in Tomado had decided that all Lean specialists and VS coaches should report directly to the Global Vice President for Operational Excellence starting August 1. Jerry was now my new boss. He came from GE and was a Lean and OpEx man through and through. Ünal also said that we would continue to work closely together as before, even though he was no longer my direct superior. On closer inspection of the organizational chart, this meant I was now on Level 3. Between me and the board of the ÄÄtch Group, there was only the level with my new boss and Tyler, the Sector President to whom my boss reported. This did not change my tasks, my relationship with Ünal, or the fun I always had – unless Lorenzo was causing trouble again.

Angelo could only support me to a limited extent during the preparation phase, so I visited Trieste more often and found a permanent hotel that offered reasonable prices even during the season. It was on the outskirts of Grado, not in the hustle and bustle. Still, the beach was a five-minute walk away in the evenings, and the restaurants in the center were ten minutes away. The hotel also had a sauna and very nice staff.

October approached quickly, and the VSA event was now imminent. We had prepared the value stream and even had to take over parts of the hallways in the plant because the value stream, documented on packing paper, was so long that it didn't fit into any meeting room in Trieste. Then came the event week. The creative phase in the first few days went very well, not least thanks to my ex-boss, who kept Lorenzo occupied with both meaningful and nonsensical tasks. This left him no opportunity to appear in other teams and influence them. We had effectively circumvented the block.

In such an event, there is also the opportunity to carry out a Kaizen directly to set an example. One evening during this week, we went to a small bar to watch football and eat pizza. Paolo, the Production Manager, and Pierro, the Operations Manager, were very nice and open-minded people who wanted to drive changes. We had known each other for a long time and had a very trusting relationship. Richard, the Advanced Manufacturing Manager from the USA, also wanted quick changes. Some watched the Champions League match of Inter Milan, while others discussed changes and ideas — things they had wanted to pursue for years, but hadn't been allowed to.

One idea the team had had for years was to shorten the line to reduce work-in-progress and lead time. The Lean leaders had recommended this several times. During each visit, they criticized that it had not yet been done. Such changes required Lorenzo's approval, which he always withheld. During the football evening, Pierro, Paolo, Richard, and I talked about it. Richard said, "If it's as simple as you say, Pierro, let's do it now." Pierro and Paolo looked at me with wide eyes – what would Lorenzo say? During this event, he couldn't prevent it; too many top managers were present. Looking at Pierro again I asked, "Can we get this done tonight and continue production tomorrow morning?" "Si, certo." he replied. I trusted him, as he knew his operation. We made a plan at the table and went through the steps (and cuts).

Then I went to Ünal and whispered the plan into his ear as he sat next to Lorenzo, fulfilling his 'task'. I asked him to keep Lorenzo engaged in conversation that evening, and he agreed. Minutes later, the first of us disappeared, then the second, and so on. The four of us drove to the plant late at night. Within 90 minutes, we optimized the line and prepared everything for the next morning – an incredible Kaizen. Just before we were about to leave, Lorenzo appeared and made a huge scene. His face was bright red, and we feared he might collapse. However, he couldn't undo the changes. It felt like the first hole in a decades-old wall, and there was light on the other side. For him, it was as if someone had completely remodeled 'his' plant without his approval. That's why he declared that if something like this happened again, I would not be allowed to set foot in 'his' plant again. My hope was that Richard from the USA had heard this as well.

During the rest of the event, we achieved more great results and presented them on Friday. Now it was about implementing the other agreed-upon measures. This was where Lorenzo came back into play. He still had all the approval rights and could slow us down in the implementation speed – which of course, he did.

Roubaix, France

To the great delight of all, the mixed-model line that we had planned for so long and intermittently in 2017 finally went into operation in the spring. This assembly line could handle twenty different products ranging from 50 to 200 kilos, all of which could be produced in batch size one. The assembly carts had large, sturdy wheels, allowing them to be pushed by hand. Everything was standardized and built from simple elements. Nothing was oversized. Back in Berlin, they would have certainly considered and bought a chain-driven conveyor system. Here, the engines were pre-assembled instead.

In Roubaix, we utilized only what was minimally required to achieve our goals — Right-Sized Equipment. This saved on acquisition costs, reduced maintenance expenses, and was easier to use. The whole process became significantly simpler. The entire area could be cleared within 15 minutes, as all fixtures and tool carts were equipped with wheels. It was a highly flexible setup that met all the demands of Lean Manufacturing. None of the other plants had ever reached such a high level. The employees in Roubaix were rightly proud of their achievements and exuded extraordinary motivation. When Tyler, our Sector President, visited France again in late autumn, he was simply amazed at the tremendous progress the p ant had made in just one year.

He recalled the words he had spoken about fourteen months earlier, "If you continue at this pace, you'll be at the top of the plant rankings next year. We once saw you as a small workshop, almost like a garage. Now I have to state, that you have transformed into a showcase facility!" It was that day, when we were at the top, that he suggested something we could hardly believe or want. He toyed with the idea of sending employees from the US to Roubaix to see our successes firsthand. However, Jan Marten asked him to refrain from this plan. We were in the process of converting another production line and required all available resources, without any Lean tourism. He laughed and said, "You're right. Keep going your way. I'll explain it to them."

Unfortunately, Ethan, our former boss, had already left the ÄÄtch Group and returned to the USA with his family a few months after the Brussels attack, unaware of this development. He had repeatedly asked Jan Marten if there was a place in the production area where he could have breakfast on the floor. Now, this place finally existed, and Jan Marten immediately sent him a picture of it. The entire layout was detailed in the standard documentation. Here, we could not only have a picnic, but also hold a staff meeting where assembly had taken place just fifteen minutes earlier. And fifteen minutes after the meeting, assembly could resume. Every item had its designated place on this line, and everything was meticulously documented. This whole situation fascinated all the other employees at the

Roubaix plant as well. Ethan was delighted with this picture and sent us his congratulations on our achievement.

What else happened

The remaining weeks of the year passed quickly. Production in the Bergisches Land had mostly been relocated, with machines and facilities partially sold or moved to Toddville and Cangzhou. Many employees were already in the transition company, and the Brezno plant had long been history. Now, a major deal involving the investors was on the table. A deal that would shed new light on the events of the preceding years, marked by plant closures in the USA, China, Germany, and Slovakia. Apparently, all this served only as preparation for a comprehensive corporate restructuring. The ÄÄtch Group was facing the decision to acquire its competitor, Dullas Parks Company. The decision was dragging on, and no clear direction had been set yet. Various scenarios were being analyzed in the interests of the investors:

1. The ÄÄtch Group acquires Dullas Parks Company and becomes a huge conglomerate, potentially leading to antitrust issues
2. The ÄÄtch Group acquires Dullas Parks Company and then splits into two public companies: ÄÄtch Group new and ZUAG Company
3. Dullas Parks Company acquires the ÄÄtch Group, and ZUAG Company becomes an independent public company

These discussions were happening in the background. For the investors, it was always true that two halves were worth more than a whole. So, there would be some kind of spin-off. Dullas Parks Company was dominant in all presentations. Even the OpEx system, called 'DPX', was regularly described as the future. Whether all this would still play a role for me, I did not know. My working life had only 22 months left.

On a more personal level, what mattered most was that we would soon visit the island again. The eventful year in many respects quickly drew to a close after the event. Shortly before the vacation, I caught a really bad cold while in Trieste, so I took a day off. The sun was shining, it was 14°C in November, and I found a sheltered and sunny spot on the beach. The next day, the bout was almost over. For this vacation to La Palma, we flew with Condor, but of course, the landing approach only reminded us of how we used to come here with Air Berlin in previous years, while enjoying a menu from Sansibar: duck breast, red cabbage, and dumplings.

Mother Nature is the finest problem solver. For millions of years, she has addressed challenges through evolution. Think of the grasping mechanism of birds of prey, the lotus effect in plants, or capillary action. When faced with a problem and seeking solutions, consider first if similar situations exist in nature and how nature has resolved them. You will find approaches that can help you eliminate your problem.

The Beginning of the Year

The holiday passed in a flash, almost too quickly for us. This year, we also planned to sell our apartment in the Bergisches Land. With the option to work from home and the HDA closed except for the OEM and service areas, there was no need to be there regularly. It only served as a brief stopover on the way to France. This year, I would only be in the Roubaix, FMIT, and Bornago plants, occasionally visiting the European headquarters in Brussels. Our outline holiday plans included driving to Roquebrune in April, traveling to Sylt in the summer, and returning to our house in La Palma for autumn and the holidays.

Roubaix, France

In Roubaix, the mixed-model line was further refined because in Lean operations, one is never truly finished. There's always a 'Future State'. That's simply the cycle of continuous improvement. It was incredible to see that in the new line, employees listened to music during assembly and synchronously moved carts to the next station. The team spirit was fantastic. We began implementing measures to introduce such a line for large and heavy products weighing up to 350 kilos. Employees were on board from the start, having witnessed the positive impact of the initial project on their colleagues. Simultaneously, we initiated the setup of a value stream for these two product lines, intended to become a permanent fixture. We had a foundation from various previous projects, but this value stream would be regularly analyzed and optimized. The goal was not to hold extensive events for value stream analysis, but instead to see it as a continuous tool.

The site was still relatively small so couldn't host large meetings with fifteen people for a week very often. All departments in Roubaix showed great interest; even the Head of Engineering approached me. He also wanted a value stream for his custom developments, beyond the two mixed-model lines. I assisted him during my regular visits. This was well received during visits by OpEx specialists from the USA. Now, they wanted to send development heads from the USA to France as well. Roubaix had firmly established itself among the top-performing plants. However, the realization remains; Lean transformation is never complete. There is always something new to learn and implement.

Bornago, Italy

My boss had another new task for me this year. Much like Ethan, his predecessor, he liked sending me to places, to tackle a challenge and solve one of his problems. His trust was immense. He knew I would tackle the task, and so we both enjoyed the work. He tasked me with planning and conducting a comprehensive value stream analysis in Bornago, similar in detail to what I had done before in Trieste at FMIT and in the Bergisches Land. The VS coach from HDA had taken over the transformation in Bornago, but it had been similarly unsuccessful there too, so I was to also set things right there. The analysis was to cover from order entry to shipment. Initially, there were some concerns, as something similar had been done less than nine months ago. They had not officially notified the Lean organization; Rüdiger had just left the tarred road, yet the potential was still there. We had to find team members who would work on the issue if I couldn't be there.

Together with the Plant Manager and Gabriele, we selected two ladies, Ariana and Rosa, as group leaders. Both would later take over group moderation in the VSA as well. Their task now was to advance preparations even between my visits. Gabriele, the Change Agent who had always prepared everything in the past, was really busy with his tasks and could only provide marginal support. After the departure of the former VS coach, Gabriele hoped he wouldn't have to prepare everything alone anymore. I managed to not only integrate Ariana and Rosa, but also steer them in the right direction. I also helped where I could, showing them how it's done and what to look out for, what information and documents they had to have. They continued the work between my visits, and Gabriele was reassured. If necessary, he would of course step in immediately and assist them. He approvingly noticed that I, together with the HR Department and the Plant Manager, was making efforts to fill the position of the second change agent, which turned out to be difficult. We received a variety of applications through the HR consultancy, but unfortunately only a few were worth scheduling in for an initial phone call.

The documentation of the value stream analysis that we prepared for the event was over twenty meters long. It just fit into the large conference room. Three walls were covered with our brown paper filled with process steps and sticky notes. We had a huge event with nearly thirty participants from Europe and the USA. The procedure was as always: discussion of the steps, marking potential problems, prioritizing the problems, developing solution approaches, and assessing their impact, then compiling a catalogue of measures with priorities and predicting the development of key figures. In the end, the mission control board was filled with cards for Kaizens, JDIs, and RIEs, with predicted values on the development of key figures, and much more.

At the end of the event, there was neither pizza nor a bowling night this time. Instead, Gabriele came up with the idea of a mini-golf tournament. And not just any tournament—but one held at a course that had previously hosted European Championships. It was a truly unique experience to play on all 18 holes in a venue reserved exclusively for us. Afterwards, we enjoyed a buffet dinner and a few drinks. It was a wonderful conclusion to a highly successful week. What a transformation, and what a brilliant idea.

Now the projects just had to be implemented. For this, we also required the second change agent, and finally filling this position again was our main task after the value stream analysis. Since summer, we had received a lot of application documents and conducted only a few interviews. The right candidate was not among them. We all agreed that we didn't want a second-rate appointment and preferred to wait. Now, at the end of the year, there were still three promising candidates in the race.

Despite my limited Italian skills, it was important to me to participate in the interviews. We opted for a division of labor; I started with the initial questions in English, as English proficiency was important for the candidate. After that, we conducted the conversation in Italian, and my focus was on the candidate's body language and micro expressions. In the end, we exchanged our impressions and agreed. The wait was worth it. Andrea was the right man for the job, an experienced Lean expert with an individual and creative appearance. With his long gray hair tied in a ponytail, he looked like an artist from Provence in France. With a wink, we said to ourselves that perhaps one had to be an artist for this position, so we hired him.

The decision was made, and Andrea started his job on December 6th. I was in Bornago to accompany him in his first days. A positive atmosphere spread. He was glad not to be alone in these days; and Gabriele was glad he didn't have the task. The department heads were glad I introduced him to them and picked him up after a few hours, packed with information to take to the next station. It was palpable that we had gained a valuable supporter.

Trieste, Italy

During the value stream analysis in Trieste the previous year, we had already optimized the production line with the highest output. In the following months, we conducted several Kaizens to achieve further progress. However, these were initial steps to set the ball rolling. We were acutely aware that more actions were needed, aiming now for a significant improvement. Our focus was on the paths and processes of this line. Everyone understood that a single line did not represent the ultimate solution for efficient assembly. Initially, we gathered motion data from the line, revealing the following facts:

- Some facilities in the line were never moved
- Orders had an approximate 23-minute lead time
- Material was delivered hourly to daily

Thus, there was a spectrum of speeds ranging from 0 to 25 movements per day. We then sought similarities in nature. What moves swiftly in some areas, slowly in others, and perhaps not at all?

Mother Nature often provides the best inspirations, and so we found a phenomenon where varying speeds harmoniously coexist: a hurricane. In a hurricane, wind speeds increase from the outside inward. Just before the eye, they are at their highest, swirling houses and cars into the air and sucking them upwards. Further into the center, the speed is nearly nil. While we certainly didn't aim to swirl things into the air, the analogy of speeds seemed a promising approach to optimize different speeds for more efficient material flow. Thus, we sketched a few concentric circles on a sheet of paper.

Based on these circles, we developed a layout that was no longer a mere line, but ultimately more of a U-cell with surrounding assembly stations. At the center of this cell were fixed installations such as testing equipment, tools, power connections, and fixtures. Around this quasi-fixed core extended the assembly circle, completed by a team in 23 minutes. Instead of conveyors, we opted for universal carts — similar to those in Roubaix's mixed-model line — on which assemblies were placed and manually moved by employees. Areas with assembled materials and smaller pre-assemblies were located on the outermost circle, with different delivery times ranging from 60 minutes to 8 hours. Thanks to this redesign, employee paths were significantly shortened, and circulating inventory could be reduced, as work content at various stations was better aligned.

We conducted simulations, intentionally introducing disruptions into the system, optimizing the layout step by step, and repeating the process multiple times until we were satisfied with the results. In close collaboration with the line assemblers and the plant's safety expert, we discussed plans and eventually persuaded them. After some final adjustments, the new layout was implemented. It was impressive to witness dedicated employees pulling together to successfully launch the new system. Within just two days, we successfully reduced cycle time and achieved a 10% increase in production output. Inventory circulation in the assembly circle could be reduced from 14 to 10 assemblies compared to the old line. Mother Nature had provided us with an idea to accelerate production.

Despite this success story, Lorenzo declined to update the value stream analysis this year, so that design could progress to the next level. I turned to Ünal to request a change in responsibilities in Trieste. He asked me for patience — one of my names, not the first or second — and promised that change would come. I trusted him. The situation could aptly be compared to a bus en route to Wonderland, with the driver unpredictably zigzagging. Passengers on the bus were divided in their seats: some content, others becoming restless. Alternatives could be offered, whether a window seat, or an aisle seat in another row. However, the bus continued its journey towards Wonderland. Those not wanting to go there had the option to leave the bus. In this case, however, everyone was striving for Wonderland, including the driver himself. Yet his erratic course persisted for too long. It was time to find him a new seat.

A few weeks later, we met for a visit in Bornago. As I spent three out of four weeks in Italy and only one in France, my company car was stationed in Italy. This allowed me flexibility to travel between the two plants near Milan and along the Adriatic coast. So, I drove from Grado to Milan and then to the plant. The tour had already begun by the time I arrived. Ünal, Lenka — Vice President for Service and Aftermarket, and concurrently Lorenzo's boss — and I warmly greeted each other. We were briefed on the progress the plant had made with its transformation and verified its reflection in relevant metrics like lead time, delivery reliability, and quality. Changes started slowly, but the tanker named 'Bornago' was now in motion. The next day, we drove with my car to the Adriatic Sea to the FMIT company in Trieste. Alongside my colleague and ex-boss Ünal, Lenka also sat in the car. She slept soundly in the back. The sounds of the Mercedes sedan facilitated it. From Verona onwards, Ünal also slept beside me; both signs of exhaustion and trust.

We arrived in the afternoon, and the meeting was scheduled for the next morning. We briefly drove to the company to check emails and say 'hello'. Then we agreed with the team in the evening on Grado Island, where I lived. We wanted to drink something in Key West, a cozy beach bar. Then we went on foot to the Pontoon Restaurant 'Al Ponte di Tripoli', where we enjoyed a wealth of fish and drank wine. It was a delightful evening that ended with warm goodbyes. Whi e Ünal, Lenka and I embraced tightly, Lenka shook hands with Lorenzo only. From Lorenzo's face and the faces of other colleagues, you could see that he took it as a personal affront.

The following morning, a meeting was held in the canteen at FMIT. All employees were present, as were the entire management team, Lenka, Ünal, the HR Department and many others. Lorenzo opened the meeting, gave a brief report on the company's current situation, and then handed over to Ünal. He made some remarks about an impending structural change, rather as a passing remark. Finally, Lenka began with words of praise for the company's growth and successes so far. The next step in terms of the ÄÄtch Group was now to create a structure like those existing in other plants of the group. All production-related departments should report directly to Pierro, the Plant Manager. Lorenzo could now focus fully cn the business of the aftermarket, service, and engineering. Pierro would now be a direct employee of Ünal and would act on an equal footing with Lorenzo, who would continue to report to Lenka.

She explained this calmly, and many employees looked bewildered. How could Lorenzo accept this? Why did he not resist his disempowerment? They realized that Lorenzo's time as the sole 'king' of FMIT was a thing of the past, and FMIT had finally arrived in the big world of the ÄÄtch Group. Decisions affecting production would now be made by Pierro in consultation with Ünal. Of course, my daily work was simplified.

We only had to involve Lorenzo when it came to changes in the service, sales, or engineering areas. Many employees were relieved, some uncertain, and it was our job to pick up the uncertain colleagues and introduce them to the new reality. Only a few resisted the changes; life went on. Those who resisted change ultimately hindered themselves and would sooner or later have to leave. Lorenzo showed no outward signs of anger. However, those who knew him better could sense that he was swallowing everything and was basically beside himself. However, he had found a new seat on the bus towards Wonderland! It was also a Kaizen, because the eighth type of waste was reduced: unused employee knowledge. In his new role, he could contribute more in the company's interest. Collaboration remained challenging, yet had a different foundation. He could no longer block changes in production. It was a step towards a new dynamic and, perhaps, an improved work atmosphere.

What else happened

Finally, spring arrived, and nothing could hold us back. We set off for the Côte d'Azur and spent our first vacation in this enchanting region. We had often perused travel reports and the hiking guide for the area. Flying via Frankfurt to Nice, we rented a car and drove past Monaco to the holiday resort Le Golfe Bleu, where our part-time apartment awaited. Settling into our rooms, we immediately savored the indescribable view from our sun terrace overlooking the Bay of Roquebrune. Our first stop was the beach, followed by a visit to Menton, and in the days that followed, we wandered through the surrounding mountains and explored the winding alleys of bustling Monaco. In Monaco, there is a high density of Ferraris, Maseratis, and Porsches, while just a few kilometers away in the old mountain villages, time seems to stand still. The stark contrasts over such short distances gave this area its' special charm. Our first two weeks flew by. Refreshed and filled with unforgettable memories, we returned home happily, already planning our next stay there.

Summer brought not only sunshine, but also an unexpected change of plans. During one of the routine six-month check-ups, a hernia was discovered, which had to be swiftly operated on in June. As a result, I spent three weeks at home. Despite the spatial change, I managed to handle some tasks quite well from my home office before embarking with my wife on a short vacation in the surroundings of Berlin. We drove to wonderful lakes in the northern and southern outskirts of Berlin – what a pity I couldn't swim in the height of summer – and took a treetop walk. Such a vacation, too, can be very relaxing and refreshing.

In July, we decided to sell my apartment in the Bergisches Land by the end of the year – a year before my official entry into passive partial retirement. With the imminent final closure of the plant in the Bergisches Land, we didn't want to wait until the last minute. At that time, the apartment was rented to a colleague from Slovenia, whose rent was covered by the company. Our goal was not to maximize profit, but to sell the apartment at a fair price. After offering it for sale through a real estate agent, we immediately encountered lively interest. The apartment, which had been my home for over a decade, eventually changed hands on December 31, 2019, for the same price at which we had purchased it.

This decision would later prove to be a stroke of luck. Nives, our tenant, had already moved out in order to return to her homeland in Slovenia by the year-end. On December 8, I returned from Bornago for Andreas' onboarding to Düsseldorf. I picked up a large delivery van from the car rental to start the move to Berlin. I spent about four hours packing everything securely with straps. With all my personal belongings packed, I drove to Berlin and left my second home for the very last time. The apartment and furniture were to be handed over to the new owner by the real estate agent — a deal beneficial to both parties. The new owner wanted to rent out the apartment immediately, thus avoiding any vacancy.

The plant in the Bergisches Land was finally closed at the end of the year. For me, it was the site that provided me with a secure job after my move from Berlin and where my development took its course. My colleagues had done everything to prevent and delay the closure. Naturally, I had not agreed with their regression on Lean issues, yet it was their option to extend operations. They deserve respect for that too. With processes crystal clear down to the last detail, as Lean strives to achieve, the site could have been relocated and closed many years ago, as evidenced by the example of Brezno. Perhaps some colleagues would have been younger then and found re-employment sooner, but at that time, older employees would also have been forced to leave, facing difficulties in the job market, just as they do now. There were many ifs and buts; ultimately, the plant gained approximately eight years of employment. And that was good. I was left with an oppressive feeling. Somehow, I was in orbit, and my launch pad on the ground no longer existed. Fortunately, I still had my 'landing permit' in several companies across Europe.

With the approaching New Year, our departure to our house in La Palma drew nearer. A week before the holidays, we set off, this time with Iberia via Madrid. While enjoying the sun and sea, we let the year fade away in the pleasant atmosphere of this island. Meanwhile, the apartment was handed over by the real estate agent. We received notice that the proceeds from the sale of the apartment had been deposited into the account. Everything was in order and went perfectly. The idea that I would already be in passive partial retirement next December felt a little strange yet also very good. However, on December 31, 2019, a news notification caught our attention. A highly contagious virus was rapidly spreading in China. We hoped it wouldn't spread as widely as avian flu or similar outbreaks. In 2017, there had been the Zika virus, and I had been very cautious then about hand disinfection and avoiding touching door handles and railings as much as possible. How this would develop further soon became known to everyone.

2020

'7 Ways: Seven Paths to Solve a Problem'

First and foremost, the number seven is synonymous with numerous paths. A problem is meticulously described, and participants are encouraged to sketch out as many ideas as possible, even the most unconventional ones, to tackle this issue. Solutions from Mother Nature also provide insights here. You will be amazed at the diversity of approaches that can be taken.

Following this, these ideas are grouped together, as they often share similarities. Then comes an evaluation phase, where the quality and likelihood of solving the problem are considered. The application of the 6 Thinking Hats tool greatly enhances the process with its structured approach. The best idea or ideas are then transformed into a 1:1 mock-up in wood and/or cardboard and tested. This is what we call 'Trystorming.'

The Beginning of the Year

Planning for the first weeks of 2020, my final working year, was clearly defined: first to Roubaix to moderate an event, then over the weekend to Trieste to pick up the car from Italy, a few days at home, followed by a planned foot operation. A hallux valgus that had slowly grown on my right big toe had to be removed; this couldn't be postponed any longer. After a recovery period in March, it would be back to the factories, then in April, we would travel again to Roquebrune to our apartment and spend beautiful days on the Mediterranean and in the Lake Alps. After that, there would be a few more events, possibly a handover, and October 31 would be my last working day. That was the plan.

Roubaix, France

After returning from La Palma, I flew directly to Düsseldorf and then onward to Roubaix. An event was imminent, focusing on reducing costs by 25% and developing a new gearbox. For this, we had planned a 7-Ways meeting – not to be confused with the 7 Wastes. We collected over thirty ideas and grouped them into six clusters. To evaluate the many ideas, we used another engaging tool, the aforementioned 6 Thinking Hats. These hats represent different perspectives: the Finance or Development departments often take on the role of 'Team Caution', offering arguments against new ideas, while other departments support them. This can lead to those voicing concerns feeling uncomfortable, often appearing as 'naysayers'. The 6 Thinking Hats help evaluate pros and cons, risks, and opportunities.

In applying the 6 Hats method[xii], each participant takes on one of the roles for a few minutes, including that of the cautious one, identifying risks. This approach ensures no one feels marginalized automatically. Teams rotate under the relevant hat, with the moderator wearing the blue hat and overseeing the process. Here are explanations of the hats:

- White Hat: The neutral and objective hat, collecting facts and information such as costs, prices, quantities, quality rates, etc
- Red Hat: The emotional hat, considering feelings and intuition. What does my gut feeling say about this proposal?
- Black Hat: The cautious hat, being critical and skeptical to identify potential problems. Manufacturing, design, or financial risks are considered here
- Yellow Hat: The optimistic hat, looking for opportunities and positive aspects. What problem does this proposal solve, are there additional benefits
- Green Hat: The creative hat, generating ideas and alternatives. Can we derive another idea from this one, perhaps even better?
- Blue Hat: The controlling hat, organizing and steering the thinking process

Each idea or cluster is evaluated by all participants from every perspective. At the end, each participant is given three to four adhesive dots to mark their favorites. Only one dot per idea/cluster per participant is allowed. It's important for all stakeholders to participate in the process to avoid one-sided solutions. The cluster with the most points is then detailed and ideally implemented as a 1:1 model for further improvement through prototype testing. This approach, called Trystorming, promotes balanced and holistic decision-making.

This event in Roubaix was once again marked by remarkable intensity and extraordinary creativity. Our ideas forge flourished, and in the end, a coordinated development plan emerged – first for cost reductions and subsequently for new development. The site surprised yet again with an extremely diverse team event.

We ventured into an escape room building, where each room posed questions to answer and tasks to solve. Everything was in French, which added an extra dimension to the experience. The fun factor was immense, as was the joy of the subsequent communal meal.

During dinner, we shared thoughts about the impending merger on March 1st between the ÄÄtch Group and Dullas Parks Company. Formally, the ÄÄtch Group and Dullas Parks Company merged into 'ÄÄtch Group New', but behind the scenes, the thinking system of Dullas Parks Company was already introduced and training prepared. It was already decided that the OpEx system named 'DPX' would now be applied. This system was highly cost-oriented and differed significantly from the behavior-oriented and Lean Manufacturing ethos of the ÄÄtch Group. Our hard-fought Lean culture, built up over the years, would no longer receive the same recognition: it was indeed unlikely that Lean Manufacturing would continue at our level.

We discussed primarily how these changes would personally affect us. Jan Marten had certain concerns, as his position was often the first to be newly filled in such cases. Raphael, on the other hand, faced the situation more calmly as a Production Manager, although he also disapproved of the DPX system's lack of Lean culture. Our enthusiasm was somewhat limited. It didn't seem to be a truly equal merger. Personally, three familiar options opened up for me:

- Firstly, I could continue working as usual, yet with only eight months left, I would essentially be a dinosaur in a new world

- Secondly, over the coming months, I could learn the new system, then apply the acquired knowledge for about four months before retiring. This seemed like an economically inefficient solution
- The third option would have been to be granted leave from the moment of the merger until the end of October – essentially eight months of paid special leave before the 33 months of paid time off began

This option would have suited me perfectly and saved the company training and travel costs. However, as we didn't know how the situation would develop, we bid our usual farewells and said 'Salut' until March.

The Return

On Friday afternoon, I set out in a rental car back to Düsseldorf. I stayed overnight at the airport and caught my flight to Milan the next noon. From there, my journey continued to Trieste in the evening. It was a peculiar time. Rumors from China about an unknown viral infection were confirmed. The virus was identified in early January as 'SARS-CoV-2', with the associated illness named 'COVID-19'. The virus spread rapidly in China and other parts of Asia, raising concerns about its potential presence in Europe as a result of an incubation period of 2 to 14 days. By mid-January, there was theoretical potential for the virus to spread in Europe.

On the afternoon of January 18th, I landed at one of the hubs to Asia, in Milan. Later that evening, I flew on to Trieste and reached my hotel with relief after picking up my car from the secure company parking lot with a taxi.

The next morning, my journey back started through Udine, Salzburg, Munich, and Nuremberg to Berlin. The weather cooperated; there was hardly any snow in the Alps, and after eleven hours, I reached home in Berlin, where my wife already waited for me. Television reports about Covid were increasingly dramatic, as it seemed. Yet, at that time, we still had no inkling of what awaited us in the near future.

Another Surgery

On Wednesday, January 22nd, I went to the hospital to have my right big toe corrected from a hallux valgus. A minor procedure compared to surgeries in the years 2015 to 2018, but it had to be done. The operation took place on January 23rd and went smoothly without complications. General anesthesia was nothing new for me. A couple of crutches supported my first steps the next day, and by Saturday the 25th, I was allowed to go home. My neighbors and wife picked me up from the clinic. Upon arriving home, I immediately assumed a horizontal rest position on a couch in the second bedroom. This would be my recovery area, as long as I asked to wear the bandage and special shoe.

Recovery progressed smoothly until January 28th. That night, I suffered from sweats, and in the morning, I felt too weak to get up. My fever persisted at 39.6° Celsius, then dropped, only to rise again. Confused thoughts spun in my head. My wife contacted the doctor, who prescribed fever-reducing medications. This condition persisted for four days. Countless sauna towels were soaked with sweat and spread on the bed. Getting up was hardly an option, and I spent about sixteen hours sleeping daily. Then, in early February, my condition began to improve. I was certain that I had contracted this novel virus, though tests were not yet available at that time; nevertheless, it turned out to merely be the effects of the anesthesia.

Over the next few weeks, I gradually regained my strength. I scheduled physiotherapy appointments from March onwards, always on Fridays or Mondays in order to allow for midweek travels. A health check for my company car was also due at the workshop. The UVV inspection was scheduled for March 6th, as my plan was to resume traveling from the 10th onwards. In early March, I already booked flights, hotels, and rental cars for the first four weeks after my illness through our travel center in Antwerp. Travel preparations were in full swing again.

COVID-19 was now spreading globally, and rumors of possible flight restrictions made us uncertain about planned travels. Friends of ours who were vacationing in the finca only just managed to return to Berlin via several detours.

Ünal's Call

On March 6th, an invitation arrived for a conference call with my boss. The assumption was that it would be about my condition, how travel would resume, how we'd manage with that dreadful virus, and other matters. The conversation took place while I was waiting at the workshop, inspecting my car. It took a completely different turn than I had expected. The merger with Dullas Parks Company had occurred on March 1st, and he wanted to bring me up to speed. Without beating around the bush, he explained to me that the situation had changed and more changes were imminent. He had special news for me: from now until the start of my passive partial retirement on November 1st, I was on 'garden leave'. Full salary, no restrictions. In American terms, they called it 'garden leave' as it implies the offer of paid time to yourself to linger in your garden.

My 'third variant' had now come into play. He also advised me to quickly go home to say goodbye to friends and colleagues via email, as once he informed HR of our conversation, my email account would be locked. There was a well-functioning protocol in such cases. The phone line would remain active for a few more weeks. My transformation from an engineering caterpillar to a Lean butterfly, just like my career, was now complete.

First of all, I called my wife and told her that I would be staying home from now on. She was initially confused, but that confusion quickly gave way to joy over the unexpected development. The long-held dream of spending more time together suddenly came true eight months earlier – what a stroke of luck! Next, I contacted my employees and closest colleagues like Raphael, Jan Marten, Gabriele, Andrea, Paolo, and Pierro, and briefly informed them of the news. My subsequent email spread like wildfire in the factories. The news caught most people completely off guard, as it had me. The many heartfelt responses touched me deeply. I was able to read them although I could no longer reply.

During the day, I cancelled all upcoming and recently booked business trips with BCD in Antwerp. A few years ago, I had already done something similar for a different reason in 2014. This decision also caused consternation there, as I was more than just a regular customer. Miss La Via cancelled everything, and we bid farewell to each other as well. As the day drew to a close, the realization set in of how quickly a decades-long career could come to an end. It became clear that there hadn't been any opportunity for me to personally say goodbye to many colleagues and the people in the hotels. This filled me with a certain amount of melancholy.

During the weekend, there were two celebrations within our circle of friends. Many had previously seen me as the one who would work until the official end. The fact that I received a partial retirement contract had already caused surprise. Now, it was the icing on the cake of my professional journey. 41 months at the same pay, including a company car and all expenses. No one felt envy; there was only joy. Our friends, who had been staying in our house on La Palma until shortly before, had only just managed to fly home to Berlin via several detours. Only two weeks later, on March 22nd, the first lockdown was introduced in Germany. Many more measures would follow in other countries. In my previous position, I wouldn't have been able to maintain my work anymore. Telephone and video conferences would have been possible, but a direct tour of the production floor to identify deviations from the norm – a crucial part of Lean philosophy – would no longer have been feasible, which was exactly the foundation of Lean; 'Go Gemba'.

The effects of Covid also meant that our planned trip to Roquebrune on the Côte d'Azur in April and May, a time when the area is particularly beautiful and has mild weather, once again couldn't take place. So we stayed at home. We had acquired it in 2017 and had only been there once so far, which was rather frustrating. I used the time for various 5S projects to make room for my large company car in our double garage, which had previously only been used for my wife's car and garden equipment. Finally, the car found its place, and I also managed to fit some workshop cabinets, a drill press, and a tool board. This completed my workshop in the garden. A small 'One-to-One Mock-Up' showed that a sauna with an anteroom would comfortably fit there. Covid was still present, and therefore, fitness studios with saunas were closed. So, I had a new project: building a sauna for us. It was completed in September and has since brought us a lot of joy and relaxation.

However, a small business problem remained – it was a well-rounded affair. The summer tires of my company car were still stored in the Italian tire shop. Between the Covid waves, I managed to pick them up at the end of June. At the same time, I could bid farewell – albeit with a 'see you later' – to colleagues in Trieste and at Hotel San Remo. On the way home, with the tires as luggage, I saw the summer lilac bloom one last time. It was in northern Italy, and immediately my thoughts went to the beginning of this episode in 2005 when I first saw it on the edges of the tracks. We had only wanted to see it four times then, but now that had extended to become sixteen. It had been eventful and beautiful. During the lockdown, I showed my wife many pictures of the place where I spent my time after work. She liked it, and so we decided to travel to San Remo or Aprilia at least once a year. We usually spend the autumn together there, and after my stay on the Côte d'Azur in May, I return to the Adriatic again.

Meetings with my former colleagues continue to be characterized by a warm atmosphere. We exchange ideas about the
changes that have occurred. At one of the meetings with old
colleagues, I picked up on a rumor. In 2008, when I received my
Black Belt certificate from Roger, the new Vice President, he was
supposed to announce the closure of the plant in the Bergisches
Land. It was put on hold because we, the ÄÄtch Group, had acquired the ZUAG Company, and this deal consumed all resources. Another plant closure simply wasn't realistic at that
time. So, he just gave me my certificate, and for the HDA site, it
meant approximately eight more years of employment for the
employees. However, as said before; this is just a rumor. Personally, it was a wonderful company for me. I had found a niche
for my desires. However, there was a master plan that everything followed.

My wife still works and prefers to fly to the Côte d'Azur. I take
the car there and use the opportunity to meet with old colleagues on the way in the Bergisches Land, Roubaix, and Mau-
beuge. Jan Marten and Raphael bought their own company and
gladly use my free advice once a year, because we have become
friends. After the Roquebrune stay, my wife goes by train to
Nice airport. My drive is from there via Milan to Trieste. Thus, I
meet former colleagues everywhere during the year and exchange ideas and also regularly see some of the hotels and their
warm staff in this way. I always said that I wouldn't miss the
loss of flying and professional status, nor the work or the feeling
of being in the rush. It's the contacts with all these lovely people from different nations, the shared lunches in the canteen,
dinners in restaurants and hotels, and team events that I miss.

At least I have been able to preserve and will continue to cherish part of these experiences. Our friends, who received one or another rejection from us during the fifteen years of commuting, are now regular companions again. It is a precious gift to be able to intensively nurture old connections again. We are very grateful for the friends who were by our side during the turbulent years of commuting and still are today. We are glad we had them and that we still have them in our lives.

At the end of such a life phase, engineers like to sum up everything that can be counted. Over the preceding fifteen years, I have visited 27 locations of the ÄÄtch Group, completed about 2,000 flights, and covered more than 2 million kilometers. My time was distributed as follows: a total of 3.5 years in the Bergisches Land, three years on weekends at home, 2.5 years in Italy, two years each in France and Slovakia, and one year on La Palma. The 15th year, in turn, was distributed across India, the USA, and other places. During my trips, I spent over a year on the way to or from the airport, at airports, in a lounge, or on the plane.

Summary

In the 1990s, I began my journey into Lean methodologies with initial scepticism, but quickly recognized its relevance beyond just the automotive industry. However, obstacles – both organizational in Berlin and personal – initially hindered my development in this field. Reluctant to leave my well-paid job in Berlin to pursue Lean, the German saying 'The shirt is closer than the trousers' perfectly captures my initial mindset.

When change became inevitable, I started self-learning in earnest. This set me apart in my new position in the Bergisches Land, where I deepened my understanding and crafted my own view of Lean. Despite numerous existing concepts in textbooks, discussing with my mentor, I explained how a self-developed perspective often endures more than one adopted without personal understanding. I didn't intend to publish it or challenge others' ideas, and my mentor welcomed this approach, encouraging me to continue.

My career didn't follow a textbook path. I developed my own strategy, learning Kanban, Supermarkets, and 'Develop people first' in a non-ideal sequence due to lack of formal training opportunities. I expanded into 5S, SMED, value stream mapping, and TPM, which was my passion in Berlin, despite minimal input. Kaizens and 3P followed, along with an arsenal of tools like Trystorming, cardboard simulations, Yamazumi charts, and more.

During my training, I increasingly realized the importance of focusing on customers and employees. Employees produce what customers pay for; they should view customer requirements as their own, and identify and solve problems. This customer-employee connection shaped my Lean perspective over the years and proved invaluable. Below, I'd like to share these insights in the form of questions and answers.

Customer Focus

- Do our products satisfactorily solve customer problems?
- Is the customer satisfied with quality, delivery time, punctuality, service, and value for money?

Employee Focus

- Managing means improving and improving means identifying and solving problems. Do we have a culture where employees are encouraged to admit mistakes, identify, correct, and prevent problems?
- Local employees know the process and problems best. They are the factory's knowledge. Utilizing this accelerates continuous improvement and turns the PDCA wheel quickly
- Instead of seeking a perfect solution, take quick, small steps
- How do we support this process? Is the target condition clearly defined to detect deviations quickly?
- Identifying is one thing, solving is another. If we expect employees to identify problems, suggest solutions, and implement Kaizens, we must develop and empower them. Thus, the motto is 'develop people first' and 'empower the people' to be able to recognize and solve problems in the customer's interest

- Problems are best identified through observation where they occur. 'Go Gemba' – Do we have Gemba Walks where employees of different levels and functions regularly go to the scene?
- 'Invert the triangle' – Do leaders support employees as servant leaders in planning and conducting Kaizens?

Lean transformations often fail because those involved don't move beyond applying instructions. They feel isolated on their journey. By considering the above questions and statements in your actions, you won't be alone on your journey.

This summary encapsulates the key ideas from this text, focusing on my journey with Lean methodologies, the challenges I faced, and the principles I have embraced for effective implementation.

Epilogue

We've learned that success isn't merely measured by numbers and profits, but by how we evolve as individuals and as a team. Lean teaches us how to overcome obstacles, foster innovation, and shape our collective future.

My hope is that the stories and experiences we've shared inspire and embolden you to forge your own paths, and to strive for operational excellence. Lean is more than just a methodology; it's a way of life. I hope that you will integrate the principles of Lean into your own life and organization, thus charting a course towards excellence.

I deeply appreciate your companionship on this journey. May your path in the world of Lean be both successful and fulfilling. Remember, movement is beneficial, mistakes are treasures, and growth and learning should never cease. Here's to a future filled with continuous improvement and success!

List of sources

i ahaslides.com; kaizen-continuous-improvement-process

ii Quote of Franz Kafka

iii Arabic proverb

iv Quote of Johann Wolfgang von Goethe

v Quote of Albert Einstein

vi Lean Publishing SMED-Methode: Shigeo Shingos Revolution für effizientes Rüsten in der Produktion

vii Quote of John Rohn

viii Travel to Slovakia   Banská Bystrica - Slovakia.travel

ix Based on: www.maschinenmarkt.vogel.de/was-ist-hoshin-kanri-die-methode-einfach-erklaert

x Quote of Bob Marley

xi Based on a Definition from the CETPM-Lexikon

xii Developed by Edward de Bono